INTO THE
LOOKING
GLASS

EXPLORING THE WORLDS OF FRINGE

SARAH CLARKE STUART

ECW PRESS

Published by ECW Press
2120 Queen Street East, Suite 200, Toronto, Ontario, Canada M4E 1E2
416-694-3348 / info@ecwpress.com

LIBRARY AND ARCHIVES CANADA CATALOGUING IN PUBLICATION

Stuart, Sarah Clarke
Into the looking glass : exploring the worlds
of Fringe / Sarah Clarke Stuart.

ISBN 978-1-77041-051-0
ALSO ISSUED AS: 978-1-77090-038-7 (PDF); 978-1-77090-037-0 (EPUB)

1. Fringe (Television program). I. Title.

PN1992.77.F75S78 2011   791.45'72   C2011-902815-8

Editor: Jennifer Hale
Cover design: Keith Berry
Images: Tree Frog © Sascha Burkard, Seahorse © Mableen, Apple © Diane Diederich
Text design: Tania Craan
ECW PRESS   Printing: Transcontinental   1   2   3   4   5
ecwpress.com

PRINTED AND BOUND IN CANADA

CONTENTS

Amid the clamor of *Lost*mania and a growing appetite among television audiences for more science fiction shows, the pilot episode of *Fringe* aired in September 2008. The opening scene, a chilling scenario clearly reminiscent of an *X-Files* episode, features a deadly virus that wipes out an entire plane full of passengers. We are then introduced to the rational Agent Dunham and, shortly thereafter, the brilliantly mad Dr. Bishop. They make a strong first impression as an unlikely pair of heroes, but their shared goal of discovering "the truth" plants the series firmly within the tradition of great science fiction, with science playing a starring role.

Recent science fiction television series tend to make the continuous search for "the truth" central to their long-term plots. Whether it is made explicit by the television creators themselves (*The X-Files'* "the truth is out there"), or the narrative is an epic spiritual puzzle (*Lost*), or questions of right versus wrong take center stage (*Buffy the Vampire Slayer*), there is a general longing for scientific, ethical, and cosmic understanding among audiences of TV fantasies. In this book I attempt to identify and explore these more meaningful notions that *Fringe* addresses but does not always make explicit. Like all good science fiction *Fringe* deals with dynamic and controversial topics using fantastic elements to convey its compelling messages.

This book is thematic in design and does not follow the series in a chronological order. As a result, one episode might be discussed in three or four different chapters, while another may receive very little attention. It closely examines many of the ideas, archetypes, and characters that make *Fringe* unique. By elaborating upon many of the narrative traditions within which *Fringe* was created, I hope this book will compel readers to carefully consider the dynamic connections that the show has so elegantly woven together.

Because my background is in literature, I naturally view television shows with literary traditions in mind. My purpose in this book is to share this viewing perspective with the reader. It is both revealing and instructive to place *Fringe* in the context of its science fiction tradition, acknowledging its literary, televisual, and film inheritance.

The reader will also notice my strong tendency to draw comparisons to other television shows, particularly *Lost*. While *Fringe* has its own unique appeal, it shares writers, producers, and fans with the island-based J.J. Abrams show, so it's fitting to compare the two. They explore common themes, including the notion of free will, the tension between faith and reason, and the mysterious nature of time.

The book is divided into three sections, each focusing on a broad element of the narrative experience of *Fringe*. The first section establishes *Fringe*'s identity as a science fiction classic, while moving the reader through the plot twists, character changes, and significant themes of season 1. It explores *Fringe*'s cinematic, televisual, and literary roots by identifying fundamental themes and character types that position it within the tradition of science fiction. This section does not address each and every episode specifically, but the content is based primarily on season 1. The second section uses the metaphor of "the looking glass" as a means to examine cultural and social problems. It also explores the notion of alternate universes, addressing what is made clear at the end of season 1: "there's more than one of everything." In addition I discuss Peter Bishop's reluctant discovery of his own connection to "The Pattern." Here I place a good deal of emphasis on the transition from season 2 to season 3, especially focusing on the two-part episode "Over There." I examine season 3's bifurcated narrative structure and discuss the juxtaposition of the two mirror-image worlds, acknowledging the significance of doubles and twinning. I also look at the interpersonal conflicts of the show and present the mirror as a symbol of self-knowledge. The final section, "The Small Screen as Looking Glass," is an examination of how *Fringe* reflects its audience and, in turn, the viewers reflect, or refract, the show. Do they see a reflection of their world in the small screen? In addition, I examine the online digital communities of *Fringe* fandom and the extra-canonical feature of the *Fringe* comic book series.

Into the Looking Glass explores the ways in which *Fringe* reveals, and sometimes critiques, the society from which it emerges. Along with many other post–9/11 television shows aired in the West, *Fringe* exposes a society's collective paranoia about an invisible web of clandestine puppet masters. It also underscores the fear of radical advances in technology and urges its viewers to ponder the ethical limitations of science. Its artful exploration of these issues against the backdrop of a compelling interpersonal drama makes *Fringe* one of the most intriguing TV shows of the last decade.

PART I

Establishing Fringe as a Science Fiction Classic

CHAPTER 1

Olivia Dunham

The Stoic Hero(-ine)

"You are the one, Olivia. Of all the children that Walter and I prepared, you were the strongest. You were always the strongest."

— William Bell, "Momentum Deferred"

The story of *Fringe* is primarily Olivia's "hero's journey."* Though Peter takes center stage in many episodes, it is Olivia's facility to "save the day" that shapes the plot. It is Olivia who has been endowed with special abilities. Essentially, she is a superhero, with her keen intelligence and sharp intuition, as well as the supernatural gifts that propel her to "Guardian of the Universe" status.

In season 1 Olivia plays the key role in saving dozens of lives, including John Scott's and her niece's. Later she saves Peter more than once. Her character inverts the traditional model of hero in which the male lead is the rescuer and the female lead is helper or victim. It is Olivia who protects and defends the world, not with intimidating martial arts moves or seduction, but rather by using her professional training and intellect to rescue those who are in danger.

The female action hero archetype has enjoyed a good deal of popularity in recent mainstream narratives, with more screen time

---

*Joseph Campbell's model of the Hero's Journey and its archetypes are used throughout this chapter as we explore this journey through a female protagonist's experience.

than ever before in film and on television. The model for this leading lady, however, has been quite narrowly defined, depicting either an extremely violent, tomboyish heroine or a conniving seductress, or a combination of both. The feminine characteristics of empathy and intuition get pushed aside in an effort to develop a heroine who is "equal" to the male hero, an effort that usually results in a replica of the man. Consider the following female action heroes: The Bride (*Kill Bill*), Evelyn Salt (*Salt*), Starbuck (*Battlestar Galactica*), and Lara Croft (*Tomb Raider*). These women, though subversive in their own ways and certainly fun to watch, are clearly trying to emulate the masculine hero archetype.

They exhibit an attractive but tough demeanor. In some cases they are extremely violent in order to compete with their male counterparts. In addition, they derive much of their power from playing into over-sexualized stereotypes. In the worst cases, they are rough, bad-mannered, unethical, and violent, all the while maintaining a sharp awareness of the male gaze.

And yet this archetype does not fit Olivia Dunham, the calm, sophisticated, compassionate, feminine female lead of *Fringe*. Her authority does not come from her physical strength or a tough emotional exterior, but from her position as a federal agent who takes her job seriously. She rarely acts like she has to prove her worth, nor does she draw attention to her position as a woman in a traditionally masculine job. She is not emotionally defensive, trying to outwit every man (or woman) with whom she comes in contact.

Olivia's story reads like the hero's journey, Joseph Campbell's model of the monomyth: she is reluctant at the outset, has a strong moral code, accepts the call to action, faces conflicts only she can battle, and is willing to give her life for greater causes. The broader term "hero" best reflects her overall narrative role. She is the hero of this journey, whether she is pursuing a bioterrorist, playing with her niece, or coping with the loss of her partner and lover, John Scott.

In the tradition of the classic hero Olivia Dunham is a solemn loner with a difficult past but an intense desire to protect the world from malevolent forces. Technically speaking she is a "heroine," but because the feminized version of this term is used so often to mean merely "leading lady" or "romantic heroine" it doesn't retain the same valiant qualities as the title "hero." Therefore, for the purpose of this chapter, I will use the term hero with a gender-neutral definition in mind.

If John Scott had not died in the pilot episode, Olivia would not enjoy the same kind of hero status that she does. It is almost a requirement for male heroes to be unattached, but it is an even greater mandate that heroic female figures be single. It would not be John Scott's status as a male protagonist so much as the presence of a romance that would have overshadowed Olivia's status as a hero. Being in love, content and attached, takes the edge off those heroines who are strongly motivated by their dissatisfaction with the status quo. Olivia's resistance to Peter's affection attests to this notion.

Like in other classic hero (and superhero) tales Olivia's childhood becomes a central point upon which the conflict turns. In many narratives, science fiction or otherwise, the hero emerges from tragic beginnings, motivated by an early trauma to believe that the world needs fixing. Sometimes the motive is vengeance or the desire to escape the past. Even though Olivia is a fairly refined female hero, with her demure appearance, calm persona, and penchant for pantsuits, her childhood was pretty rough. As it becomes clear by the end of season 1 that young Olivia was used as a subject for a sketchy drug trial, the picture of her past grows increasingly dismal.

Olivia's unwitting participation in the cortexiphan trials at the Jacksonville navy base initiates her into a world of danger at a very young age. Walter and William Bell expose Olivia to treatments that have "unforeseen consequences," both good and bad. Although the drug is toxic to many other test subjects, cortexiphan allows Olivia to develop supernatural abilities, qualities that elevate her heroic status. In "Ability" Nina explains to Olivia that "Doctor Bell theorized that the human mind, at birth, is infinitely capable . . . and that every force it encounters — social, physical, intellectual — is the beginning of the process he referred to as 'limitation,' a diminishing of that potential." Through scientific ingenuity, Olivia's human limitations have been diminished, which makes her, quite literally, superhuman.

Olivia's abilities range from telepathy to universe-crossing. William tells Walter in "Over There, Part 2" that she is the best thing they ever created together. This suggests that Olivia is herself a science experiment — the ultimate product of fringe science. But by engendering superhuman abilities in her, Walter and Bell have limited her human qualities. Perhaps her stoicism is a side effect of these synthetic components; the drugs that make her more than human have also buried some of her most basic human emotions, and this is why she has trouble accessing romantic passion.

Olivia's character serves as a microcosm of the relationship between the natural world and technological advances. She illustrates how a great scientific discovery can achieve spectacular results while also limiting our sense of humanity or disconnecting us from the natural world. This is an important theme in many science fiction stories: the disembodiment and mechanization of the human being. (This idea is explored in more depth through the shapeshifters, and in a later chapter, we will discuss in greater detail what it means to be human.) Olivia's experience is not far removed from the life of a cybernetic organism. A cyborg is simply a person composed of both biological and artificial parts and, arguably, the chemical makeup of Olivia's brain is partially man-made.

Olivia's experience is akin to heroes such as Spider-Man or Batman, whose powers are borne of freak accidents or tragic events. In season 2's "Jacksonville" Olivia visits her old preschool and the memories of a terrifying experience come flooding back to her. It seems that exposure to cortexiphan allowed her to tap into an unknown source of power and become pyrokinetic; she created a large fire in one of the labs. This incident must have left a remarkable impression on three-year-old Olivia, though she did not remember it until Walter brought her back to the site of the trauma.

The rest of her childhood wasn't much better, though her problems are more commonplace. When young Olivia finally stands up to her stepfather after years of abuse, she demonstrates how, even at the tender age of nine, she embraces the role of the hero. She protects the weak: her emotionally distraught mother and vulnerable younger sister. Because Olivia's mother never called in the authorities to protect the family from abuse, Olivia felt compelled to take matters into her own hands, so she shot her stepfather with his own gun. She became a "soldier" in order to protect and defend others from the horrors that she witnessed; Olivia knew then that she wanted to work for law enforcement. It could be argued that enduring the abuse of her stepfather molded her into the hero she was to become.

After recovering from his injury, her stepfather disappeared and Olivia never saw him again. But each year he sends her a birthday card, a reminder that he's still out there. "I should've killed him," she tells Peter in "The Cure." "I know that rationally he's not responsible for all of the bad things in the world, but he is responsible for some of them." Coupled with the cortexiphan trials, the abuse suffered on the home front created a strong sense of responsibility in Olivia. What might have destroyed other children turned her into a warrior. Undeniably her status as a hero is the direct result of a dark, disturbing past, experiences that not only provided her with emotional strength but with genuine superpowers.

Olivia's experience with John Scott could also be included in her "difficult past" narrative. When we first see Olivia she is enjoying relative bliss in the arms of her lover, John. By the end of this episode John is dead and Olivia has learned that he completely deceived her. She becomes disillusioned and angry, priming her even more to become a hero, as she explores the limits of her emotional strength. Without this "final straw" Olivia's powers may have never been reawakened. Certainly she would not have met Walter or Peter, the key figures guiding and accompanying her on her hero's journey. John Scott's death shakes Olivia's foundation and calls to her attention a series of challenges that can only be addressed with her unique abilities. Thus, through suffering, she is initiated into a monumental adventure.

In the following sections we will explore the different facets of Olivia-as-hero to see where she fits in the tradition of heroic female archetypes.

The Female Warrior
Olivia, the Soldier

In "Olivia. In the Lab. With the Revolver" Sam Weiss tells Olivia that she's "a soldier, a protector" by nature. He keenly notes that she "practically wear[s] a uniform." When he comments that she never wears primary colors he's not exaggerating: at one point the audience gets a glimpse of her closet where her outfits, neatly lined up, are seemingly identical, all in black or shades of gray. She rarely is seen wearing anything other than a dark pantsuit and white blouse or a navy blue FBI jacket. She has been referred to as an unwitting soldier for ZFT in the "coming war." David Robert Jones tells her that she was abducted so ZFT could test her ability as a "recruit." And when it comes to her role as warrior, William Bell literally expects the world of her: he is preparing her to become the defender of the universe.

Those who precede her in the "female warrior" category range from Athena in ancient Greek mythology to *The Matrix*'s leather-clad Trinity to Buffy the Vampire Slayer. The *X-Files*' Agent Scully is a clear precursor to Olivia's character, not only in terms of her occupation as a detective-soldier but in her reserved nature. Though Olivia's not by any means a martial artist, she has demonstrated physical proficiency when it comes to chasing down criminals, escaping captors, and outwitting opponents in the few hand-to-hand combat encounters in which she has engaged. And, of course, she knows how to handle a gun.

However Olivia does not seek out violence or find satisfaction in battle the way that Xena does, nor is she a self-identified "slayer" or combatant. Certainly if innocent lives are at stake she will not hesitate to hunt down and detain (or kill) the guilty party. She has a strong moral code and her loyalties lie only with the "greater good." When she learned that John Scott was working for the wrong side, for instance, she at once set aside her romantic feelings to lead the mission pursuing him ("Pilot"). In this way she is a just warrior, defending good at all costs. Even as a child she was clear-headed about the notions of right and wrong, no matter who was involved: protecting her mother from her stepfather meant standing up against the family's provider in the name of justice.

Olivia demonstrates her warrior status again and again, saving the world from untold horrors. Just by accepting the assignment to the Fringe Division, however reluctantly, Olivia takes a courageous step toward the role of heroic soldier. Her battles take her into gruesome crime scenes and chilling circumstances. In "Bound," for example, she pilfers the vials of a potential bioweapon before making her great escape, which enables Walter to figure out what is happening to the victims. In this episode Olivia repeatedly puts her own life on the line in order to capture a double agent. Later in this same episode

Olivia visits Mitchell Loeb's house, again putting her life on the line, this time to expose Loeb's betrayal.

In "The Transformation" both Peter and Olivia knowingly put themselves at risk by going undercover to procure the antidote to a horrific virus and, more critically, to identify a cell of bioterrorists and bring them into custody.

In "Ability" Olivia's courage is tested when she faces a task that no one else can perform: David Robert Jones has attached a toxic bomb to the roof of a downtown skyscraper, and it supposedly will emit poisonous gas for miles if it explodes. Though she doesn't have complete faith in her own abilities, Olivia orders everyone else off the roof to remove them from immediate danger, but she stays behind to try to dismantle the bomb. She is willing to risk her life, especially if it means saving an entire city.

In *Athena's Daughters* Frances Early and Kathleen Kennedy explore the role of the "woman warrior," citing Buffy the Vampire Slayer, Xena, and Seven of Nine (*Star Trek: Voyager*) as exemplary models of this archetype in modern popular culture. Early and Kennedy's descriptions of female warriors undoubtedly apply to Olivia: "If the stories she tells enable fans to re-imagine and reclaim the heroic narrative for young women, then the new woman warrior is a potential ally to the feminist project of reinventing the world" (10).

The Mother as Hero

Olivia, Defender and Guardian

Typically in the male hero's journey the motherly character is an object who serves him — a well-regarded figure but still just another mile marker on his trail. But the female hero appropriates this archetype and transforms it into the subject, incorporating the positive characteristics of a maternal figure into its persona.

President Roslin of *Battlestar Galactica* is a prime example of this model in recent television history. Her job is to guide and protect all of humanity as matriarch of a lost race of people wandering through the universe in search of a home. Buffy also serves as a model of maternal strength, as a nurturing figure for her friends and protector of humanity in general.

When it comes to playing a maternal role, Olivia balances her individual relationships with the needs of a larger community. Her evenhanded approach to conflict compels others to instinctively trust her, including one of the most powerful men in the world, William Bell. He has entrusted Olivia with guarding the gate to the other side and, presumably, saving the entire universe. The enormity of this task creates in Olivia a sense of responsibility for all of humankind.

But Olivia also plays a maternal role on a less epic scale. She is strong and supportive of her sister, Rachel, and almost serves as a second parent to Ella in the wake of Rachel's separation from her husband. She not only jokes and plays with Ella, but she also shows genuine maternal tenderness, as illustrated when the little girl falls asleep in Olivia's arms. The intimacy exhibited within her family reveals that Olivia is just as powerful on a personal level as she is battling evil and saving the world.

Ella isn't the only recipient of Olivia's motherly instincts. In "Inner Child" Olivia develops a strong connection with a frightened young boy who is found sealed underneath an old building. The boy is mute, but Olivia seems to understand his thoughts. She is the only one who can make him feel comfortable in his new environment. Like a new mother with an infant, she is completely in tune with him. He refuses to eat anything until she coaxes him into trying yellow M&M's (though admittedly not exactly the food of choice for moms). He is relaxed and happy when Olivia is around but will not cooperate with any other adults.

It is clear that Olivia's passion operates within the model of nurturing protector rather than lover or Muse (see below). Unlike with some female heroes, Olivia is slow to anger and not overly sensitive. But the emotional connection that she develops to the innocent victims of crime is strong and deep. Her protective nature is what motivates her. In a rare display of self analysis, Olivia explains her motives to Broyles, revealing why she exposed Dr. David Esterbrook, a well-regarded "senior officer of a multibillion dollar conglomerate." She lays it out in clear terms — who she is and why she does what she does: "I understand that you think I acted too emotionally. And putting aside the fact that men always say that about women they work with, I'll get straight to the point. I am emotional. I do bring it into my work. It's what motivates me. It helps me to get into the headspace of our victims . . . See what they've seen. Even if I don't want to, even if it horrifies me. And I think it makes me a better agent" ("The Cure").

The Muse and Temptress as Hero
Olivia, the Goddess of Love?

The temptress-as-hero (or temptress-as-villain) is a fairly common archetype in adventure stories, and for good reason: there is power in sensuality and physical attraction. We see exhibitions of sexual power played out in popular action narratives frequently, whether the female character is an adversary and temptress of the male lead, or the central figure, one whose "kick-ass" qualities make her all the more appealing to male audiences. Consider Nikita, Mrs. Smith (*Mr. and Mrs. Smith*), Catwoman, and Six (*Battlestar Galactica*).

An even more common female lead archetype, one that is often combined with the temptress role, is the romantic heroine or Muse. Most stories, no matter how masculine in aesthetic, have at least one romantic heroine. Traditionally adventure narratives have been told with a male hero as the central character and one of the major defining moments of the traditional hero's journey is "getting the girl" — the man's dangerous acts of bravery win the love of a beautiful woman. Convention dictated that a leading lady cast in a film about a male hero, for instance, would be automatically relegated to the status of damsel-in-distress.

In *Fringe* this archetype is rejected. There are plenty of examples of Olivia fighting, chasing, and escaping on the one hand, and nurturing, guiding, and protecting on the other, but the instances of seduction are few and far between. This does not mean that she doesn't have this very powerful weapon on hand, however. We've seen her whip it out on occasion, and quite easily too. In "The Cure" she approaches David Esterbrook under the guise of a peer at a social function. She stands close to him, engages in the kind of intense eye contact we rarely see from her, and most significantly she pretends to empathize with his ideology. She tries to soften him up to get information from him and he is successfully deceived. Clearly she knows what it takes to win the affection and trust of a man, if only to collect evidence for a case.

From time to time Olivia uses this same false display of romantic interest on other unsuspecting men, but always with a clear objective in mind, for the "greater good" of her job and the victims she's protecting. But she never flirts for the fun of it or to inflate her own ego.

But undoubtedly Olivia's key personal obstacle is that she is not emotionally available when it comes to erotic love. In season 3 her inability to open up to Peter becomes a central conflict. It has been apparent all along that he has feelings for her, but their chemistry, especially in season 1, is almost nonexistent, mostly because of Olivia's guarded nature. To be fair, it is reasonable that Olivia could only reveal her sensual side under false pretenses. Her most recent relationship before Peter was based on lies, after all.

In season 2, just when Olivia and Peter seem to be getting somewhere in their relationship, Olivia's fear of intimacy jumpstarts her latent ability to identify people from the alternate universe, exposing Walter's deeply held secret. In "Jacksonville," as Peter and Olivia are going out for drinks together, she sees him glimmer and instantly knows that he's from the other universe. It's a specific blend of emotions, the combination of fear and love, that allows Olivia to identify something or someone from the other side. This discovery, of course, eventually sidetracks their budding romance, especially when Peter leaves her universe altogether to return home in "Over There, Part 1."

His departure awakens something in Olivia and compels her not only to take action and save her man, but also to voice her feelings, no easy task for Olivia. The reason she gives Peter for returning home — "you belong with me" — ignites their romance and sets the stage for the bizarre love triangle of season 3.

When "Fauxlivia"* steps in and takes over where Olivia left off, Peter follows right along, perhaps believing that Olivia has finally come to terms with her intimacy issues. The "emotional quantum entanglement"** that ensues is almost more than Olivia can bear. Fauxlivia is the unscarred version of Olivia, the one who, among other things, still has a mother and was never treated with cortexiphan. According to Olivia, Fauxlivia is the kind of person who laughs easily and even wears dresses on occasion, implying that she, Olivia, could never be like that. She holds Fauxlivia at arm's length, trying to distance herself from what she most fears: vulnerability and passion.

Olivia's position is typical of the male hero. Her strength lies in her ability to rescue her beloved even if it means risking her life. But when it comes to intimacy and exposing her feelings, she's at a loss. She can battle monsters and villains without a single tremor of fear, but when it comes to a simple kiss, Olivia is filled with terror. Ultimately it's Fauxlivia who propels Olivia into a serious confrontation with her fears. Olivia is furious with Fauxlivia's intrusion into her life, but it is precisely this intrusion that kicks Olivia's romantic passion into high gear. In Jungian terms, Fauxlivia is the shadow self that works to unravel the most practical intentions of the ego. She stirs up the emotions that Olivia would otherwise continue to repress. In "6B," after Peter and Olivia prevent a trans-universal cataclysm together (one that was fittingly triggered by a strong connection between a man and a woman), they begin to work out their own emotional entanglement. Perhaps emboldened by Peter's sentiment that most people (including him) dream of spending a lifetime with the person they love, Olivia stops repressing her Fauxlivia side, much to Peter's delighted surprise.

Olivia: Guardian, Defender, and Muse

The character of Olivia Dunham has greatly contributed to the continuing establishment of the female action hero archetype, and she has expanded its definition to include an even more complex female lead. The "tough girl" warrior is obvious in Xena, Starbuck from *Battlestar Galactica*, and Kate Austen from *Lost*. All of these women represent the Amazon or Artemis figure, the feminine hunters and warriors. Olivia has taken the archetype to a new level, the "strong female character" who recognizes the value of intellectual maturity. She's not a mere duplicate of the male version, as many female heroes tend to be characterized, simply adopting the masculine narrative, nor is she a hyper-sexualized object using seduction as the source

---

* Although "Fauxlivia" does not accurately describe the alternate universe's identity, it seems to be one of the more widely used names for her, along with Bolivia and Altlivia. She is certainly not fake or false, nor is she necessarily "bad" or "alternative" to Olivia. But for the sake of consistency, I will refer to her character as Fauxlivia.

** Walter uses this term in "6B" as a scientific theory grounded in Einstein's work.

of her strength. Olivia is not overly emotional, but she's sensitive when the occasion arises. Because she plays such an even-keeled, reasonable character (one long-criticized for being "wooden"), her moments of vulnerability, anger, or lust are that much more compelling. Though she is "haunted" as Peter says ("Over There, Part 2"), she is not vengeful or hateful. In fact this may be a key reason why fans were so completely underwhelmed by her character in season 1: Olivia's no drama queen. She tries her best to be impartial, honest, and painstakingly reasonable. Like her "fringe science" predecessor, Agent Scully from *The X-Files*, she is rational, practical, and quietly passionate, in contrast to the man who helps her along her hero's path — the quirky, impractical Walter Bishop.

CHAPTER 2

WALTER BISHOP

THE MAD SCIENTIST

"So you're telling me . . . what? My father was Dr. Frankenstein?"
— Peter Bishop, "Pilot"

Walter Bishop is the quintessential mentally unstable man of science. Initially, his "madness" is given greater weight than his scientific ability. His sanity is in question long before he appears in the scientist's typical setting, the lab. He is first introduced while still in the grip of involuntary detainment. An asylum for the criminally insane is a place of tedium, drug-induced stupor, and mental decay. For a gifted scientist accustomed to unlimited exploration and access to the most advanced technology, this opening setting underscores a tragic backstory.

It is the grin of a madman that Olivia Dunham sees when she first steps into Walter's room at St. Claire's Hospital. Slowly turning to face her, Walter reveals an unkempt beard and a bleary gaze. This is the first glimpse that we get of the legendary Dr. Walter Bishop, a man charged in the death of his lab assistant but deemed unfit to stand trial. Presumably he was more than just an absent-minded professor. His was the profile of a megalomaniacal genius — a danger to himself and the rest of the world.

Olivia comes to St. Claire's to question Walter about his work on tissue regeneration, hoping to save John Scott's life. Peter waits in the lobby, obligated to be present during the visit but unwilling to reconnect with the father who essentially abandoned him and his mother. In this context Walter's expression takes on a treacherous quality, and Peter's objection to discharging him from the facility seems fairly reasonable. Walter's first words to Olivia — "I knew someone would eventually come" — are both eerie and puzzling. How much does Walter know? Why doesn't he seem surprised that Olivia, a stranger, is that "someone"?

But Olivia is not easily spooked. In Walter she recognizes a sense of good intention and compassion. Further he's the only person in the world who can potentially save John Scott's life. She is prepared to put her faith in this man, despite his strange history and questionable ethics.

The mad scientist is not usually the good guy. One of the more famous mad scientists in both literary and cinematic history, Dr. Moreau, is both crazy *and* malevolent. His practices are terribly cruel and unethical, and he never shows remorse for his monstrous creations or the wellbeing of his test subjects. On the other hand, geniuses can be fairly complex characters. As explicitly illustrated in the *Strange Case of Dr. Jekyll and Mr. Hyde*, these men (indeed, they are usually male) have more than one dimension to them. First, there is the curiosity-driven calculating side that, if unchecked, can lead to destructive, unscrupulous practices. Then, there is the emotionally intelligent side, something that Walter seems to cultivate in season 1. His newly found personal connections, especially to Peter, help him consider the ethical implications of a rapid advance in science and technology and its effects on a personal, and even spiritual, level. In "Midnight" Walter admits to another scientist, Nicholas Boone, that he sometimes wonders how his own "scientific trespasses" will be judged. "If indeed there is a soul," he explains, "we must consider that there is still time for redemption."

Walter Bishop exhibits aspects of both the protagonist and the troublemaker. He sincerely wants to assist the FBI and Olivia. His intention is to help solve mysterious cases that require biological and technological expertise but sometimes, in the thrill of curiosity, he forgets to put the welfare of the victims (or patients) first. He allows his passion for science to take priority over human life. In many cases this side of him arises in the evidence of his past research. When he discovers that the ZFT manifesto was written on his own typewriter, for instance, Walter knows that he might be fighting against scientific practices that he initiated but can no longer remember. Like Dr. Jekyll, the monster dwells within Walter and in his past. He must struggle with himself to overcome the worst tendencies of the mad scientist.*

Legendary Mad Scientists

"And just for the record . . . one mad scientist is my limit."
— Peter, "Midnight"

There is a long tradition of fictional scientists and academics who allow their work to drive them over the edge. H.G. Wells' Dr. Moreau and the Time Traveller, Jules Verne's Professor Von Hardwigg, Robert Louis Stevenson's Dr. Jekyll, and William S. Burroughs' Dr. Benway are just a few of the mad geniuses guilty of a rash of sins against both humankind and nature. They are known for "playing god," engaging in dangerous experiments that threaten the lives of many and experimenting on unwilling human subjects. The following are brief descriptions of three famous mad scientists and how they compare to the practitioners of fringe science on television.

Dr. Frankenstein

Walter Bishop's most recognizable literary forebear is Mary Shelley's Victor Frankenstein. Peter makes the comparison to this nineteenth-century character early in the series, during a conversation with Olivia, and it raises some important questions. If Walter has engaged in unthinkable experimental practices, will viewers be able to connect with him? Is this a bad guy or a good guy? Is Peter justified in turning away from such a man, or has Peter coldly abandoned his poor, weak, mentally ill father?

The similarities between Walter and Frankenstein lie primarily

---

*Later, in part 2, we will explore how Walter must not only face the actions of his younger self but also his own double. In seasons 2 and 3, he will have to confront the Walter of the parallel universe, or Walternate.

in the fact that their passion for science destroys those who are close to them. The monster murders Victor Frankenstein's five-year-old brother; his good friend, Henry Clerval; and, most tragically, his wife, on their wedding night. Similarly Walter's wife and son are both negatively affected by Walter's "scientific transgressions." Because of his arrest and institutionalization his wife is left to raise their son alone. She eventually commits suicide, and Peter becomes estranged from his father and emotionally disconnected from others. Walter feels betrayed by his good friend and partner, William Bell, and their friendship dissolves while Walter is locked up at St. Claire's. Walter's reckless practice of science also kills a young woman: his assistant dies in a lab fire and he bears the guilt for it.

In *Frankenstein* (1818) the relationship between the creator and the monster serves as a metaphor to illustrate man's shaky relationship with advancing technology. Victor Frankenstein is unremitting in his scientific objectives, but when he finally sees his creation come to life he is horrified. The experiment in reviving the dead ends in the scientist's own devastation.

Walter is certainly not the only "Frankenstein" in *Fringe*. In fact many of the Massive Dynamic scientists and the followers of ZFT are modeled on this archetype. In their race to be the most cutting-edge innovators, they disregard the destructive powers that could be unleashed by the innovations themselves. As Nina Sharp tells Agent Dunham in the pilot episode, "We reached the point where science and technology have advanced at such an exponential rate for so long, it may be way beyond our ability to regulate and control them," admitting that "the monster" has already been unleashed.

Dr. Moreau

The title character in H.G. Wells' *The Island of Doctor Moreau* (1896) emerges as an allusion in two different episodes, "The Transformation" and "The Day We Died." Two unrelated characters, Conrad Moreau and "Moreau," are both scientifically inspired men with questionable integrity. The original Dr. Moreau was a lonely man. Before he founded his strange community on a remote island, he was banished from his scientific circle in England. He was exposed as an unethical researcher who performed gruesome vivisections on animals. The narrator explains, "He might perhaps have purchased his social peace by abandoning his investigations; but he apparently preferred the latter, as most men would who have once fallen under the overmastering spell of research. He was unmarried and had indeed nothing but his own interest to consider" (33).

This "overmastering spell of research" seems to regularly creep into Walter's mind. At the scene of a crime, when other investigators are repulsed by the grotesquely mutilated bodies, Walter doesn't even attempt to conceal his sense of awe and excitement. He is often cheered by a surprising chemical change or a strange growth that he has never seen before. The tragic nature of the deaths does not appear to concern him, especially in early episodes.

To a far greater extent, Dr. Moreau possesses this same cold manner, inspired by an unrelenting curiosity. Dr. Moreau left England to establish an elaborate research project on a small island where he used different species of animals to create "superior" hybrids. The resulting creatures are hideous but possess the capability of speech and intelligence comparable to that of humans. The procedures to transform them, however, inflict torturous amounts of physical pain. The narrator, a castaway on the island, reports that the screaming of the test subject (a puma) is incessant and he finds out later that the creatures refer to the lab as the doctor's "House of Pain." Their newly acquired intelligence causes them further torture, a chronic mental anguish that remains long after their surgeries. They have the ability to consider their own existence, the injustice of their situation, and the shame of their disfigured bodies. Dr. Moreau creates them and then abandons them. He does not take responsibility for their ongoing misery. He pursues these experiments for his own scientific glory.

One episode that clearly alludes to Dr. Moreau's practice is "Unleashed," wherein Walter's past research resurfaces. When a hybrid creature is released from a local laboratory, Walter recalls his prior work in "radical transgenics," a theoretical examination of cross-breeding between different species. The hybrid monster found wandering the city and procreating is huge, destructive, and hostile to humans. It typifies the Moreau-like creature that rises up against its creator. This event serves as a clear warning to the mad scientist: be careful what you research.

The same can be said about the cortexiphan trials. Walter and Bell significantly altered the children in the Jacksonville daycare experiment and then left them to deal with the long-term effects on their own. As adults, these test subjects were a danger to themselves and to others, starting spontaneous fires, inciting homicides and suicides, and even causing cancer in others. The unforeseen consequences of the cortexiphan case are devastating, but Walter can only see the damage in retrospect. In the moment, the exhilaration of a possible scientific breakthrough blinds him to the negative possibilities of such extreme alterations. Like Dr. Moreau, Walter lacks the capacity to empathize with his subjects; he does not value their humanity, at least not until much later in life. And as much as he does finally come to regret the negative side effects of his experiment, he and Bell still view Olivia's ability as a product of their genius: their greatest creation.

Dr. Jekyll

The Strange Case of Dr. Jekyll and Mr. Hyde, a novella by Robert Louis Stevenson first published in 1886, provides us with two elements similar to Walter: a scientist famous for his drug use and a man with a hidden monster within. Dr. Jekyll develops a drug concoction that can essentially split the personality of a human being into two distinct personas. He uses it to liberate himself from the strictures of morality and civilization. It changes both his physical appearance as well as his ethical constraints, allowing him to unleash his passions — whether murderous or lustful — on unsuspecting victims without guilt. Certainly Walter has not shown any signs of intentional malice, but he does exhibit traits of the amoral scientist. Further, his misdeeds of the past are not yet fully revealed. We don't necessarily know what Walter is capable of, but we do know that he has, wittingly or unwittingly, played a role in the creation of monsters, both figurative ones and real-life creatures.

The initial contrast between Walter and Walternate (Walter's alternate universe counterpart) is striking. Throughout seasons 1 and 2 we see Walter as a gentle, compassionate man with a strong desire to correct some of his ill-guided scientific projects from the past. Walternate reminds us that Walter was once an arrogant, self-serving man, a brilliant scientist with a god complex. Walternate also reveals the possibility for corruption and bitterness in Walter himself by serving as a mirror that reflects the Mr. Hyde characteristics in Walter. For example when all of the cortexiphan test subjects die under Walternate's care he is completely callous, revealing his absolute disregard for human life, but when he refuses to experiment on children we can see just how unethical Walter was in his own cortexiphan trial. If even Walternate wouldn't "cross that line," then Walter is truly lacking integrity.

Walter's Transformation

Walter's progression from dependent mental patient to an autonomous, if eccentric, employed scientist is rapid. Season 1 shows Walter gaining emotional strength as new dimensions to his personality are revealed. In his portrayal of Walter, John Noble has done an excellent job adding depth to this character, but in the first several episodes of season 1 Walter's quirky antics seem to ring a bit false. Noble was playing the stereotypical mental patient. But once the layers of Walter's history are established, allowing Noble to delve into a unique take on the mad scientist archetype, things get interesting.

It is in season 1 that Walter's character changes the most. In many ways, Walter starts out like a child. He is given a new life when he is released from St. Claire's, but he must relearn everything about the outside world. On his way home the first day, he exhibits childlike behavior; he is unable to maintain a clear line of thought or even regulate his bladder. At night he finds it difficult to sleep without hearing the song that one of the mental patients would sing every night, "Row, Row, Row Your Boat." And to Peter's great annoyance, Walter babbles in the middle of the night, reciting the decimal points of pi in order to soothe himself to sleep. In the lab Astrid and Peter act in cooperation to keep Walter focused on the work at hand, and in public places Peter cannot leave Walter alone for fear that he will wander away.

But, all the while, change is taking place in Walter. Before leaving the hospital he dramatically transforms his appearance by shaving off his beard. He demands access to his lab and updated materials and equipment. After several weeks of living in a single-bedroom hotel with Peter he requests a separate living arrangement, citing his need for personal space. At one point he even finds the strength to return to St. Claire's as a way to help Olivia solve a case and save a child's life ("The Equation"), of which Peter later tells him, "What you did, by going back into that place, was very, very brave."

In many ways Walter is the centerpiece of *Fringe*'s conflict, both as a problem and a problem-solver. Because of his inventive, if sometimes unfocused, ideas and the access that he has to his earlier innovations, he is vital to meeting the FBI's objectives. Olivia and her division depend on Walter to help them solve seemingly impossible cases. The dynamic, multilevel set that serves as Walter's basement lab at Harvard is the center of *Fringe*'s narrative world. But both he and his lab also tell a history of the Pattern, the collection of cases assigned to Olivia. He has played a role in creating the central conflicts posed by the Pattern, but he is also the central force in developing solutions.

Peter plays an essential role in Walter's ability to function at such a high level, first as a guardian and interpreter but eventually as a partner in scientific innovation. And here we come to the great triumvirate of *Fringe*, the glue that holds together the personal drama and deepens each character individually: Walter, Olivia, and Peter, with Walter at the center of this trinity. Although Olivia believes that she was the one who initiated the FBI's link to Walter and who reconnected Peter with his father, it is actually Walter who first touched the lives of Peter and Olivia. Long before Olivia's John Scott case, Walter bound them all together in a plan with far-reaching consequences.

In "There's More Than One of Everything," the season 1 finale, Olivia finally confronts Walter about the cortexiphan testing. Walter, in an unprecedented display of remorse, weeps in front of Olivia. This scene is a culmination of his character arc over the season; Walter grew to consider the implications of his practices, both those he could remember and those he had forgotten. Now able to maintain deep emotional bonds with both Peter and Olivia, he must reconsider his tendency to engage in "mad science," a feverish and hyper-creative kind of work but one that is potentially blinding and destructive.

CHAPTER 3

ZFT

THE CLANDESTINE OPERATIVE

"A black horizon approaches. Our scientific advancements have
so dramatically outpaced those of the human soul that man, a
creation . . . defined by passion and greed, now stands at the
base of [a] pyramid of knowledge which expands heavenward
with no regard for the . . . frailty of its foundation."

— Excerpt from the ZFT Manifesto ("Ability")

In the *Fringe* universe, ZFT is a terrorist group that propagates its
agenda by way of scientific breakthroughs. The name itself —
Zerstörung durch Fortschritte der Technologie or "Destruction Through
Technological Progress" — reveals the extent to which the work of
mad scientists pervades this show. In season 1 all of the scientists
linked to biological attacks or human experimentation have a connection to ZFT. Even William Bell and Walter are associated with the
group and seem to have had a hand in the creation of the manifesto
and/or funding the entire operation.

When Broyles first recruits Olivia to work with him, he explains
that a series of strange events is happening all over the world.
Throughout season 1 the Fringe team believes they are tracking an
organization of villains responsible for this phenomena called the
Pattern, but as brutal as some of their experiments are, it is never
clear whether these are truly the "bad guys." The events of the amorphous Pattern are finally revealed to be linked to the other universe
and its shapeshifting invaders. In any case the group that affiliates

itself with the cause to defend "our world" is a loose web of scientists responsible for or linked to the Pattern, wittingly or otherwise.

The desire to advance science to an apocalyptic precipice permeates the narrative and affects all of the characters' lives. At least five of the characters in this chart are dead by the end of season 1, all killed in the name of science. All of them have brought grief, terror, and even death to others because of their involvement in bioterrorism. Some of them have engaged in horrifying human experimentation or brought their destructive technology into public spaces, endangering the lives of many. Though not all of them have been trained as scientists, they all push themselves beyond the pale of sanity, using scientific progress to justify unthinkable acts.

These men are motivated by an obsession with science or they are urged into action by the charisma of their leaders. As explored in chapter 2 the narrative conflicts of *Fringe* are driven to a large extent by the passions of mad scientists. On the corporate end, William Bell has established a worldwide conglomerate based on the work of "mad science" and the desire to push technology to its limit. ZFT, an organization committed to technological advancements and the practice of unrestricted scientific experimentation, is clearly supported by Bell too; Massive Dynamic is a chief player in the Pattern. This leads us to a mysterious contradiction: David Robert Jones, the ring leader of ZFT in season 1, was originally rejected by his own scientific circle, including Massive Dynamic and William Bell, but he is furthering the dictums of William Bell's manifesto. Or is he just altering the "word of Bell" to support his own agenda? In any case the increasingly complex realm of ZFT is a key source for understanding the overall plan of *Fringe*'s narrative. The shadowy history of this organization is inextricably linked with the history of William Bell. Understanding this secret society might reveal the exact nature of Bell's involvement in the unraveling of the universe.

The Tradition
In many ways the underground organization archetype is similar to that of the "evil corporation." In science fiction the secret society usually operates very closely with the corporate conglomerate, a model we will discuss in the next chapter. Sometimes a clandestine element

can be found within a large company acting as the secret, nefarious force behind corporate interests; other times there is just an implied relationship between big business and the impassioned soldiers of a subversive cause, as is the case with ZFT and Massive Dynamic in *Fringe*. The Dharma Initiative in *Lost*, for instance, was funded by the all-powerful Hanso Foundation, a firm with suspicious connections and a stake in all sectors of life, including major warfare. Even more suspect were the Others, a group with shifty motives who had representatives all over the world but seemed almost invisible to government and law enforcement. In *Fringe* William Bell, founder and CEO of the biggest corporation in the world, has repeatedly been linked to the international bio-terrorism group ZFT.

To examine the "clandestine operative" more broadly we should take a look at the array of fictional examples from popular narratives. Bokononism, for instance, is the fictional religion created by Kurt Vonnegut in his critically acclaimed novel *Cat's Cradle* (1963). The followers of Bokonon are forbidden to practice their religion according to the governing powers of San Lorenzo, the central setting in the book. Bokonon's teachings consist of silly poems and profound, if cynical, passages such as "So I said goodbye to government / and I gave my reason: / That a really good religion is a form of treason" (118). Later in this chapter I will explore how, like the disciples of a dogmatic religion, some followers of ZFT commit acts of betrayal toward family and government in the name of their group's ideology.

Another notable operative is the Knights Templar, a real organization dating back to the Crusades, but also featured heavily in Dan Brown's popular novel *The Da Vinci Code* (2003). The Knights Templar was also mentioned in the Indiana Jones films and *National Treasure* (2004). In reality, the Knights Templar was a monastic order with a legendary web of underground cells dating back to the twelfth century when they established a military stronghold during the Crusades. They were wiped out by the French monarchy in the fourteenth century but their legend has long outlived the organization. Popular fiction continues to mythologize the Knights Templar, playing on the notion that the Knights are not only still with us, but wielding great power throughout the world. They are guardians of the group's ancient secrets, codes, and holy objects. Though not always the case, they are commonly depicted as villains.

Other secret societies include the "fight club" from the novel of the same name by Chuck Palahniuk; *Heroes*' international covert organization, "The Company," made all the more secret with Primatech, the paper company that serves as a cover; W.A.S.T.E. in Thomas Pynchon's *The Crying of Lot 49*; HYDRA, the terrorist organization intent on world domination in the Marvel Comics universe; the Order of Aurelius from *Buffy the Vampire Slayer*; the Order of the Phoenix and Dumbledore's Army in the *Harry Potter* series; a special race of people with telepathic abilities from Isaac Asimov's Foundation Series; and Torchwood in the *Doctor Who* mythos. This brief list demonstrates just how pervasive secret operatives are in popular narratives.

In real life we usually think of secret societies as being grounded in radical political and philosophical doctrine, as with the Branch Davidians or the Ku Klux Klan. They are established as networks to support causes that are either illegal or unpopular, and the followers keep a low profile to avoid regulation from governmental organizations. Their central issue is that the public authorities will not address their grievances; they must take matters into their own hands. Both secretive and cause-driven, *Fringe*'s ZFT group is a quintessential clandestine organization, but it deals in science and technology rather than political power or religious freedom. Its followers do have a zealous quality, but their faith rests squarely on the promise of science and technology. "Everything we know about these guys suggests that they're zealots," Charlie tells Broyles in "Midnight." They are suspected of a wide array of terrorist activities, from the Glatterflug Air incident (the virus unleashed in the airplane at the opening of the series) to David Robert Jones's attempt to cross universes in pursuit of William Bell ("There's More Than One of Everything"). Broyles tells Olivia that the group has an unknown number of cells operating all over the world.

Season 1: The Far Flung Connections and Alleged Associations
In season 1 the ZFT thread is ever-present but the actual name is not mentioned until episode 7, "In Which We Meet Mr. Jones," when Pattern-related events are connected to a single group. In these

earlier episodes we can only speculate that the extreme scientific experiments are in some way supportive of the general objectives of ZFT, although this is never firmly established. In the pilot episode Richard Steig, a former employee of Massive Dynamic, is seen at the airport driving away from the Glatterflug incident. In a prior scene his identical twin, Morgan Steig, is infected with an airborne virus that quickly spreads to the other passengers and crew, instantaneously melting their flesh and killing them. There is no concrete link between Richard Steig or his brother and ZFT, but we do know that Richard was in contact with John Scott, someone who certainly knew about ZFT. Scott was certainly involved with the group, if only in an undercover position.

In this first episode both Massive Dynamic and the military become associated with questionable modes of scientific research. When Walter is investigating John Scott's case and the Glatterflug incident he notes that, decades earlier, the exact same toxin was being researched for its potential use in the Vietnam War. Viewers learn early on that the source of new science and technology for ZFT often originates with the U.S. military and Massive Dynamic.

In the next episode, "The Same Old Story," Claus Penrose seems to be working under the tenets of some sort of clandestine group, though a clear link to ZFT is never made. He is continuing research that was begun with Walter, at a time when the U.S. Army was looking for a way to quickly cultivate human soldiers. Penrose continued the work and successfully developed several clones, including his "son," Christopher. Penrose's ultimate goal for this rapid growth research is at first unclear, but it falls in line with ZFT projects that are later revealed, like the weaponizing of humans or the synthetic cultivation of soldiers.

In "The Ghost Network" federal agents Evelina Mendoza and Grant Davidson are accused of an affiliation with Pattern-related events and/or ZFT. Mendoza is on a public bus when a toxic gas is released and then solidifies into a resin-like compound, trapping and killing the passengers, including the agent. But it is Matthew Ziegler, an assassin likely working for ZFT, who opens the canister and releases the toxic gas. His goal is to find a microchip (which, unbeknownst to him, Agent Mendoza has surgically inserted in the palm of her hand for safekeeping) that has information on it vital to ZFT. The organization for which he's working is serious about concealing their plot. ZFT inspires a certain zealotry and sense of duty reminiscent of the most unyielding terrorist organizations. Nina later confirms the microchip is one of many Massive Dynamic has found.

"The Arrival" features mob killer John Mosley trying to procure information about the mysterious metal cylinder that surfaced in a construction site under the careful watch of the Observer. Like Ziegler, Mosley is unwavering in his task, torturing and killing several people for the sake of this strange cylindrical device. There is no evidence that he is working for a group, but his technical understanding of the mind-reading device and his undying determination to get the cylinder suggest that he isn't just a mafia man. He seems to have a vested interest in the mysterious cylinder, which appears to be an extremely advanced piece of technology. He must also know about the Observers, which raises suspicion about a relationship between ZFT and the Observers.

In "Power Hungry" Dr. Jacob Fischer is researching the weaponization of humans. To find willing subjects he establishes a self-help center, to which the vulnerable Joseph Meegar falls victim. This utter disregard for ethical protocol demonstrates Fischer's strict adherence to the principles of ZFT. He's clearly a fanatical disciple of radical scientific progress. After abducting and strapping down Meegar to a lab table he says, "Look what science has made you: special."

In "The Cure" David Esterbrook takes advantage of vulnerable patients suffering from Bellini's lymphocemia, a (fictional) terminal disease, so that he can apply them with radiation and turn them into human bombs. Esterbrook is the head of INtREPUS, a pharmaceutical company, and it is not clear how close his connections are to the ZFT cells.

Characters affiliated with ZFT: William Bell, Walter Bishop, Nicholas Boone, Marshall Bowman, Grant Davidson, Ryan Eastwick, Sanford Harris, Daniel Hicks, David Robert Jones, Mitchell Loeb, Samantha Loeb, Raul Lugo, Conrad Moreau, John Mosley, Joanne Ostler, Joseph Smith, Richard and Morgan Steig, Isaac Winters, Matthew Ziegler

Characters with possible links to ZFT: Cameron Deglmann, David Esterbrook, Jacob Fischer, George Morales, Claus Penrose, John Scott, Nina Sharp, Dr. Bruce Sumner, Jonathan Swift

ZFT Activity

The plots of these first six episodes of *Fringe* are never explicitly linked to ZFT, even after the organization is mentioned. Most of the nefarious schemes in the remaining episodes of season 1 are more cohesive and tie directly to ZFT. These emerging connections make the narrative more interesting, much more compelling than the seemingly standalone monster-of-the-week episodes that had dominated the show to that point. The ZFT thread helps to escalate the stakes of the drama by making clear the nature of the force the Fringe team faces.

"In Which We Meet Mr. Jones" introduces viewers to two key players: David Robert Jones and Mitchell Loeb. Though it is not revealed until the end of the episode, FBI Agent Loeb is a loyal follower, or perhaps just a well-paid employee, of David Robert Jones, the purported leader of ZFT at this point in the narrative. Jones, former employee of Massive Dynamic, is serving time in a German prison for stealing government intelligence. According to Nina he is a disgruntled researcher who has an ax to grind with William Bell.

When Jones attempts to get some information from Joseph Smith, a suspect in a shipping fraud case that Mitchell Loeb is supposedly investigating, Smith becomes a central target for the Fringe team. His background in science and frequent travels abroad make him a likely candidate for ZFT involvement. Since Smith is not in voluntary contact with Jones, it is clear that he is estranged from the group, or at least that particular cell. Later, in "Midnight," we learn that things don't usually end well for defectors of ZFT and such is the case for Mr. Smith.

Mitchell Loeb, it turns out, has aligned himself with Jones, and his plans are revealed in "The Equation" and "Safe" when we see what he and Jones have in the works. First they abduct a child virtuoso who, by way of musical composition, is able to provide Loeb with the solution to a complicated mathematical problem. When Loeb inputs the solution into a special computer it allows him to physically pass through solid matter. In "Safe" it becomes clear that Loeb and Jones want this technology to locate isolated components of a machine located in various safe deposit boxes. None other than Walter himself created it, and he hid it in pieces in several different locations, places he can no longer remember. The machine would allow anyone to travel instantaneously through space and/or time. Jones wants Loeb to reassemble it and use it as a means to escape from Wissenschaft Prison. One of Loeb's partners in crime for this project is Raul Lugo, an old friend of John Scott. Is this yet another clue that John Scott was deeply involved with ZFT?

The possibility of large-scale biological warfare is posed in "Bound" when the country's leading epidemiologists are assassinated by ZFT. Olivia's abduction takes us into a ZFT hideout, a place that exhibits all the characteristics of a mad scientist's lair. It's not the first makeshift lab we've seen — the ZFT cells seem to have safe houses all over, underground and in abandoned warehouses. The setting adds a sense of horror to what this covert group is doing. An old, decrepit building is a scary location to practice science, especially if human subjects are involved. Later when Olivia identifies Loeb as the instigator he cryptically tells her, "Do you not understand the rules? What we're up against? Who the two sides are?" What rules is Loeb referring to? Who established the rules? And further are the "two sides" the two universes? If so, does this mean Loeb is potentially a hero? Even by season 3 Loeb has not returned nor have any other ZFT agents. The Fringe team could certainly use their help if trans-universal warfare is what they have been training for.

ZFT is never mentioned in "The Transformation" but Broyles asserts that a suspect named Conrad Moreau was allegedly involved in "half a dozen biological attacks" and adds that "he's been manufacturing biological weapons and distributing them on the black market for years." This guy sounds like a key player in ZFT, but the general tone of this episode suggests that there is another incentive for getting involved in ZFT: money. Although science plays its usual central role, the presence of organized crime transforms a normal monster-of-the-week episode into a high-stakes undercover heist. The trafficking of biological weapons is big business, and Olivia and Peter are in over their heads when they meet with the sellers.

Marshall Bowman and Daniel Hicks seem at first to be deeply entrenched in this world, but after Olivia discovers their identity as NSA agents, she realizes that ZFT's reach is much broader than she initially imagined. ZFT's access to things like DNA-altering serums is a frightening notion.

In "Ability" a strange relationship emerges between Olivia and Jones. It is clear that Jones wants her to know that she is part of something bigger, that she is one of the soldiers mentioned in the ZFT manifesto. But why? What is Jones's plan for Olivia in the long-term? At first he just seems like one of those villains who singles out a particular authority figure to torment, but in retrospect we can see that there must be some connection to Bell and Walter, some shared history that involves the development of Olivia's special abilities.

This is also the episode when Peter and Walter finally get their hands on the manifesto, courtesy of their bibliophile friend Markham. Over the phone Peter explains to Olivia that the manifesto "reads like a happy combo between an anti-science manifesto and a call to arms." If Peter ever read Walter's official lab notes (the set of documents created for the official *Fringe* site in season 1) he might find a striking similarity between the style of the manifesto and Walter's distinctive writing voice. Even though Walter believes that the book was written by Bell, he probably had more to do with it than he can remember.

The transgenetic manipulation seen in "Unleashed" suggests the work of ZFT but neither Dr. Robert Swift nor his associate Cameron Deglmann is explicitly connected to a group. In contrast Dr. Nicholas Boone reveals quite a bit about ZFT in "Midnight." He admits to the Fringe team that he worked for the clandestine organization until he found out about the unethical nature of some of their practices. His attempt to defect from the group resulted in an attack on his wife, Valerie. They infected her with a virus that turned her into a vampire-like monster that goes on murderous rampages in search of spinal fluid. When the Fringe team finds him Boone is frantically trying to develop an effective antidote, one that ZFT is withholding. In exchange for help finding and curing his wife Boone provides Olivia with intelligence on ZFT, including the shocking allegation that William Bell is funding the organization. Boone also reveals that the scientists involved are primarily concerned with exhibiting their own cutting edge research to other scientists no matter the consequences. According to Boone all of these horrific experiments are a way for them to "show off."

Following John Scott, Mitchell Loeb, and Grant Davidson comes yet another federal agent associated with ZFT: Sanford Harris. In "The Road Not Taken" Harris works with Isaac Winters in the weaponization of Susan Pratt and her sister, Nancy Lewis. This is not the first time these twins have been victimized by men with close links to ZFT. Walter and Bell's cortexiphan trials made the sisters "special," and now they are being targeted. If only Walter could remember his own role in the experiment, he could protect Susan and Nancy. Through their story the terrible negligence of Walter and Bell is truly revealed.

In this episode Walter begins to understand his connection to the Pattern. The shocking discovery that the manifesto was written on the typewriter in Walter's lab is the first solid piece of evidence that connects Bell and Walter to ZFT. When Olivia confronts Walter about his involvement in all of the ZFT-connected events, he admits that he and Bell were trying to prepare the children for the future but he still doesn't have a clear handle on what they were planning. The irony emerges as he reads aloud from the manifesto's chapter on ethics: "Our children are our greatest resource. We must nurture them and protect them. We must prepare them so they can one day protect us." And yet it seems preposterous to think that Bell and Walter ever valued those cortexiphan children as their "greatest resource." It is obvious that they have not been protected, and no one has prepared them to control their abilities, let alone to participate in a war.

The final episode of season one is the culmination of David Robert Jones's narrative. The objectives of ZFT as a whole are unclear but Jones, the leader of one of the more active cells, makes it his mission to travel to the other universe. Over the course of several episodes this serves as the group's central objective, ending in the death of Jones. The powerful device that was hidden inside Nina's arm is a necessary component in Jones's construction of a gate to the other universe. This is a technology supposedly created by Bell; however it seems evident that Walter was the only one to ever use a portal to the other side, a machine he developed when Bell was traveling abroad in 1985. This mode of crossing over is apparently the most destructive to the fabric of the universe. Even Walter has refused to ever use it again. He knows the danger, and, in fact, the central objective of the Fringe team in this finale is to prevent such destruction: if Jones successfully crosses over, the consequences could be cataclysmic.

Their other goal is to ensure that Jones doesn't murder William Bell. When Jones finally finds a stable opening to the other side, Walter thwarts his plan and closes the inter-universe portal just in time, slicing Jones in half and killing him as he attempts to cross over. But why does Jones want to murder Bell in the first place? Sure, he was angry about a spat fifteen years before, but is it possible that Jones wanted to become the undisputed leader of ZFT? Bell may very well be the organization's high priest; perhaps Jones was attempting some sort of coup, a violent shift of power from Bell to himself. This would explain why the manifesto was altered — to undermine the authority of the original author and shape the organization's ideology.

The Manifesto

Where do the laws of a clandestine organization originate? Many times a religious text is sufficient as a "book of rules"; it is reinterpreted to fit the group's fundamental objectives. But often there is a single author who creates an original document to clearly establish the organization's doctrine. Such is the case with ZFT's manifesto, with William Bell as the alleged author.

The manifesto is crucial to understanding ZFT, even if, as Walter claims, the followers have altered its original meaning. In the copy that the Fringe team procured someone has removed the chapter on ethics and, therefore, obscured the entire message ("The Road Not Taken").

In the alternate universe this same manifesto is a widely read best-seller, presumably written by Walternate. This gives rise to a number of questions. If Walternate actually *is* the author then it would follow that Walter, not Bell, wrote the same text on this side. However with so much back and forth between the universes, who's to say that each universe has its own author? It's possible that either one or the other (Walternate or Walter) wrote it, or that Bell was the single author and brought it over to the other universe and, for whatever reason, shared it with Walternate. But it doesn't seem likely that Bell wrote it by himself. Usually when Walter attributes something to Bell, it turns out that Walter was involved too.*

Even so it still seems most likely that Walternate, or at least someone in the alternate universe, wrote the zFT book, simply because the text mentions that those from the other universe were the first to traverse worlds: "The unknown truth is that the means to cross over have already been discovered by beings much like us but whose history is slightly ahead of our own." Since the entire plot revolves around Walter's initial invasion of the other side, it stands to reason that this could only have been written from the perspective of the alternate universe, even though we've always assumed that the altverse is more advanced than the over-here-verse. Further Walternate's signature tone is reflected in the text. It says that "only one side will prevail. And it will be either us or them." We already know that Walternate is ready to fight no matter the cost to the other universe.** Walternate is also likely to comment that the coming war is "a battle of survival," as the manifesto argues, and to call children "our greatest resource." Though certainly not a sentiment particular only to Walternate, he's very concerned with the welfare of children and especially bitter about not being able to protect his own son.

That said, Walter's writing voice is also reflected in the manifesto.

* Like when he said that he had nothing to do with initiating the cortexiphan trials and yet, as we know, he played a key role in experimenting on children.

** His polarizing style of leadership is not unlike a recent U.S. administration that led its country headlong into a war, telling other nations that they were "either with us or against us."

Much of the document reads like the ravings of a madman, and some of the points are incomplete or incoherent, similar to Walter's thought process. In addition, Walter's lab notes from season 1 are comparable to the language used in the manifesto. But, of course, the two Walters could reasonably share a similar style of writing.

Most notably Walter-esque is the metaphor used to describe the universe. Only Walter would compare it to a bowl of pudding. It was pudding, after all, over which Walter obsessed while at St. Claire's, making a point to tell Olivia how "dreadful" the butterscotch pudding was. In season 3 Astrid draws Walter away from Peter's bedside with the temptation of this particular dessert ("The Last Sam Weiss"). The manifesto states that the world we know is just the "skin on a bowl of pudding," an observation likely made by someone with a very peculiar fondness for pudding.

The manifesto also explains that what we perceive as reality is just a tiny little "membrane" in the larger scheme of things (the multiverse) and that other beings, much like us, exist in an alternate universe. At this point it is unclear whether "they" are the inhabitants of the original universe (Olivia's world) or what we have been referring to as the alternate universe (Fauxlivia's world). But it is unquestionable that, from the author's perspective, these Other people should be considered adversaries, and that there is no hope for diplomacy between the two worlds: they are "not of our world and as such should be treated as enemies."

Parts of the text clearly support the case that it was written in the other universe, but others seem to negate this fact. The author's point that the Others' arrival will wreak great havoc in the universe, ending in irreversible damage, suggests that he (the author) must be from the alternate universe since it was Walter who made the initial breach. But the author also notes that some of these enemies are already living among us, which refers to the shapeshifters who have infiltrated the original universe.

The following summary of the manifesto could reflect authorship from either side: an apocalyptic war is unavoidable, but our government is not prepared for this kind of armageddon. As such, special soldiers must be trained to fight in this war and the "unknowing" must be guided in the right direction. Only a few bloodlines are equipped to fight in this "battle of survival." A selection process called the "gift of continuance" will choose those who "are gifted at the molecular level."

Most notable is the author's insistence that ethics and rules of social behavior will not apply to this process in which "morality has no place." This disturbing sentiment doesn't sound like something Walter would say, at least not in any of the episodes prior to season 3, but we should consider the fact that Walter and Walternate are not all that different. In fact in "6B" Walter admits to Nina that, given the same circumstances, his decisions and judgment are eerily similar to Walternate's: "I'm arguing that we do exactly what he did. What sort of person does that make me?" Walter, as head of one of the biggest corporations in the world, feels the weight of responsibility that comes with great power in this episode. As executive of Massive Dynamic he holds a position comparable in status to Walternate's job. It is probable that Walter is just as inextricably connected to ZFT as he is to Massive Dynamic, considering that the two organizations are completely entangled.

CHAPTER 4

Massive Dynamic
the corporate Conglomerate

"Did I invent ZFT? Flight 627? The North Woods Group? John Scott? The Pattern? The whole thing is a hoax. It's all a smoke screen so Massive Dynamic can do whatever it wants — to whoever it wants. Do you understand that? Massive Dynamic is Hell . . . and its founder, William Bell, is the Devil."

— George Morales, "The Dreamscape"

That a powerful, ethically shady corporate entity is operating within the mythology of a J.J. Abrams creation is unsurprising. Look at the Hanso Foundation and Paik Industries in *Lost*. Or consider *Alias* with its international criminal organization, Alliance of 12, a multinational clandestine group with far-reaching control. Then there is Massive Dynamic, the most mysterious high-tech company on television. A puppet master corporation is a staple of the darker components of science fiction: something always goes awry when a wealthy sociopathic sponsor gets mixed up with science or when a mad scientist finds himself in a position of great economic power.

But where does this theme originate? What inspires the mystery and suspicion that surrounds large corporations in real life? Is it the potential they have to control the minds of their consumers? It's true that Facebook has access to some fairly intimate details of its users' lives and that Google has become a panopticon of the earth, continually re-photographing every street around the globe. Then there are the retail giants aggressively targeting children and adults alike, telling us what new gadgets we can't live without. Unlike George Orwell's totalitarian world in his dystopian novel *1984*, we don't need to worry so much about the government engaging in mind control. Rather it is the corporate conglomerates that are training, teaching, manipulating, monitoring, and studying everything we do. Or, as Neil Postman famously argued in *Amusing Ourselves to Death*, Aldous Huxley, not Orwell, correctly prophesied the future in *Brave New World*. In the foreword to the classic text on the vacuity of consumer culture, Postman neatly summarizes its central point: "As [Huxley] saw it, people will come to love their oppression, to adore the technologies that undo their capacities to think" (xix).

In *Fringe*'s pilot episode Agent Charlie Francis notes the overbearing supremacy of privately controlled institutions compared to the dwindling power of his own state-funded operation. In a conversation with Agent Dunham he contrasts their own lack of influence as government agents with Massive Dynamic's corporate muscle: "We're supposed to protect the world, where one breath of the wrong air can incinerate you from the inside out. I mean, how do we protect people when corporations have higher security clearances than we do? When we're not fully briefed on half the things that we're investigating? You know, when the truth is . . . we're obsolete." Does this reflect the real world? Do other institutions, including family, religion, and education, pale in comparison to the allure of big business?

Let's consider Huxley's prophetic novel more closely to see if it reflects modern-day life. In *Brave New World* time is recorded not in relation to a religious figure (A.D.), but in connection to the death of Henry Ford (A.F.). Religion has been replaced by consumerism. These characters are controlled by the most enthralling propaganda of all: promises of instant gratification and eternal contentment. They are slaves to their own pleasure. In the real world we may not measure time in terms of the birth of mass production, but it does seem that retailers mark the big holidays for us, determining when Christmastime begins and ends. Through sentimental advertising they instruct how and when to express our love for others. For many families, the Disney Corporation has more influence on family tradition than, say, Memorial Day or All Saints' Day.

And, like the society in *Brave New World*, typical modern-day consumers are in essence ruled by the instant gratification they receive from consumer goods: the latest gadgets, new clothes for every new season, a deluge of devices for mom and baby, an array of toys for the children, and an endless supply of information and entertainment.

But unlike the automatons of *Brave New World* many consumers are still concerned about the "masterminds" behind the most prosperous companies. When a clever, innovative college student is catapulted to CEO of a multibillion-dollar corporation, everyone starts paying attention. When private businesses begin to profit by selling genetically modified food, opposition soon follows. No matter how much they love its technology and/or the affordability of its products, many consumers question the large corporation that is pocketing great profits.

It's justifiable to have reservations when huge companies acquire small, local businesses, or to be skeptical of large corporate interests in general. But imagine if Google, Disney, Dow Chemical, Microsoft, and General Dynamics were joined under one roof, with only one CEO and one set of stockholders. That would be Massive Dynamic. Software companies like Google, Apple, and Microsoft, or biotechnology firms like Genentech, are the only businesses that come close to what we see in *Fringe*. There is no single company (to date) that is comparable to the fictional Massive Dynamic, but the idea of a corporation with its "hand in everything" is a thing to be feared . . . and always a popular trope in science fiction.

Nina Sharp

Massive Dynamic is first featured when Olivia's attempt to speak with William Bell ends with a meeting in Nina's office instead ("Pilot"). Despite William Bell's name being thrown around as the "wealthiest man in the world" as founder of Massive Dynamic, Nina Sharp is truly the face of the company. She clearly knows everything that goes on behind the scenes, but she never reveals more than necessary. In an interview, Blair Brown, the actress who plays Nina, commented on the nature of Massive Dynamic: "Like most big corporations, they have their good side and they have their evil twin." Nina is the chief operating officer (COO) and Walter Bell's "right hand" as he says in a letter at the reading of his will (an ironic comment, considering that Nina is missing her right forearm). It is implied that her relationship with Bell was also romantic in nature. The Massive Dynamic website describes her as one of the founding partners and says that she "has overseen the firm's rise from feisty start-up to multinational conglomerate."

The first private conference between Olivia and Nina brings to light one of the key components of a successful company: its image in the public eye. Nina reveals that Richard Steig, the instigator of the Glatterflug incident, is a former employee of Massive Dynamic and may have stolen some of its research. But she warns Olivia that if the FBI exposes the company in a negative light, Massive Dynamic will take swift legal action against them.

At this same meeting Nina also shows Olivia her robotic arm, explaining that she "owes her life" to Massive Dynamic and the work of William Bell. She is at once the faithful, dedicated employee and the power-wielding executive. She claims that the injury to her arm was the result of cancer, but later Walter reveals a different story. At this point Nina is either covering for William Bell and Massive Dynamic, for Walter, or, more likely, for both. She is also invested in portraying Massive Dynamic as a virtuous company.

Nina's relationship with Olivia is an interesting one — she is both protective and hostile toward her. Even by the end of season 3 Nina continues to be a morally ambiguous character, never revealing her true intentions. Is she an antagonist or just an enabler of the mad scientists in her life? She clearly defends the righteousness of her company's cause and the technological promise that their products hold, but she also is well aware of the dangers that drastic advances in man-made devices can unleash. She tells Olivia that science and technology have advanced beyond the capacity of humans to maintain it ("Pilot"). Is this a sincere warning or is Nina just making excuses for not taking responsibility for, and control of, her company's more hazardous inventions? Many of Massive Dynamic's research projects are inadvertently leaked by estranged employees. The company's innovations always seem to wind up in the wrong hands. Are these accidents or is it all part of William Bell's (and Nina's) larger plan?

William Bell and His Double?

In season 1 William Bell doesn't appear on screen until the finale, "There's More Than One of Everything," when he summons Olivia to the alternate universe. He tells her that a war is coming and that she must be the keeper of the gate and a soldier for her universe. Though he is profiting at an unprecedented level, Bell and his fellow citizens of the original universe will all pay a great price for all of the new gadgets and advances in science that he has introduced.

William Bell's rise to success and Walter's fall from grace were simultaneous. And yet the original vision of the company, the central source of Bell's success, was Walter's idea alone. Bell says, "Creating Massive Dynamic was not my idea, Walter. We both talked about borrowing this world's technologies to help our own" ("Over There, Part 2"). Could Bell and Walter actually be the same person, or does Bell only exist in the alternate universe? After all, we've never seen him in the original universe with the exception of a brief cameo in a flashback of Walter's ("Grey Matters"), a possibly unreliable memory.* Perhaps Walter somehow was the owner of Massive Dynamic all along and William Bell was just an alter ego created to prop up the company while Walter was locked away. Bell supposedly started up Massive Dynamic in 1992, three years after Walter was charged with murder and sent to St. Claire's. But it was previous to this incident that Nina lost her arm to the alternate universe. Walter was chiefly responsible for Nina's arm, so wouldn't he naturally be the one to fix things? Perhaps this alter ego, if it *is* only that, is a foreshadowing of what's to come for almost all of the characters: their doppelgängers. Walter has his double in Walternate, of course, but what if he's already been operating within the structure of an alternate self, and the alternate universe is just a reflection of what's been happening all along in Walter's extraordinary mind? Bell is the practical, organized, coherent answer to Walter's fuzzy-minded eccentricity. And the two men do share the same initials. Bell propels Walter to greater heights and, once Walter steps in for Bell at Massive Dynamic, he seems to become more closely associated with the Bell persona. If nothing else, the two men achieve a kind of balance usually reserved for the

---

* Aside from his spiritual possession of Olivia.

doubling of one individual character; they are representation of the split self.

Other Massive Dynamic Employees

As mentioned in the previous chapter, David Robert Jones worked for the company at one point in time; he was one of the first employees and was supposedly close to William Bell. He was fired from his job, but Nina never reveals the details of this incident. The company's lab scientist, Brandon, though not featured in season 1, becomes a key player in later episodes, welcoming the Fringe team into the Massive Dynamic labs to explain some of the finer points of time travel and molecular instability. Other employees mentioned throughout the series are Richard Steig, the former researcher who was involved in the Glatterflug incident in the pilot episode; Mark Young, who jumped to his death from the Massive Dynamic high rise after he believed that he was being wounded by a swarm of butterflies; and Dr. James Carson, the aerospace scientist who was responsible for exposing his "son" to the company's research on mind control ("Of Human Action"). This boy Tyler Carson is actually one of many "Tylers," clones subjected to Massive Dynamic's experiment in which a scientist acts as guardian to a cloned child.

Products and Research

J.J. Abrams once described Massive Dynamic as "a company that seems to own everything." But what does Massive Dynamic do exactly? What are their signature technological advancements? Their boastful slogan "what *don't* we do?" suggests a sense that Massive Dynamic wields far more power in more fields than any other company in the fictional universe of *Fringe*. Its branches include biological and medical, computing and communications, environment and energy, aerospace and transportation, and life and leisure. As noted earlier, Massive Dynamic is an amalgamation of at least five very different real-world companies.

Massive Dynamic's products, marked with an "M," can be seen in the background of various scenes: in the pilot episode there are the plane engines and the satellites, in "The Arrival" we see the Massive Dynamic construction crane, and in "The Same Old Story," the electronic pulse camera. Other research is mentioned in passing, usually with the implication that it can be traced back to William Bell's original designs (which can, in turn, be traced back to the alternate universe). Massive Dynamic's website provides details about their cutting edge technologies in ludic science (videogames), which "progressively erase the line between the virtual and the real," and special effects. They "promise to revolutionize commercial transport" and to reduce travel time, making "near-instantaneous travel a reality in your lifetime." In communications and computing they offer such futuristic concepts as artificial intelligence and synthetic biology. Like Walter, Massive Dynamic also has the technology to obtain information from the brains of the recently deceased. When they first bring in the body of John Scott, a lab attendant informs Nina that he has been dead for five hours. "Question him," Nina commands. The casual way in which she makes this request suggests that this is a regular occurrence, but it gives rise to a host of questions about this company. What kind of research are they doing on the human brain? What do they know about human consciousness that they are keeping to themselves? In what manner did they discover this information? What are the company's ethical guidelines on human experimentation?

Like interrogating people from beyond the dead, a notion that is revisited in several episodes, other concepts that emerge from Massive Dynamic's labs are usually both highly advanced and ethically questionable. In addition it's hard to know whether the work originated in this universe or the alternate one. It turns out that Bell is guilty of a good deal of plagiarism, but the extent to which he has appropriated the other world's technology is still unknown.

In any case almost all of the scientific innovations (or abominations) that the Fringe Division is called on to investigate seem to be linked to Massive Dynamic in one way or another. In "The Dreamscape" the drug responsible for killing the Massive Dynamic employee and then George Morales was formulated at one of the corporation's labs. In the pilot episode it is a former employee with knowledge of the company's research who infects the people on the airplane. In "The Cure" there is an implication that Nina Sharp may have something to do with the unscrupulous pharmaceutical company, INtREPUS, which is using humans as lab rats. And most significant, David Robert Jones, supreme leader of bioterrorist group ZFT, is a former (disgruntled) employee of Massive Dynamic. His propagation of radical scientific and technological advancements seems to be inspired by, if not stolen from, his employer. According to Nina quite some time has passed since he was employed there, so it's hard to say what research he actually took. In "Midnight" Dr. Boone, a well-accomplished scientist who claimed to be working for ZFT, reveals in a video that William Bell is responsible for the horrific effects of all of ZFT's work. Boone claims that Bell is funding the whole operation.

Other Influential Businesses in Fringe
INtREPUS

INtREPUS is a pharmaceutical company owned by David Esterbrook that specializes in "prenatal gene therapy, human-animal hybridization, and viral warfare," according to Charlie's investigation in "The Cure." It appears to be a rival of Massive Dynamic's pharmaceutical division. They experiment on patients suffering from Bellini's lymphocemia by implanting radioactive, time-released capsules in the bloodstream. The capsules can then be activated remotely, at which time the victim and anyone in close proximity dies from exposure to high levels of radiation. Like Claus Penrose in "The Same Old Story" INtREPUS is in the business of preparing human beings to be soldiers, assassins, and even bombs. This is decidedly the epitome of an "evil corporation," experimenting on unwilling human subjects and then throwing them out like garbage, or sending them out as unwilling agents of destruction.

To a lesser extent William Bell and Walter did the same thing to their cortexiphan subjects. Though it was before they were organized as a company, Bell and Walter used the cortexiphan kids to further their own research and glorify themselves as scientists. Later Walter would attempt to use the outcome of this experiment to prevent a war with the other side by trying to send Peter back with Olivia.

Kelvin Genetics and Swift Research

Kelvin Genetics is a small pharmaceutical and biotech firm sponsored by the U.S. Army. Walter and William Bell worked on some of their projects in the 1980s. Its activities were supposedly overseen by DARPA (Defense Advanced Research Projects Agency), a governmental organization responsible for developing new technology for the military. Walter claims that during his time with Kelvin Genetics he developed a method for hybridizing animals but, as with many projects, he never followed through with it and suspects that the research fell into the wrong hands.

In "Unleashed" we see the consequences of this kind of research. Swift Research has taken the existing theories about radical transgenics and applied them, creating a monstrous hybrid reminiscent of the creations of Dr. Moreau. In this episode animal rights activists break into a Swift Research lab to release the animals. Inadvertently they let out a dangerous experimental creature.

The Convention of "Evil Corporations" in Science Fiction

What is it about the private sector that inspires suspicion in the general public, making individuals imagine that the worst case scenario is being played out behind closed doors? The mystery and shadow that surround real-life corporations is replicated in science fiction narratives to illustrate these fears, and sometimes these fictional entities shed light on what could happen within real corporate conglomerates. The dangers of an overly corporatized society range from what we currently experience in terms of aggressive marketing and dishonest trading to an all-out corporate-controlled government that wields its powers over all citizens.

Notable fictional companies include Lex Luthor's profitable corporation in the Superman stories; *Blade Runner*'s Tyrell Corporation (which produces lifelike androids designed to work as slave labor); Wolfram & Hart, the demonic law firm from *Angel*; and Weyland-Yutani, the unambiguously evil corporation from the *Alien* film series. Lunar Industries from 2009's *The Moon* is another organization that implements projects with terrifying implications. In this film an employee astronaut, who has been working in solitude on the moon for several years, uncovers Lunar Industry's nefarious plans for him. *Robocop* offers a depiction of how society might look if entire nations were operated by a single company. In this world the government has become corporatized and Omni Consumer Products runs all aspects of its citizens'/customers' lives. It is in charge of everything, including the proliferation of social deviants. The government funds criminal organizations and law enforcement equally to keep things balanced and to keep police officers employed.

"All the Myriad Ways"

A comparable entity to Massive Dynamic and a possible inspiration for the scientifically advanced corporation can be found in Larry Niven's short story "All the Myriad Ways." In this narrative, first published in the 1970s, Niven explores the psychological implications of Hugh Everett III's Many-Worlds Interpretation. In 1957 Everett postulated that all outcomes of a "quantum experiment" are happening simultaneously and that all possible variations of the future are continuously branching out. In other words, every time we make a decision, another world opens up where we made the opposite decision and continue our lives with the consequences of that choice.

In "All the Myriad Ways" an increasingly powerful company, Crosstime Corporation, finds a way to cross parallel universes and return with highly advanced technologies. The company earns incredible profits as it patents these finds. They continue to send pilots to other worlds, compounding their profitability.

The growing corporation and its wealthy founder are at the center of this multiverse plot. Like William Bell who pillaged the other universe for its technology, the head of this company, Ambrose Harmon, has reaped the benefits of "crossing over," becoming extraordinarily wealthy in a short period of time. At the beginning of the story Harmon is found dead and Gene Trimball, a police detective investigating his death, tries to wrap his mind around the multiple universe theory.

Trimball slowly discovers that, for some reason, unrestrained access to other universes has led to an upsurge in violent crimes and suicide, especially suicides of the Crosstime pilots. There are dark consequences to these journeys. The investigators at the scene of Harmon's death determine that his was also a suicide; it was reported that he just walked off his balcony.

As Trimball investigates the high suicide rate among Crosstime

Corporation's employees, he searches Harmon's business accounts for clues. He can't seem to find any plausible motive or an underlying cause for the rash of cases. But he does know that the "universes of alternate choice" have something to do with it. Unlike in the world of *Fringe*, traversing universes is public information, a notion embraced by all. Crosstime discovered the portals and has claimed exclusive rights to this kind of travel and to all of the inventions that result from it. The company holds all of the patents to "lasers, oxygen-hydrogen rocket motors, computers, strange plastics — the list was still growing" (171).

Trimball, "convinced as he was that Crosstime was involved in the suicides" (173), is concerned that the city's murder rate is increasing too. People are engaging in violent crime at unprecedented rates, usually without a clear motive. Trimball characterizes the behavior as a virus, a toxin for which Crosstime and Ambrose Harmon are solely responsible. The company has destroyed the world by pushing technology to a point where morality is irrelevant to the common person. The company has exposed the world to the notion that every possible outcome of every decision exists in other realities. The idea that there exists a version of oneself who will always make the *other* decision leads to mass mayhem. Ambrose Harmon, founder of all these might-have-beens, kills himself because "if alternate universes are a reality then cause and effect is an illusion. You can do anything and one of you will, or did" (175).

In *Fringe*, according to Bell, he and Walter had always intended to develop a company by growing rich off borrowed technology from alternate universes. Knowing their affiliations with other science fiction writers — Walter supposedly knew Arthur C. Clarke personally and William Bell claims Isaac Asimov is an old friend — it's likely they were friends with, or at least readers of, Larry Niven. But if they were indeed familiar with this short story, they certainly did not heed its warnings. Massive Dynamic's advanced technology comes at a high price, the highest price of all — the entire universe.

A Massive Network of Influence

The most intriguing mysteries that still remain are questions about affiliations between Massive Dynamic, ZFT, and the state. How are they connected and who authorized their cooperation? And to further connect the dots: what is the relationship between the Fringe Division and Massive Dynamic or, more precisely, between Nina and Broyles? What are the motives of Massive Dynamic, a company that already "owns everything"? Since Massive Dynamic does have so much power over military and communications, should citizens be concerned that their country is overly corporatized? How much control does Massive Dynamic really have over millions, maybe even billions, of lives?

CHAPTER 5

The End of the World
IMPENDING WAR AND DESTRUCTION

"A storm is coming, perhaps the last and worst storm of all. And when it is over, I fear there will be little left of our world."
— William Bell, "Momentum Deferred"

Like many science fiction narratives *Fringe* serves as a cautionary tale about the perils of unrestrained technology. The threat of man-made catastrophic events looms large in the world of *Fringe*; a shadow of potential doom continually hangs over the FBI team as they work against the clock to rid the world of dangerous genetic experiments and bioterrorism. The fear of an uncertain future has been woven into each episode; the possibility of an apocalypse is a notion made quite clear in the ZFT manifesto.

There are two types of cautionary tales when it comes to apocalyptic narratives: one features self-destruction and the other is fueled by aggression from outside forces. Both of these threads exist in *Fringe*. The heroes of *Fringe* are called upon to keep radical technological and scientific advances under control, but they will also have to confront a kind of warfare unprecedented in the history of their universe.

Fringe addresses the very human fear that life as we know it can end at any time without warning. A sense of "high alert" mounts with each episode and there is a continuing preoccupation with potential mass destruction. For followers of ZFT this "world's end" scenario is inevitable, and for the alternate universe, it is already happening.

But what is the significance of this doomsday theme? The notion that the world must be saved certainly makes for exciting fiction, facilitating the emergence of a hero. In *Lost*, for example, the recurring notions of a coming war and "the end of everything" give the characters a higher purpose and inspire heroic acts in many of them. Reading or watching narratives with this apocalyptic possibility helps the audience leave trivial matters behind, as they consider a more noble purpose, if only in the fictional world. In *Fringe* Olivia's calling to be a guardian of her own universe opens up a much broader role for her as the narrative's central heroine. Before joining the special team she was saving humanity one case at a time as a federal agent, but now she is called to save the whole world at once. These elevated stakes — and the epic scale of the task — bestow greater meaning on the narrative. As science fiction critic Eric S. Rabkin points out, "The modern popular literature of the end of the world continues humanity's permanent questioning of its place and its permanent quest for a reason to exist" (*The End of the World*, vii).

Guns, Germs, and Human Error: Catastrophic Endings
Ice-Nine

At the apocalyptic moment of Kurt Vonnegut's quirky novel *Cat's Cradle*, the narrator realizes that the mishandling of a single scientific "advancement" has brought things to the ecological tipping point. He describes the apocalypse as simply the shutting of a door: "There was a sound like that of the gentle closing of a portal as big as the sky, the great door of heaven being closed softly . . . the sky darkened. Borasisi, the sun, became a sickly yellow ball, tiny and cruel" (174). No large-scale war caused this world's end; rather, it was the work of a peculiar scientist and the carelessness of his children who were responsible for keeping his technology safe. Dr. Felix Hoenikker, also one of the (fictional) creators of the atomic bomb, was commissioned by the army to create a compound that would prevent soldiers from having to walk through mud during battle. Though it seems a trivial problem compared to the larger issue of warfare itself,

Dr. Hoenikker busied himself with the research, eventually creating ice-nine, an isotope that is solid at room temperature. It can instantly transform a muddy bog into a solid surface, but it can also "freeze" anything it touches, including human beings. It becomes apparent that this technology is far more destructive than the atomic bomb, which arguably *did* end the world for a particular population.

Throughout the story there is a pervasive fear that ice-nine will get into the wrong hands. Sure enough, it is human error that proves to be the undoing of the whole world. A simple mistake, a small spill into the ocean, transforms the world into a solid blue-white ball of ice-nine, causing a sweeping eradication of most of Earth's population. Among the inhabitants of San Lorenzo only a handful survive, and most are quick to commit suicide shortly after the transformation. This shocking notion, that one scientist could be responsible for such widespread devastation, is also central to *Fringe*.

Obliteration by Microbe

In Margaret Atwood's novel *Oryx and Crake* (2003), one of the main characters, a brilliant geneticist, creates a pandemic when he develops a rapidly spreading virus that is unleashed under the guise of a mandatory prophylactic. He comes close to annihilating the human race, and his apocalypse is very much an intentional one. Like the adherents of ZFT in *Fringe*, Crake believes that the world is on a fast track to self-destruction, and he decides to take the end of humanity into his own hands.

Before exposing humans to the virus, Crake creates another race of creatures, ones that are immune to the disease; they are also less intelligent and more peaceful than human beings, making them better suited for maintaining a healthy planet. They are genetic hybrids and would probably be of great interest to someone like Walter Bishop.

The tinkering of one scientist brings about a quick end to the world; the virus wipes out all but a few pockets of people. Crake's best friend, "Snowman," survives, responsible for leading the simple-minded "Crakers" into their new existence. And this is how the novel opens, with Snowman surrounded by a gaggle of green-eyed children. This scenario, the threat of a strange post-apocalyptic race of Earthlings, lingers in the subtext of *Fringe*. There is a strong possibility that the mechano-organic shapeshifters could overcome the human race. Like Crake the scientists affiliated with ZFT might welcome such a drastic upheaval. After all the central goal of their movement is "destruction through technology."

Bioterrorism

The X-Files, an obvious precursor to *Fringe*, with its focus on the FBI and its fascination with strange science, has its share of cautionary tales about man-made destruction. In the episode "Pine's Bluff Variant" domestic terrorists are responsible for releasing deadly organisms into a movie theater, killing fourteen people by way of an aggressive flesh-eating disease. The implications of this attack are frightening, especially since this militia group seems to be moving fast, ready with another attack on a bank the next day. What kind of fear and paranoia might something like this incite in the real world?

In *The Real Science Behind The X-Files* Dr. Anne Simon discusses the actual possibilities for this kind of warfare. She provides interesting real-life examples of the development of genetically engineered weapons. In 1992, for instance, it came to the international community's attention that the Soviet Union had been producing and stockpiling "twenty tons of plague bacteria, twenty tons of smallpox virus, and hundreds of tons of anthrax bacteria" over a period of twenty years (285). Thirteen years before, a small leak that virtually went unnoticed caused the deaths of sixty-six residents in the community of Sverdlovsk. At the time the Soviet government explained it away by identifying meat from anthrax-infected animals as the problem, but later it was revealed that the victims were exposed to several different strains of anthrax. According to Simon this means that "the Soviets were actively seeking ways to render the current anthrax vaccine impotent" (287). This is just one example of biological warfare programs. For about thirty years the United States government engaged in all kinds of biological experiments for the military until 1972 when they, along with more than 100 other nations, signed a treaty promising not to develop or stockpile microbial or other biological toxins.

But similar to the fictional ZFT and the group in "Pine's Bluff Variant" there are real threats from non-governmental organizations that have the means to produce biological weapons. Simon uses the example of Aum Shinrikyo in Japan, a group responsible for releasing sarin nerve gas in Tokyo's subway system, killing at least a dozen people. But since Simon's writing many terrorist cells have emerged across the globe, all of them with the potential to use these silent weapons. "Odorless, tasteless, easy to produce, and very cheap — it is no wonder that so many experts on terrorism are concerned," argues Simon. The small scale experiments that take place in enclosed spaces (the subway, a theater) are just the beginning of potentially catastrophic events. The fear that humankind will be the death of this world is not just a fanciful idea in science fiction. It is a real fear, more relevant in the twenty-first century than ever before. Whether pollution, overpopulation, or nuclear war is the cause, the danger is clear.

Let's now take a closer look at how the end of the world motif is played out in individual episodes of *Fringe*. The threat is ever-present, but sometimes just below the surface of the narrative.

Season 1: Threats on the Homefront

So what world-ending weapons has the Fringe team been able to unearth? In season 1 alone the innovations of science and engineering that have been unveiled as harmful technology include genetic mutation, radical transgenics, time travel, manipulation of solid matter, lethal psychosomatic disorders, radiation, telepathy, electromagnetism, viral contagions, and human weaponization.

In season 1 it is ZFT that threatens the safety of the world, or so it seems to the Fringe team and the numerous victims of ZFT's mysterious feats of scientific experimentation. If the Fringe division's speculation is correct, the organization is likely responsible for most Pattern-related events, and in this section I will discuss how they threaten global stability and the future of humanity. Based on the virulence of each of their technological exhibitions, it is plausible that any one of their schemes could have devastating consequences.

First of all let's consider the radical genetic mutation, the kind that we see in "The Transformation." Like the pilot episode this one begins in the passenger section of a commercial jet. A panicked man, Marshall Bowman, is in the bathroom looking at himself in the mirror; his nose is bleeding and a tooth falls out. Suddenly quills rapidly begin growing from his spine and it becomes clear that he is no longer human. Bowman is the victim of a "designer virus" that operates by rewriting the genetic code of those who are infected. Once he is fully transformed into a monster, he attacks everyone on board and the plane crashes. After investigating the site of the crash and learning more about the virus, Olivia and Peter embark on an undercover mission in an effort to apprehend a major weapons dealer. The virus and its antidote are being trafficked on the black market.

The consequences of developing and spreading such a contagion in the real world would be catastrophic. Assuming that this virus existed, the makers of such an organism could (if they so desired) infect any number of people and rewrite their genetic codes. If this were an airborne virus it could turn an entire nation of people into a swarm of gnats, or a group of mediocre soldiers into an army of blood-thirsty, bulletproof mutants.

Another possibility in the field of genetic mutation is what Walter calls radical transgenics, the product of which we see in "Unleashed," an episode featuring a monstrosity of a hybrid. Part bat, part "parasitic wasp," and part Gila monster, this transgenic creature is inadvertently released by an animal rights group when they break into a local laboratory to liberate the animal test subjects. It is interesting that one of the participants of this "liberation" is Jonathan Swift, namesake of the great satirist who might encourage such subversive acts. It recalls Swift's misanthropic texts, suggesting yet another cautionary signal to keep technology and "progress" in check.

Though Walter blames himself for this monster's existence, the men who were involved in the actual development of the hybrid are Robert Swift (Jonathan's father) and Cameron Deglmann. If they are affiliated with ZFT it is likely that Swift Research is profiting greatly from this work. The engineering of powerful organic machines that will quickly reproduce would be quite beneficial to a terrorist organization, even if the animal was used simply to incite fear in the group's enemies. But it would also wreak ecological havoc, considering it lacks a natural predator and has a strong genetic code designed for a high rate of survival.

In order to raise strong soldiers and weaponized humans, ZFT

INTO THE
LOOKING GLASS

has invested much of its research in experimenting on unsuspecting subjects. At the end of season 1 Peter and Olivia find evidence that William Bell's involvement in ZFT is closely linked to his cortexiphan trials on children. As mentioned earlier there are other cases of the cultivation of soldiers, such as the research featured in "The Same Old Story." In that episode Dr. Claus Penrose is trying to perfect an experiment that began when he worked for the United States Army (with Walter). The one thing he cannot alter is the subjects' rapid aging — without a certain hormone the synthetic humans tend to survive only a few days.

This research poses an important ethical question: would the army have continued this research if they *could* control the aging process? They would be able to create millions of clones, an unlimited supply of soldiers to defend and perhaps conquer the entire world. In the wrong hands this kind of technology could turn a small militia into a dominating force, one that could overturn central governments. Consider too that Claus Penrose escapes capture; he is out there somewhere, perhaps cultivating an army. If he succeeds he could quite possibly change the entire nature of humanity. Would these super clones be "real people"? Would they replace the weaker, if more individually unique, race of human beings? What kinds of rights would they have? If Penrose's ambitions echo those of Crake, the bioengineer in *Oryx and Crake*, his "children" might be able to repopulate the world in the case of an apocalypse.

As they are portrayed in *Fringe* bio-weapons such as flesh-eating bacteria, airborne viruses, and genetic manipulation pose serious threats to the entire human population. The manufacturing of microbes for purposes of destruction is certainly no small matter. Indeed if human beings do have a natural predator capable of destroying whole populations it is most certainly disease. The rapidly spreading toxic organisms are centrally featured in many apocalyptic narratives because the threat of bioterrorism is real. But according to Mitchell Loeb and others associated with ZFT there is an even bigger threat on the horizon. Loeb tells Olivia that he is just a soldier in a larger war, a struggle in which the enemy is more unrelenting than any virus.

Seasons 2 and 3: The Threat of "Foreign" Invaders

It cannot be ignored that the ZFT manifesto identifies something else as the threat, something that makes their "terrorist" activities pale in comparison. The followers all seem to share in common a confidence in the severity of the threat and a sense of military duty in their own efforts to thwart it. Though the leaders if ZFT are not clear about the force they are fighting in season 1, seasons 2, and 3 clarify the impending danger.

The following quotation from the ZFT manifesto was read as a voiceover by Walter in "Ability," but, as noted in chapter 3, it likely was written by Walternate.

> The negative aspect of such visitation will be irreversible both to our world and to theirs. It will begin with a series of unquantifiable natural occurrences difficult to notice at first but growing, not unlike a cancer, until a simple fact becomes undeniable: only one world will survive. It will either be us or them.

In season 1 ZFT carries out small-scale experiments, using enclosed public spaces as their laboratories and exposing only a few to the freakish products of their innovative bioengineering. Why are they doing this? Why expose a plane full of people to a flesh-eating air-borne toxin? Why alter a man's DNA so radically that he turns into a monster? If these experiments serve a higher purpose, one that involves fighting an unprecedented force, what kind of enemy are they anticipating?

Preparing for War

In a short video on Fox's official *Fringe* site titled "Just the Facts: The Coming War," *Fringe* executive producer J.H. Wyman suggests that the alternate universe might be waging war not just for revenge but to take over and inhabit the original universe and abandon their own dying world. This is the premise of many alien invasion movies, where the people of an uninhabitable planet are looking for a new, more hospitable home, something like Earth. The fear of destruction by extraterrestrial forces is a science fiction staple, but *Fringe* largely avoids alien stories. Instead the "foreign" threats are copies of the original characters; the "aliens" are people from an alternate universe.

In "Momentum Deferred" William Bell informs a skeptical Olivia that she has been prepared as a gatekeeper and soldier of their universe. Throughout season 1 it seems that the hazards confronting the Fringe team are contained in ZFT's activities, but Bell is worried about threats on a much larger level.

Taken together William Bell's warning of impending war, the scenario of the cortexiphan "soldiers," and the ZFT manifesto paint a picture of imminent doom. They also tell us that William Bell's involvement with ZFT was one of necessity. In fact it was probably William Bell who began the organization, disseminating cutting-edge scientific research via Massive Dynamic. In this way he develops defensive forces with advanced training and the materials necessary to fight a world more technologically savvy than our own.

William Bell, a regular traveler between universes, apparently has been trying to fix things ever since Walter initially opened the door to the other universe. It is Bell who brought over the technology from the more advanced world to his own, therefore growing an extremely profitable company. In the meantime he was also possibly funding ZFT, sending out former employees and new research to set up defenses all over the world — a clandestine group of scientists and engineers. Granted, many of these ideas are speculation, but they clearly explain why Bell has done what he's done. It also justifies much of the seemingly nefarious schemes ZFT carries out. If we are to consider that the experiments are small trials (or sometimes just accidents) to test their defense system against the other universe, ZFT's crimes don't seem as horrendous. It doesn't explain their zealous intolerance or the means by which they carry out some of the experiments, but it does clarify the severity of their mission.

In narratives like H.G. Wells' *War of the Worlds* the apocalyptic threat comes from an alien force and the humans have no power to stop it. Martians invade Earth and destroy humans in order to take over the planet. The end of the world seems imminent since the alien race is much more advanced than Earthlings, but it just so happens that the Martians are destroyed by tiny microbes. They lack the immune system to ward off certain Earth-bound illnesses. Thus, by chance, the world does not end and the Martians are defeated. There was no plan in place to use bio-warfare in *War of the Worlds* but in light of *Fringe*'s "war" it certainly seems like a good idea for them to consider it.

In "The Road Not Taken" one of the witnesses Olivia and Peter interview talks about the ongoing conflict between the United Federation of Planets and the Romulans, a race of people in *Star Trek* usually characterized as the antagonists. Though this witness believes that he is Spock and is obviously a bit crazy, his discussion of the fictional war foreshadows the epic scale conflict that is in store for this universe.

It is interesting to consider how the ZFT manifesto functions differently for each universe as a call to arms. As explored in the chapter on ZFT, it is unclear who actually wrote the document or if the same person was the author for both universes. Was it Walter and Walternate? William Bell and Walternate? Just Bell (whose altverse counterpart supposedly died in a car accident)? It's interesting to see how differently the two worlds respond to the manifesto. The document states that there is another universe whose history is slightly ahead of "our own," where people have learned to cross universes. But to which universe is this statement targeted? It has always been assumed that the alternate universe was slightly ahead of ours in their technology, but it was Walter, from the original universe, who figured out how to cross over. So if the end of the world is coming by way of invaders from another universe, which universe actually initiated this "unavoidable" war? If it is inevitable, then which universe will be "torn to rags" as the manifesto so vividly describes?

CHAPTER 6

ETHICALLY PROBLEMATIC SCIENCE AND TECHNOLOGY

"I crossed into another universe and took a son that wasn't mine. And since then not a day has passed without me feeling the burden of that act."

— Walter, "White Tulip"

One of *Fringe*'s most significant recurring themes is the exploitation of science and engineering for questionable purposes. Almost every episode grapples with the ethical problems that arise from the application of radical advances in science and technology. I have already discussed this trope in the previous chapters as it directly influences "mad scientists," the end of the world, and organizations such as ZFT and Massive Dynamic. But in this chapter I will focus intently on the moral implications of rapid scientific progress. Walter Bishop's life is a clear demonstration of how some human innovations, however brilliant, can lead to devastating consequences. As much as he atones for his transgressions, the negative effects of Walter's (and William Bell's) research are far-reaching.

Human Experimentation

In *Fringe* it is nonconsensual human experimentation that most effectively demonstrates the ethical offenses emerging from the pursuit of scientific advancements. Even in fiction involuntary human experimentation, especially when painful and harmful, is always morally offensive and difficult to watch. But it's much harder to process when the victims are real people. Many real-life ethical transgressions, committed by doctors and scientists in the name of progress, are revisited or reinterpreted in *Fringe*'s rather brutal dramatizations of human testing. The history of medicine is riddled with comparable cases, and it can be instructive to review some of them to help establish context for the fictional scenarios in *Fringe*.

In 1951 the U.S. Army and Dow Chemical began a clinical study to examine dioxin, a toxic carcinogen and component of Agent Orange. They wanted to test its effects on human skin as part of the military's herbicidal warfare program. Dow Chemical factory workers who were exposed to the substance had been developing skin problems and the company wanted to test for other potential harmful side effects. Led by Dr. Albert Kligman from the University of Pennsylvania, this experiment involved injecting seventy prisoners of Holmesburg State Prison with dioxin. These men, mostly black, developed skin lesions that went untreated for several months. Kligman led this and other dermatological testing for more than twenty years, from 1951 to 1974. After Kligman's death in 2010, the *New York Times* reported that his subjects "were paid to test a variety of substances that included deodorants and shampoos as well as radioactive, hallucinogenic, and toxic materials on behalf of more than thirty pharmaceutical companies and several government agencies." Allen Hornblum, author of *Acres of Skin*, a book exposing the Holmesburg Prison clinical trials, said that Kligman "turned Holmesburg into the Kmart of human experimentation."

In the 1960s at Willowbrook State School in Staten Island, New York, mentally disabled children were intentionally infected with viral hepatitis in a research project conducted by Saul Krugman of New York University who was working on a vaccine for this virus. The agreement that was signed by the parents of the test subjects was allegedly not clear about the exposure, and many parents, desperate to have their children admitted to the facility, agreed because the only spaces available were in the experimental wing. Some sources note that Krugman told parents that the children would be given vaccinations when, in fact, he fed the children an extract of the virus made from the feces of other infected patients. Surprisingly the research was sponsored by the Armed Forces Epidemiological Board, Office of the Surgeon General, U.S. Army and approved by the New York State Department of Mental Hygiene. Though Krugman's practices were widely determined to be unethical, he still became the president of the American Pediatric Society in 1972.

Beginning in the 1930s the infamous Tuskegee syphilis experiment preyed upon hundreds of unsuspecting test subjects. In this sadistic clinical study doctors intentionally withheld treatment for 400 impoverished black men in Tuskegee, Alabama. In most cases the patients were given placebos, pills with nothing more than aspirin in them. Researchers were testing to see the effects of syphilis on the human body, even long after — twenty-five years to be exact — the discovery of penicillin. The research lasted from 1932 to 1972, at which time seventy-four of the test subjects were still alive. One hundred and fifty of the men had died of the disease or syphilis-related complications, forty of their wives had contracted syphilis, and nineteen of their children had contracted congenital syphilis. The U.S. Public Health Service was responsible for this experiment. Dr. John Heller, head of the Division of Venereal Diseases, once reported, "For the most part, doctors and civil servants simply did their jobs. Some merely followed orders, others worked for the glory of science."

All of these projects were carried out in the name of science and in some cases "just to see what happens." I offer these stories to illustrate how the unethical research practices portrayed on *Fringe* have precedents in the real world; they have happened right here in the United States, backed by large agencies with great authority.

Violating the Code

Scientists tacitly agree to a certain set of ethical standards or make a pledge similar to that of the Hippocratic Oath that doctors take before they begin practicing. After the brutal human experiments of Nazi Germany's concentration camps were revealed, the Nuremberg Tribunal established a set of laws for medical experimentation on human beings. The Nuremberg Code states that practitioners of science must abide by ten basic tenets when using humans as subjects of clinical studies, with the voluntary consent of the subject as the first and most important tenet.

If we acknowledge that ZFT activity or Pattern-related events are basically science experiments on a large scale, then of the first twenty episodes of *Fringe*, at least fifteen illustrate violations of the Nuremberg Code. For each tenet of the code quoted below I have provided a fictional example of its violation in *Fringe*, applying real-world ethics to fictional breaches of conduct. The ethical issues that arise with the human experiment cases in "Power Hungry," "The Cure," "Midnight," and "The Road Not Taken" are hardly subtle. These episodes demonstrate one of the most serious breaches of ethics that a medical professional or research scientist can make: inflicting pain and suffering on unwilling individuals.

In "Power Hungry" Dr. Jacob Fischer deceives Joseph Meegar into believing that his clinic provides treatments for individuals with low self-esteem to "unlock their hidden potential," when, in reality, Meegar is used as an experimental subject. Without his knowledge Meegar is electrically enhanced by Fischer's experiment. He is unable to give consent for something that was never fully disclosed, and yet the code of ethics states that "the voluntary consent of the human subject is absolutely essential."

Meegar's case is just one of many research projects associated with Dr. Fischer. Broyles describes Dr. Fischer as a doctor of biotechnology who is "wanted in four states and three countries for illegal human experimentation." Fischer is guilty of an array of nonconsensual experiments, including one case in which a subject "was pumped full of stimulants and kept awake for a solid year, fed on a steady visual diet of horrific images."

Though Meegar is walking around freely when the episode begins, Dr. Fischer is not finished with him. When we see Meegar strapped to a bed, pleading to be let go, it's becomes apparent that Dr. Fischer has absolutely no regard for his "patient's" life or health. Human experimentation to such a degree is reminiscent of the infamous medical testing performed by Mengele in the German concentration camps. Like the test subjects of the Nazis, Meegar is viewed as less than human, valuable only as a science project. His mother's death is just another casualty in the Dr. Fischer's quest to "improve" humanity. Meegar is a prisoner, fully cognizant of the tortures in store for him. Like both Walter and Walternate, Dr. Fischer can no longer empathize with the subjects of his work. He tells Meegar, "Look what science has made you: special," when it has only destroyed Meegar's life. Fischer is far more concerned about his own status as "special." When the Fringe team finally tracks them down (by way of homing pigeons, no less) Meegar's physical suffering ends but his mental anguish will continue.

Olivia and her team have seen numerous cases in which human test subjects suffer from terror, pain, and even death. The ethics code stipulates that "the experiment should be so conducted as to avoid all unnecessary physical and mental suffering and injury," and yet in "The Cure" suffering seems inextricable from the experiment itself. The opening scene shows two men emerging from a van in the middle of the street, where they abandon a young woman, Emily; it is obvious that she has been abducted, terrorized, and possibly brutalized. Disoriented she wanders down the street and into a diner where one of the employees, concerned about the girl's wellbeing, contacts a police officer. She tries to explain her circumstances but she comes across as delusional, claiming that her abductees injected her with a blue substance and then a red substance, a possible foreshadowing of impending danger on a much larger scale. Is it possible that the chemicals represent the blue and red worlds?*

Olivia's last-minute rescue at Esterbrook's facility reveals the most heinous circumstances of human experimentation ("The Cure"). Our real-life examples of the justification for human testing don't compare to Esterbrook's reasoning, but Claire's fear and helplessness mirror what any unwilling test subject would feel. Once again Olivia swoops in to save the victims of ego-driven scientists.** Both Claire

---

* Is this what happens when the two universes react with each other? We know that what happens to Emily is a gruesome display of blood and gore: her head explodes all over the glass door of the restaurant as she attempts to escape. Is this what will essentially happen to the two universes? At this early point in the narrative, do the writers already have such a clear grasp on the symbolic significance of these colors?

** Little does she know at this point that she's lived through her own trauma at the hands of such a scientist.

and Emily suffered from a disease that was "treated" with capsules of radiation injected into their bloodstream. Recall that this treatment was administered by one of David Esterbrook's partners in crime, Dr. Nadim Patel, a medical professional entrusted with protecting and promoting his patients' health. Instead Patel helps turn them into human bombs. This is an extreme version of the Tuskegee syphilis experiment in which more than one authority was to blame, but ultimately it was the doctors who were responsible for the treatment of their patients. Perhaps he forgot that his objective should be to "do no harm," not to "see what happens if . . ." When Olivia finds out that David Esterbrook is behind this inhumane experiment, she confronts him about transforming human beings into weapons. Esterbrook even mentions he has a client in mind for his "product." Emily was the experiment and Claire, the final product.

Many times in *Fringe* the experiment or research is carried out in the basement or backroom of someone's home, certainly not adhering to the guideline that "proper preparations should be made and adequate facilities provided to protect the experimental subject against even remote possibilities of injury, disability, or death." In "Midnight" Nicholas Boone runs Lubov Pharmaceuticals out of his kitchen. Over the years he has ordered several strains of bacteria and viruses from the CDC for his "research" as well as RUD-390, "a chemical compound used in the construction of biochemical weapons." When the Fringe team raids Boone's home, the sight of the lab is chilling. Animal corpses (for clinical trials) litter the home; the team finds him in a wheelchair working on the spine of an unidentified creature. As far as we know Dr. Boone isn't working on any human test subjects, but ZFT has victimized his wife by injecting her with a virus that turns her into a spinal-fluid-thirsty monster.

Eventually Dr. Boone comes to be seen as a victim, rather than a perpetrator of unethical practices, but his initial willingness to participate with such an organization certainly demonstrates how the man becomes the monster. The confusion between human and beast is not merely a conflation of terms, as Frankenstein's monster has become synonymous with Dr. Frankenstein. In Boone's case, a human — his wife — is actually transformed into something inhuman. In his lab notes in another monster episode, "Unleashed,"

Walter fittingly quotes Friedrich Nietzsche: "Battle not with monsters lest ye become a monster."

The violation of the test subject's free will is common in the episodes that deal with human experimentation. The only time that a test is ended according to the subject's will is when the test subject has the wherewithal to overcome the lab team with physical force and escape like Olivia does on more than one occasion. And yet the code of ethics makes it clear that a subject should be able "to bring the experiment to an end if he has reached the physical or mental state where continuation of the experiment seems to him to be impossible."

Additionally "the scientist in charge must be prepared to terminate the experiment at any stage, if he has probable cause to believe, in the exercise of the good faith, superior skill, and careful judgment required of him" that the project may injure or kill the subject. Walter and William Bell are both guilty of pushing experiments far beyond the limits of good and "careful judgment." The effect of administering cortexiphan to young children resulted in not only extreme fear and discomfort *during* the experiment, but long-term side effects that included the deaths of many subjects. "To say that they are permanently damaged would be an understatement," says Olivia to Bell about the condition of the cortexiphan test subjects ("Momentum Deferred").

In "Bad Dreams" we meet Nick Lane, a former mental patient with a substantial insurance policy from the military. He has been labeled "hyper-emotive" and has the ability to influence those around him based on his own emotional state. When he's happy, others in close proximity become happy too; when he's depressed, others feel the same. But what is most interesting about Nick is that he was one of the young test subjects from the daycare center in Jacksonville (which may explain why he has a suspiciously lucrative insurance policy from the military). Nick is aware that, as a child, he was being prepared to become a soldier in a war against a parallel universe.

In this episode Walter denies culpability in administering the drugs to children but still justifies the experiment as a worthy cause: "It worked on perception. Carlos Castaneda, Aldous Huxley, Werner Heisenberg all focused on one single elementary truth. Perception is the key to transformation." The side effects of this theoretical notion, however, "result in injury, disability, or death to the experimental subject." Walter and Bell have created a being who has no control over his powers of transformation nor any understanding of the purpose of his hyper-emotion. He unwittingly causes the deaths of several people, deaths for which Bell and Walter must take responsibility according to the Code of Ethics.

In "The Road Not Taken" we see another two victims of the cortexiphan trials: Susan Pratt and her twin sister, Nancy Lewis. Their case seems to recall Josef Mengele's concentration camp experiments, if only because they are twins. Mengele is infamously known for the torture he inflicted on thousands of twin siblings, with the objective of advancing eugenics research and furthering genetic studies. It is an interesting choice to use on a set of twins in this drug trial. Did Walter and Bell have a special plan for these girls, or perhaps believe that their similar genetic code would make them stronger? But both girls, like the rest of the cortexiphan subjects, grow up with little knowledge of their participation in these trials. As a result they have no means of understanding, let alone controlling, their powers.

One sister, Nancy Lewis, eventually learns to master her ability, but only after being abducted by double agent Sanford Harris and strapped down to a chair like a prisoner. With Olivia's help she is able to use her enhanced mind to kill Sanford and save herself. But Nancy's sister is not as fortunate. The opening scene of this episode features an increasingly agitated Susan Pratt ultimately exploding into flames on an urban street corner. She and her sister were both endowed with the power of pyrokinesis, the ability to set fire to things using their minds.

By the end of this episode Olivia has pieced together enough evidence to expose Walter's unethical practices, and she has reason to believe that Bell is closely affiliated with the appalling activities of ZFT. When Walter tries to defend his motives, claiming he didn't intend to harm anyone, Olivia becomes visibly angry. She is likely horrified by his inability to take responsibility for his actions. Though his remorse is evident in this scene, his lack of ethical clarity at the time of the experiment is gravely offensive. She makes it very clear for him, "You were drugging children. Three-year-old children, Walter. Why did you do it?" Walter believed he was preparing the kids to become soldiers. Perhaps he believes that his experiments fell within the scientists' moral code and would "yield fruitful results for the good of society, unprocurable by other methods or means of study," but what exactly did Walter and Bell have in mind as a "fruitful result" of such an experiment? Unlike Walternate's trials in the other universe, this project was undertaken without any clear knowledge of an impending war. Both Walter and Bell crossed a line that, even under the most desperate circumstances, Walternate would not cross. Granted Walternate has his own serious issues of personal integrity: for one, he is completely unconcerned about the deaths of the adult test subjects in his own cortexiphan trials. But experimenting on children is something even *he* refuses to do. This brings up an interesting point about the so-called line. Why is it always Bell who encourages crossing the line, and Walter who always pays the price for following through? We are somewhat justified in seeing Walternate as the bad guy, considering he attempted to kill (and vivisect) our Olivia, but it is Walter who performed abusive experiments on children and it is Walter who made the first trans-universal breach. Is Bell some sort of devil on Walter's shoulder? Walternate doesn't seem to suffer under the influence of this sort. At a meeting in 1985, shortly before the first Peter dies, Walter arrogantly announces to the military personnel that "as scientists, we must embrace every possibility. No limitations. No boundaries. There is no reason for them," yet Walter will soon find many reasons.

Long-Term Consequences

The other major issue that concerns ethicists in terms of advances in science and engineering is formulating weapons or viruses that could fall into the wrong hands and cause widespread destruction. Ironically it is Walter who says to Dr. Alistair Peck, "It is not our place to adjust the universe" ("White Tulip"). He is referring to Peck's desire to travel through time and change the past, but the larger concern is that any kind of scientific research, if mismanaged or abused, could potentially change the universe in a negative way. Already having implemented his own "adjustments" to the universe Walter appears to have learned his lesson at this point. As Eric Rabkin points out in his commentary on apocalyptic narratives, "One way or another we have always wanted to know too much, have made our

Father-Gods jealous, have risked changing the world and, thereby, inevitably, changed it" (*The End of the World*, vii).

A chapter on ethics in science is never complete without several references to the Nazi research implemented during World War II, and so we will explore one more aspect of the regime's scientific "advances." After all we can't ignore "The Bishop Revival," in which Dr. Josef Mengele's work becomes closely associated with Dr. Robert "Bischoff," the Bishop patriarch. Genetically targeted warfare is at the center of this particular episode, as is the Bishop family history and legacy of questionable scientific practices. The idea that Walter's father was working under the Nazi regime, albeit as a spy for the Allies, and developing a weapon specifically designed to identify victims according to their genetic makeup is quite a lot to process, for both Peter and the viewer. Further it's frightening to think that it might have been Peter who inadvertently released the research to the killer, simply by selling his father's books ten years before. If nothing else "The Bishop Revival" is the portrait of a family whose genius far outreaches their sense of responsibility. Engaging in such dangerous, groundbreaking research requires a certain level of conscientiousness and discretion, not only for the scientist but also for anyone who has access to his work, which in this case includes two subsequent generations — Walter's and Peter's. Walter realizes the full weight of this liability when Peter reveals that he sold the books. "The very thing [my father] was trying to stop, you put back into the world," Walter tells his son. Yet again the unforeseen consequences of a Bishop science project is coming back to haunt Walter, and this time it's not so much the research that he regrets but his failure to protect it — "my father's work is killing people." Luckily for Walter's conscience, it turns out that the fault doesn't actually lie in Peter's security breach, but the implications of this possibility are sobering, to both Peter and Walter.

In 1984 a set of guidelines for researchers was developed called "The Uppsala Code of Ethics for Scientists" and published in the *Journal of Peace Research*. It is prefaced by a skeptical viewpoint about the worthiness of an advancement of weapons: "it is doubtful whether it is ethically defensible for scientists to lend any support to weapons development." Had Walter abided by the following parameters established at the Uppsala convention and carefully assessed "the consequences of his research," the two universes would not be waging war on one another.

1. Research shall be so directed that its applications and other consequences do not cause significant ecological damage.
2. Research shall be so directed that its consequences do not render it more difficult for present and future generations to lead a secure existence. Scientific efforts shall therefore not aim at applications or skills for use in war or oppression. Nor shall research be so directed that its consequences conflict with basic human rights as expressed in international agreements on civic, political, economic, social and cultural rights.
3. The scientist has a special responsibility to assess carefully the consequences of his/her research, and to make them public.

"Unleashed," an episode in which Walter hunts down the dragon-like creature in the underground sewer system, is an illustration of the catastrophic potential that this kind of experimentation can yield. Walter blames himself for contributing to the creation of the hybrid monster that has escaped from a testing lab. The creature is responsible for the death of a scientist, a college student, and two animal control employees. Even more problematic is that it has the capability to reproduce by using humans as hosts for its larva. If it successfully reproduces it could quickly take over the city.

Dr. Cameron Deglmann, a pioneer in the field of transgenics, shows up when he gets news of the alarm at his lab. He sees the animal rescuers and says, "*Tell me you didn't open that door in there.*" The irony of this quote is lost on them, but to the keen viewer it is a good way to sum up the message of this episode: they've opened a door that could lead to destruction through their unethical scientific projects. Walter bears the brunt of this guilt even though he wasn't directly responsible for the incident. He makes it his mission to find the hybrid, in order to obtain DNA that will complete his antidote for the infestation of Charlie.

In this episode the consequences of a scientific act are clear and very dangerous. Though Walter wasn't responsible for this particular creature, his research has undoubtedly contributed to the field of "radical transgenics." Walter confronts his scientific responsibility by personally hunting down the hybridized animal.

According to his lab notes Walter accepts full responsibility for unleashing hybridized monsters: "I knew what I wanted. To turn Greek myth into modern reality. To create life like no one had seen before. To play God." But he also makes the point that if human beings didn't push the limits of technology, we would all be "huddled in caves with only skins to cover us."

Here he seems to be nodding in the direction of the Prometheus myth, in which the titan Prometheus is concerned with the betterment of mankind, and ultimately steals fire from Zeus to bring it to the people. Fire, of course, is a basic form of technology, and this myth is usually used to signify the human desire to push the limit of technological advances.

Walter realizes that his research purposes were not exactly altruistic; he was motivated, rather, by the desire to exhibit his own powers: "I didn't seek medical cures or better food or safer energy. I sought only to prove that I could, to find the limits of the possible . . . to gain knowledge." Also a mythological concept, the tree of knowledge represents sin: the desire to know what God knows. The idea that "playing God" is a sin against nature continues to emerge throughout the series.

In "The Same Old Story" Dr. Penrose is found to be guilty of cultivating human beings. This experiment, one started when he was working for the U.S. Army, has gone awry and his "son" Christopher is victimizing regular human beings to retard his aging process. In "Midnight" Dr. Boone, former agent of ZFT, regretfully considers his own research and his "scientific trespasses": "I often wake up at night, frightened, with the understanding that there are things Man shouldn't know." This anxiety about knowing too much or going too far demonstrates the conflict between the desire for rapid progress and a sense of humility. Humans are curious by nature and fascinated by the things we can accomplish, but at the same time we should be cautious about indulging our curiosity beyond a certain responsible limit. The consequences of such rapid advances in technology can be far reaching and extremely destructive.

CHAPTER 7

Time Travel
BUGS IN AMBER

"All time is time. It does not change. It does not lend itself
to warnings or explanations. It simply is. Take it moment by
moment, and you will find that we are all . . . bugs in amber."

— *Slaughterhouse-Five* (Kurt Vonnegut)

In "Safe" Walter remembers what he was hiding in all of those vaults
targeted by Mitchell Loeb's team: a time machine. Walter's original
purpose for the machine was to find a "brilliant" Swiss doctor who
had died in 1936. Dr. Alfred Gross was the only one known to be
capable of curing young Peter's seemingly terminal illness. Walter says
that he never used the machine, "But the science behind it, in theory,
it would work. In theory it could retrieve anyone from anywhere."

Once Loeb's team finds all of the pieces and assembles the contraption, they use it to move David Robert Jones from the German
prison to Little Hill, a field located outside of Boston. Evidently the
machine is handy for instantaneously moving through space, as well
as traveling great spans of time.

This chapter will not address whether Walter's teleportation
machine, or time travel in general, is conceivable theoretically or otherwise. Rather it will explore the notions of temporal displacement in
other fictional narratives and see how *Fringe* compares. *Fringe*'s idea
of the time-space continuum largely focuses on alternate realities (see

chapter 10 on parallel universes), but there is one episode in particular that demonstrates the various conventions of fictional time travel in a single universe, "White Tulip." To explore how time travel operates in *Fringe*, I will examine this noteworthy episode in detail.

Many time travel stories illustrate the notion of traveling *forward* in time, a concept that is theoretically plausible. But the events that take place in "White Tulip" pertain to moving backward in time and changing prior events, therefore creating new "loops" of reality. Altering history is a key issue for time travel stories, one that can complicate a plot line to such an extent that audiences sometimes are left perplexed by the "rules" of time travel.

The Eternals versus the Observers

The End of Eternity (1955), Isaac Asimov's futuristic novel, tells the story of an organization of male humans, "the Eternals," who observe and make changes to the course of human history through the twenty-seventh century. So the fictional concept of a select group of men chosen to travel around in time for the benefit of humanity is nothing new.

Let's review the characteristics of the Observers in order to draw comparisons between them and their science fiction predecessors. In "August," a revealing episode about the nature of the Observers, Brandon explains to Olivia how time is perceived by this odd group of bald white men. Apparently the strictures of time do not affect the Observers; they travel back and forth in time, as he demonstrates with a bit of water and a glass tube. First he shows how most people view time as a tube in which water flows only one way, from one end to the other, offering the viewer an important lesson in the nature of time and how we should think about it in the context of the show. When he fills the glass tube with water again, blocking both ends this time, we can visualize how the Observers operate. By contrasting our linear understanding of time with the Observers' more holistic approach to the course of human history, Brandon identifies the Observers as a completely different race of beings and offers a new understanding of their role in the lives of Peter and Walter. The demonstration perhaps lends some insight into what the observers can and cannot do, but also opens up numerous possibilities about who they really are — aliens? Superhumans? But the central question still remains: what is their objective? As Brandon explains, "These guys show up at important moments, Um, historical, technological, scientific." But why? He also notes that their appearances, relatively speaking, are few and far between: in the past 5,000 years, there are only two dozen recorded sightings. So why do they repeatedly appear in the lives of the Fringe team? And how does Brandon know so much about them?

In the same way as the Observers, the Eternals from Asimov's story are able to travel "upwhen" and "downwhen" through history, entering the temporal world at any given point. They are able to make small changes to events in history with the purpose of diminishing human suffering, but ultimately they learn that their "tweaking" has put Eternity itself at risk.

Similarly the Observers seem concerned when one of them gets too involved in the events of human history. At one point the original Observer, known as "September," says that "he has said too much" to Walter, afraid that he will have an impact on history with unintended consequences ("There's More Than One of Everything"). The Observers' contact with humans is supposed to be limited to watching, and yet both September and August have created "irregularities" in the course of events. Indeed September steps in several times, attempting to fix his mistake. Unlike the Eternals who intentionally make small "reality changes," the Observers are largely there simply to watch and possibly keep record of what people do.

But the central conflict around which *The End of Eternity* develops is the very issue of making these changes. Eventually the Eternals meet another race of time travelers who have consciously chosen *not* to inflict alterations upon the past. It turns out that the Eternals, by impacting the past even in small ways, are contributing to a major catastrophe. This seems to be the moral of more than a few time travel stories: changing or preventing events in the past, though the traveler has good intentions, will either have no effect (as events will "course-correct") or make things much worse. "White Tulip" shows the futility of trying to improve history or, more compellingly, the hopeless nature of trying to rectify personal wrongs. This episode, late in season 2, is the series' finest demonstration of time travel and a superb example of *Fringe* storytelling in general.

"White Tulip"

The structure of "White Tulip" consists of several time loops; the writers use the device of time travel to illustrate four different scenarios of approximately the same storyline. Dr. Alistair Peck, the time traveler, is the only witness aware of the changes. It's possible that there could be an untold number of these scenarios, depending on how many times Peck actually traveled back in time trying to get his "reality change" to work, but viewers see only four of them.

Peck, an astrophysicist working at M.I.T., is blinded by grief and guilt after losing his fiancée in a car accident ten months earlier. The episode focuses on his effort to change the past and, as a byproduct, change Walter's future. Its structure is unique in that it offers four different scenarios of the same course of events; in essence it introduces the idea of alternate universes. By traveling back and forth in time Peck seems to create multiple realities, although every time he goes back, he thinks that he is "resetting" things. But is it possible that he's just visiting worlds that were already there and revisiting decisions he's already made?

Loop 1

The first loop establishes what we consider the "original" timeline. As such, this first storyline is covered in the greatest detail. We first learn that, somehow, Dr. Peck's attempts to travel through time have resulted in the deaths of many train commuters. As Dr. Peck exits the train this first time around, a digital clock is visible directly above his head with a sign that says, "Get there in no time," a foreshadowing of what's to come. Time itself is this man's major obstacle, and, as an extremely gifted physicist, he seems to think he can manipulate it and somehow change history.

In a parallel storyline Walter is struggling with the issue of Peter's origin: should he tell Peter that he's from "the other side"? Like the man on the train Walter is struggling with the past, a common point of conflict in time travel stories. Olivia has already guessed Walter's secret and is pressuring him to tell Peter. Walter is attempting to embrace the past and forgive himself, something that the physicist cannot do. In the next scene we see Walter carefully composing a letter to Peter, explaining Walter's past misdeeds and revealing Peter's origins. Walter cannot bear the thought of losing Peter again, but he knows that it is only a matter of time before something (or someone) will bring it to Peter's attention. After some investigation the team figures out that Dr. Peck has been driven to madness by the idea that he might be able to change the course of events. During the FBI raid Peck returns to his apartment and is surrounded by federal agents. He disappears in front of their eyes and travels back in time, in another attempt to alter history.

Loop 2

In the next loop everything transpires like the first timeline except that this time Peck does not return home. He continues his work at a lab in a different location, where he has already moved much of the important equipment. The fact that Peck has created a new timeline has implications for the overall mythology of the show. Walter has explained that each decision we make creates a new branch in the ever-expanding tree of history. So is that what we're seeing here? Just *one* of those decisions played out in multiple scenarios? If this is the case, does it mean that there are more Fauxlivias and Walternates (and even alt-Peters) in an infinite number of parallel universes? Is Peck creating separate timelines (or universes) or he is just momentarily disturbing the original universe, allowing a fray of scenarios to play out, eventually blending together again and ending up on the same path? If so, could the red-verse and the blue-verse eventually blend together peacefully, making one big, happy purple-verse?

In the meantime, Olivia visits Peck's former colleague at M.I.T. Dr. Carol Bryce, who explains that Peck was working on particle acceleration and the creation of wormholes, but that none of his colleagues could comprehend or appreciate much of his research. Peck ended up resigning the year before but left his journals with Dr. Bryce who, in turn, hands them over to Olivia's investigation.

Back in Walter's lab it becomes clear (once again) that it was Peck's time travel that killed the passengers and drained all of the train's electricity; traveling through time requires a massive amount of energy (in reality, one would need the amount of energy equivalent to the explosion of a star). Another discovery leads to the notion that Peck is trying to undo an event in the past: the death of his fiancée, Arlette. Walter finds a note in the back of his journal called "The Arlette Principle" and becomes worried that if Peck killed dozens of people by traveling only twelve hours, that he would kill hundreds of people by traveling ten months into the past. The next scene is the apex of the episode and the most compelling bit of dialogue we've seen in *Fringe*. Once they find Peck again, Walter is adamant about speaking with him. In an interesting heart-to-heart between the two "mad scientists," Peck reveals his grief and the motives for all he's done. If he had only gone with Arlette to do their wedding shopping, he believes that she would still be alive. "I know it wouldn't have happened," he desperately tells Walter.

The conversation takes a different turn when Walter mentions his own experience and the guilt he bears for playing God. "Until I took my son from the other side, I had never believed in God. But it occurred to me . . . that my actions had betrayed him and that everything that had happened to me since was God punishing me." This scene reflects the moment in "Peter" when Dr. Carla Warren warned Walter not to "tamper with" things that humans should not know. Walter tells her that there is "only room for one god in this lab and it's not yours." But Walter has been changed by his experience of crossing the line that shouldn't be crossed. He fears that Peck will suffer similar consequences; just because he *can* do it doesn't mean that he should. Peck's final point, that God *is* science ("God is polio and flu vaccines and MRI machines and artificial hearts"), illustrates the notion of faith in a new light. Peck's understanding of God as science is actually more religious than it sounds. The idea that the divine dwells in everyone and everything is common to many faiths. Therefore the notion that God is a field of study — art, music, gardening — is not exactly a godless thing to say. Once the narrative is again reset, Walter's "religion" is in the hands of Dr. Peck and science.

Loop 3

In the next sequence the Fringe team is once again trying to find Peck. He is at his apartment finishing up his new, improved equation when the investigators surround his home. At the last minute he escapes but not before he addresses a letter to his colleague at M.I.T. This time he travels to May 18, the day his fiancée was killed, and climbs into the car with her, but it's too late — the accident still happens, and this time it kills them both.

Loop 4

When the next thread restarts, there is no mention of Alistair Peck or time travel; instead we see Walter at his desk at home, writing the letter to Peter. When the mail is delivered Walter opens an envelope addressed to him. Inside is a single hand-drawn white tulip. Drawn by Alistair Peck ten months before (and sent through Dr. Bryce at M.I.T.), this message delivers two different meanings. To Walter it is a sign of forgiveness and a nudge to tell Peter the truth. It also bolsters Walter's notion that there is a god, one who is paying close attention to him. On the other hand the viewer knows (and Peck knows) that the only reason Walter received such a letter is because of Peck's own technological innovation. The illusion of God, therefore, is sustained in this gracious act. Technology *is* God. The relief of forgiveness that Walter needed came from another human being through the medium of a man-made machine.

Lost, *Slaughterhouse-Five*, and Time

Time travel is a tricky narrative device, one that has turned many a plot line into a tangled mess. Though readers are forgiving when it comes to imaginary scientific principles, if the rules of time travel are not clearly established by the author (or TV writer) the audience easily catches the holes in logic.

In *Lost*, for instance, the rules are clearly stated but difficult to wrap one's mind around. It was established that the characters could not change history when they traveled back to the 1970s and lived "there" for three years. By living among other people they seemed to be affecting history, but only a history they thought they knew. The viewer must accept the notion that "what happened, happened." If Sawyer became the head of Dharma security when he went back in time, then that is the way that the course of events always happened. Nothing has changed, essentially, because history is completely reset, and it is only our perception of history that changes with the new information we now have. No alterations to reality can be made — the survivors cannot undo the plane crash that will occur in 2004, nor can they prevent any of the many deaths they've seen on the island. There are no Eternals or Observers here. In one scene where the writers cleverly explain their rules of time travel to the *Lost* audience, Miles explicitly states the rules to Hurley after one of the survivors, Sayid, traveled back in time with them and shot a young Ben Linus, a boy who would grow up to be their enemy on the island in 2004. As in *Fringe, Back to the Future* is referenced as adhering to a contrasting theory, when Hurley worries that they will start disappearing because they'll actually prevent their own existences. Miles explains in no uncertain terms, "You can't change anything. Your maniac Iraqi buddy shot Linus. That is what *always* happened."

Consider the model of time as conceived by Kurt Vonnegut in *Slaughterhouse-Five* (a novel that is key to fully comprehending *Lost*). Like the Observers, the extraterrestrial Tralfamadorians in Vonnegut's story see all of time at once, like an entire mountain range. This is in contrast to Earthlings, who can only view one point at a time as if they see only the bit of mountain range on which they are standing. When the main character, an Earthling named Billy Pilgrim, asks the Tralfamadorians how the universe ends, they reply, "We blow it up, experimenting with new fuels for our flying saucers. A Tralfamadorian test pilot presses a starter button and the whole universe disappears." Billy, of course, wants to know why they don't simply prevent the pilot from pressing the button if they know about its devastating consequences. The answer? "He has *always* pressed it and he always *will*. We always let him and we always *will* let him. The moment is *structured* that way" (117). Earlier in the story Billy had learned that Tralfamadorians believe that we are all trapped "like bugs in amber" (77) and that each moment is structured in a definitive way. It's strange that neither Walter nor Walternate has ever attempted to travel back in time to prevent the abduction of Peter or, even better, to cure both Peters before they became fatally ill. Perhaps they know they would never survive the radiation levels caused by the journey in time. But what about the Observers? Can't they go back and change things, considering they've been getting so involved in human history anyway? Is it possible that they've already tried? If we ascribe to the Tralfamadorian point of view, this is just the way things happen — one Peter died, the other was taken, Walter is guilty, and the alternate universe is subsequently falling apart. This is the way it was always supposed to be, and any attempt to change things was always a part of the overall scheme.

PART II

INTO A GLASS DARKLY

CHAPTER 8

THE FATHER, THE SON, AND THE TRANS-UNIVERSAL MACHINE

"I don't belong here. But I don't belong there, either."

— Peter, "Over There, Part 2"

In times of family distress it's fairly common for children to wonder if they are actually from another family, perhaps inadvertently switched at birth or secretly adopted. Young or old, everyone occasionally feels that they, like Peter, "don't belong." As Elizabeth Bishop tells young Peter, "Sometimes the world we have is not the world we want" ("Subject 13"). The alternate universe in *Fringe* reflects the feeling that we might be happier if events had transpired differently, that maybe things would be better if only we had a different job or spouse or education. Peter's trans-universal life illustrates these common human longings.

Newly abducted from the other universe, young Peter is almost certain that Elizabeth and Walter are not his real parents. He doesn't know how to articulate what he has experienced, telling his mother that he's from the world "at the bottom of the lake." He is confident that his parents are deceiving him but, as an eight-year-old child, he has no means to prove it. At his age it's easy to mix up fantasy and reality, and the delirium from his illness further obscures the distinction between the two. In time he will learn to let go of this "fantasy," in the same manner that most children give up their illusions of fairies and talking animals.

Young Peter earnestly believes that he came from a world that is situated much like Wonderland — underground. He feels as though he fell down the rabbit hole when he and Walter broke through the ice, only to be pulled through to the other world by a magical creature: the Observer. Once Peter regains consciousness and recovers from his illness, he sees his new reality much like Alice viewed her looking-glass world. This world resembles his own, but, just like the words in Alice's books, everything goes "the wrong way."

Things certainly *do* go the wrong way for Peter and his new parents. Within only a few years of Peter's abduction Walter is hauled off to St. Claire's. Not long after that Peter and his mother are forced to leave Cambridge because she can't afford the mortgage on their house. After Peter moves out he wanders in and out of odd and high-risk jobs and is frequently arrested for his involvement with organized crime. Shortly after moving abroad Peter learns that Elizabeth has committed suicide. Her grief and guilt have led to her actual self-destruction. It is at this point that the story of *Fringe* opens: in the middle of a father-son relationship devastated by grief, deception, and disappointment.

Despite his dark past Peter initially appears to be a goodhearted guy; his shady dealings in the Middle East and alleged connection to the mob are at odds with the character we see. At the same time he is clearly bitter about his father's seventeen-year absence. He's also continually frustrated and embarrassed by Walter's lack of common sense. Walter is the only person who can really get a rise out of Peter, who otherwise plays it cool. In the pilot episode Peter is visibly angry when he finds out Walter is going to put Olivia in the water tank to perform a questionable procedure that may or may not help her access John Scott's memories. "This man will kill you!" he shouts, fully believing that Olivia is going to die at the hands of his father. When she agrees to participate in Walter's experimental tank-submersion project, Peter is aghast: "He is insane and you're insane for following him."

Though Peter's demeanor is usually easygoing, he does have a dark side, one that first begins to materialize when the secret of his origin is revealed at the end of season 2. In "Reciprocity" this shadow self emerges once again, quite shockingly, when we discover he is murdering shapeshifters. Though many characters have alluded to his shady pre–Fringe team past, this mysterious dimension to him doesn't really ring true until this episode, in which he kills the "mechano-organic" hybrids without remorse and conceals his actions from everyone.

Squeezed between the hero and the mad scientist, Peter generally plays the role of communicator and moderator, absorbing the shock of the things that Walter says and urging Olivia to access her emotional side. After so much wandering he seems to have found his place and a makeshift family among Walter, Olivia, and Astrid. But when he discovers that he actually is from the other universe, his sense of home with the Fringe team is destroyed. Further, he realizes that he's been deceived by his own father.

The major crisis that Peter was forced to suppress so long ago — his abduction — is revealed in "The Man From the Other Side." When he is finally given a chance to escape this wonderland "at the bottom of the lake" after so many years, and return to where he belongs, things don't improve like he imagined they would when he was a child. Nothing fits into place and his identity begins to unravel. He doesn't belong entirely in one world or the other. He realizes that his distress arises from both worlds and that, to some extent, he belongs to both universes, to both Walter and Walternate, Olivia and Fauxlivia. Will he be able to join together the two sides in a way analogous to how he has mediated between Walter and Olivia (or arguably Walter and the world)? Since his heart is in both places, can he reconcile the universes' differences and allow them to come together in some sort of harmony?

Sins of the Father

At its core Peter's story is one of loss — his own and his parents' (those of both Peters). It's about the loss of a child, by death on one side and abduction on the other, but it's also about Peter's own sense of emptiness. He lost his other half, his reflection or shadow self. In the fictional world of parallel universes, what impact does losing one's alternate self have on an individual? It is possible there is a permanent imbalance of the self, or even the universe, when one version of a person dies. Not only did Peter lose his real parents, he also had to live with the void left behind after the other Peter's death. Essentially he was the shadow of the "original" Peter, at least in his parents' eyes. As the surviving child he would never be able to compete with the dead one or fulfill his parents' expectations. The Bishop family felt a great sense of internal estrangement: they were isolated even when they were together. Elizabeth made it clear to Walter that she wanted Peter returned to his own world immediately, a clear sign that she would never fully accept the new son. Even her words, while encouraging to Peter, undermined Walter: "be a better man than your father."

The abduction of young Peter is the central conflict of the series, the pivotal disaster that moves the entire plot along — in all directions. In "Peter" Walter tells Elizabeth that though their son is dead, they can take comfort in the fact that in some other universe another Peter will grow up and live a happy life. But when Walternate fails to see that he has created the disease's cure, Walter can no longer merely "take comfort" or move on. He must take action so that the other Peter can live the life Walter wished for his own son. Walter never intended to keep Peter: he brought the medicine to save him, but the vial broke during the crossing and he felt he had no choice but to bring the boy back to save his life. Walter's actions are extraordinary, considering what he was willing to risk for a son who wasn't his.

Parent-child bonds are a powerful thing. When Walter and Elizabeth have a living, breathing version of their son back in their arms, how can they let him go again? The first thing Elizabeth does when she sees Peter is check that he is breathing, something parents of young infants do, fearing that the child, so newly alive and yet so vulnerable, might stop breathing. To Elizabeth this is Peter's rebirth and a chance to be near her son, if only temporarily.

But the alternate Peter quickly shows he is not *their* Peter. Crossing over affects both universes — on a personal and a cosmic level. On this side the "soft spots" become weaker because of Walter's breach. On the other side giant chasms in the universe begin to form, manifesting as "micro black holes," vortexes that begin to erode the alternate world. As a reflection of the world at large falling to pieces, the personal lives of both Walternate and Walter begin to deteriorate. Walternate's marriage fails because of Peter's disappearance, and Elizabeth, on this side, is wracked with guilt and remorse over what Walter has done, finding it extremely difficult to lie to Peter and watch him endure such confusion and grief.

Walter and Walternate are both capable of immense creativity but also terrible destruction. The loss of a child propels Walter to commit an act that threatens the entire universe, and the loss of Walternate's child eventually brings about harsh governmental controls and, far worse, the declaration of a trans-universal war. Walter knows what he did was wrong and that he created the "first crack in a pattern of cracks, spaces between the worlds." But he defends his choice to Olivia by asserting, "You can't imagine what it's like to lose a child" ("Peter"). Walternate frequently talks about "the cause" and "the greater good," but it is clear that his motives are also personal: his actions stem from losing Peter. When a young and distraught Olivia crosses over and shows him a drawing of Peter, Walternate quickly begins the crusade to get his son back and destroy Walter's universe ("Subject 13"). In "The Abducted" Walternate tells Colonel Broyles that "there's no crime more heinous than the theft of a child." Though it initially appears that Walternate is paying closer attention than Walter to the needs of the universe as a whole, in fact, Walternate is confusing "tragedies of unimaginable scale" with the loss of a single person. Like Walter he is unable to distinguish his personal emotional needs with the best interest of the rest of the world.

Fathers and Sons and Science

The father-son dynamic, which plays a central role in *Fringe*, is frequently interwoven with the theme of dangerous technology. Reckless practices in the development of new technologies are used to underscore the conflicts between parent and child. For the Bishop family these issues span multiple generations: in "The Bishop Revival" Walter safeguards his own father's formula for a dangerous toxin for many years, only to find out that his son unwittingly sold it to a bookstore. In an interview with Stuart Fox at PopSci.com, J.J. Abrams explained that it was his own grandfather who first inspired his interest in science and technology. He and his grandfather, the owner of an electronics company, "would spend hours building and soldering things. As a young kid, it's so inspirational to see that you can build things that aren't made by the hand of God, that you can attach the motor to a wire and make something work." Though Abrams' experience was a positive one, it's telling that he uses the term "hand of God," conjuring the image of the patriarch-engineer as creator, wherein the clever human takes the place of God.

One of the most relevant classic stories to Peter and Walter's relationship is the story of Daedalus and Icarus. The theme of parents and children suffering the negative effects of technology is explicit in season 3's "Os," an episode that underscores this connection by paying special attention to this myth. Essentially the tale of Icarus, which Walter explains in "Os," is about a father who uses his genius to save his son.* Daedalus and his son, Icarus, are trapped in a labyrinth of Daedalus's own making. He had constructed it for King Minos to house the great Minotaur beast. Daedalus knows that he and his son are in great danger if they remain in the labyrinth — but how to escape? Known for his brilliance and innovative genius, Daedalus engineers wings for himself and his son and attaches them to their bodies with wax. They will be able to fly to freedom, but before they leave the labyrinth Daedalus warns his young son that he should not fly too close to the sun or too close to the water. Despite his father's words of caution Icarus, "drawn by desire for the heavens, soared higher." The warmth of the sun softens the wax and Icarus falls to his death. When Daedalus sees his son's lifeless body he "cursed his own inventions," much like Walter frequently regrets the consequences of some of his most brilliant innovations.

In "Os" when Walter arrives at the scene of a bizarre burglary he

---

* Walter is known for uttering the most appropriate (and sometimes inappropriate) literary and culture references to express his delight. For a man who has spent all of his adult life in the sciences, he's certainly well schooled in creative works of fiction; some of his most brilliant ideas are inspired by fictional or religious texts. In season 1's "Walter's Lab Notes," he references several works, from the Prometheus myth to *Macbeth* to Edgar Allan Poe's "The Bells." As Nina says it is his "boundless creativity" that makes him special. He notes the connection between his creative imagination and scientific exploration in "Unearthed" when he says to a close-minded, doubtful priest: "Please allow me a moment to entertain my fantasies. They often lead to a truth."

exclaims, "They glanced up and saw Icarus floating through the sky and, taking him for a god, they stood still in wonder." The dead man he sees floating in the sky is the victim of yet another scientist-father who is trying to save his son, a young man confined to a wheelchair. When they finally catch this scientist Walter sums up the message of the myth nicely, for both the scientist, Dr. Krick (a fitting name for a pioneering scientist), and the audience: "Daedalus crafted wings for his son, Icarus. So he could fly away. So that he could be free. The wings he gave him wound up killing his son." Indeed, if anyone understands the ramifications of dangerous technology — and of intervening in the course of nature — it is Walter Bishop.

This brief sermon is quite clear, but its message is swiftly cast aside when Walter demands to know how Dr. Krick "defied the laws of physics" and created the extraordinary compound that gives man the ability to fly. Though he uttered his words of caution only moments before, it is difficult for Walter to stop searching for answers. Without William Bell he often feels incomplete and less than brilliant. He needs to know that he still has the intellectual power to manipulate technology and fix things. It seems more important than ever that Walter save his son, or at least understand the danger that Peter might be facing. Walter is still very much a Daedalus. And why shouldn't he devise plans to save his son and the world? After all it was Icarus who flew too close to the sun, not his father.

"Os" is not the series' first episode to pair controversial science and father-son relationships against the backdrop of Walter and Peter's reconnection. In "The Same Old Story" Dr. Penrose searches for a way to help one of his genetically engineered sons to survive; both he and his son Christopher engage in the inhumane harvesting of a certain growth hormone. The case of Dr. Tyler Carson in "Of Human Action" dramatizes another bizarre mad-scientist-dad scenario. An adolescent boy discovers that he has the ability to control other people's minds. At first it appears his father, an employee at Massive Dynamic, subjected his son to his own cutting-edge research. It turns out that the boy's entire existence began in a Massive Dynamic lab. He is Dr. Carson's son only as a part of an elaborate experiment begun fourteen years earlier.

From the pilot episode onward father-son tension, further

exacerbated by the notion of dangerous technology, drives the story on *Fringe*. Walter's secret, Walternate's vengeance, Peter's sense of betrayal, Peter's feeling of responsibility toward his father: they all stem from a technological mishap. The machine itself is a major source of contention between Peter and Walter, even before they know the extent of its significance. In "6955 kHz" the two clash over Peter's work on the device with an exchange that ironically swaps characteristics from father to son. It is Peter who is advancing technology, perhaps even "crossing the line," and Walter who is cautioning against it as "playing with fire." Like a typical mad scientist Peter feels bonded to the device — "it came alive in my hands" — and cannot ignore the rush of curiosity that comes with his gift of engineering genius.

Peter's Destiny

More so than any other character on *Fringe* Peter's life seems controlled by destiny, a force embodied by the Observers. They call "the boy" a key figure in how things are "supposed to happen." Peter's mysterious connection to the machine seems preordained, and the machine itself appears as an object of religious mysticism. Though Peter is a self-described skeptic, there is a spiritual element to his involvement with the two universes. Once he travels to the future and back he seems touched by his new wisdom, inspired to unite the two worlds ("The Day We Died"). He is almost like a messiah figure, ordained to lead the people into a new era or usher in the end of the world.

It is possible that Peter understands his fate but has not articulated it yet. Though he's generally a logical person, his faith in a certain path is growing. He emphasizes the "feeling" he got when he first touched the machine in "Over There, Part 2." His involvement in the shapeshifter deaths suggests that he has found his mission and can see his destiny laid out before him. By the end of season 3 it is clear that the creator of the machine and the "creator" of Peter are the same man. This time the strong link between technology and fatherhood is illustrated in epic proportions.

If the mystical bowling alley manager, Sam Weiss, is right, then Peter's romantic life is the key to the survival of the universes. Though Peter is originally from the other side, he and Olivia are a more fateful pair than he and Fauxlivia. Even as children their connection was strong when they met in that enchanted field of tulips under the Florida snow, back in 1985, and talked about changing the world using only their imaginations ("Subject 13").

In the pilot episode, when Peter and Olivia first meet as adults, they don't remember their childhood encounter and get off to a rocky start. Peter wants nothing to do with her investigation, but she forces him to cooperate by threatening to divulge his whereabouts to "certain people." However Peter soon becomes as committed to solving the mysteries as Olivia, and his working relationship with Olivia develops into an affection that takes its time blossoming into passion. Theirs is a partnership that goes far beyond the limits of the job. Without significant others they have formed a kind of family — the two of them and Walter. When Olivia is injured in her return from the other side in "A New Day in the Old Town," Peter is right by her side to comfort her when she wakes up in the hospital. Similarly she is there to greet Peter when he wakes up from the injuries he sustained on the bridge in "The Man From the Other Side." But that is the last time they see one another before things get complicated.

Raging Against (and With) the Machine
In *Fringe* genius is highly prized; the show regularly features brilliant minds exhibiting their powers in acts of creation and destruction. The scientists' inventions are awe-inspiring, even when these creations have frightening ramifications. Might *Fringe*'s glorification of genius be illustrated in the concept of the mysterious machine? This device, which seems to be almost an extension of Peter, is the quintessential work of technological genius, one that might just ignite the "singularity" (a concept that will be explored in the following chapter). Like a scientist or engineer this machine can create and destroy; it is at once creation and creator, man and God.

In the modern world the solutions to our current problems (especially the educational, medical, and professional ones) seem to lie in the promise of technology. For *Fringe*'s First People the machine was the secret of life, "the key to the universe," as Walter says ("6955 kHz"). That belief could be reflective of the outlook of our industrialized society, which is in the midst of the information age and places so much hope in technology. New innovations are an endless source of inspiration for humanity but also the cause of so much unintended destruction. Is it possible that we could (or we already have) created a machine that could destroy everything?

The First People are characterized as a highly technologically advanced society and the creation of the machine has been attributed to them. Although the book, *The First People*, indicates that they referred to the machine as "the Vacuum," it is officially termed the Wave-Sink device on Walternate's plans but more commonly called "the machine" by both characters and fans alike. It has a dual nature: the capacity to create and to destroy. In Walter's lab notes for "The Road Not Taken" he mentions the two names for the Roman god of fire: Vulcan and Mulciber. Fire is commonly considered the quintessential technology, the one that catapulted man into civilized existence. But Walter points out that, like the machine, it has the dual nature to construct and destroy, perhaps embodied by the two dualistic personas of this Roman god.

The most significant aspect of the machine is that it needs a human being in order to operate, and not just anyone will do. It requires Peter, relying on his unique DNA sequence. The machine is like an inversion of the cyborg, a primarily organic being that fully resembles a human but is enhanced with mechanical parts. This "Vacuum," on the other hand, appears to be mostly a mechanical device enhanced by a human component. Peter's life has been deeply affected by fringy scientific innovations — the original machine that Walter developed to cross universes, Walter's dangerous experiments in the lab, and most significantly the universe-uniting machine. The overbearing presence of technology in Peter's life has changed the organic nature of his family. His father, driven by the need to control the universe with man-made devices, has thrown the natural world out of balance. By extension it has changed the family dynamic and completely eclipsed the mother-son relationship. In the season 3 finale Peter uses the destructive technology of the machine to reverse the effects of his father's work. With the machine's power he brings the two universes together, hoping that the two opposing fathers can reconcile with one another. The machine is a device of destruction — Peter uses it to tear holes in the universe — but can it also serve as a creative force?

CHAPTER 9

TECHNOLOGY AND HUMANITY

"Patricia Van Horn was living with a shapeshifter for two years.
She must have noticed something different."
— Peter, "Do Shapeshifters Dream of Electric Sheep?"

Recent advances in genetic replication and synthetic life are beginning to realize the kinds of things once seen only in science fiction. A scientist producing new life in a lab is no longer something confined to the realm of fantastic man-makes-monster stories. We are now within reach of the abilities to build an organism from the ground up and enhance life with artificial intelligence. What does this possibility mean for life as we know it? Will the definition of "human life" be complicated by these new technologies? In *Fringe* the shapeshifters serve as an exemplary metaphor for the convergence of technology and humanity. But before we delve into that, it is important to first explore what it means to be a fully organic human being, if such a thing even exists.

The Mystery of Human Life

In "Unearthed" Walter once again exhibits his willingness to embrace the unknowable and to broaden his understanding of the essence of life. When he tells Peter, "No one truly knows the nature of human consciousness," he's preparing Peter, as well as the viewers, for a mind-bending possibility: the disembodied "floating" consciousness, otherwise known as a spirit. It is surprising that a man of science such as Walter chooses the term "spirit" to describe what happened to Andrew Rusk after his death.*

But it seems there is no better word to use when talking about the energy of the human mind. Soul, spirit, consciousness, memories — words used to describe our "true" selves as distinguished from our physical bodies. Generally a person of scientific persuasion argues that this consciousness cannot operate separately from the physical structure of the brain. But not Walter. He is very open to the idea of an invisible spirit-like energy escaping from the body after death, though he never provides an explanation of how it could be scientifically possible. In "Os" things really get strange when the "energy" of the deceased William Bell uses Olivia as a living host. Walter explains Bell's theory as "soul magnets," which will be covered in more detail later.

If we could prove the existence of the soul, then it might be easier to identify exactly what it means to be human. But what is a soul? What do we mean by human consciousness? A cluster of memories and knowledge? The unique chemical makeup of an individual's brain? Does one need a whole body to be considered alive? If a person's "spirit" is located in the brain, it seems plausible that a human head, supported by a mechanized system, could technically pass for a human. Yet we consider a brain-dead person — a live body without a functioning brain — as fully human. Not only should we ask ourselves what it means to be alive, but also what does it mean to die. How do we define the moment of death: when the brain ceases functioning or when the heart stops?

Some people argue that death occurs when the soul leaves the body; scientists have tried to measure this separation of physical and spiritual matter. The myth that the human soul weighs twenty-one grams was given quite a bit of consideration back in 1907 when Dr. Duncan MacDougall published this finding in *American Medicine*, after conducting a flawed experiment on six terminally ill patients. Even though only one of the six subjects was conclusively recorded

---

* It should also be noted that in "6B," Walter denies the possibility of ghosts.

as losing twenty-one grams at the time of death, the idea that the spiritual world may be subject to the laws of physics proved to be a popular one, and it became a common belief that the soul weighed twenty-one grams.

The practice of reanimation has been explored in more than one episode of *Fringe*. In "Unearthed" the reanimation scenario is spontaneous: when Lisa Donovan comes back to life she is inhabited by two souls — her own and Andrew Rusk's. In "Marionette" Roland Barrett, a scientist who has studied cell regeneration, plays God by "resurrecting" Amanda Welsh, a girl whose suicide he refuses to accept. He reassembles her various parts by seeking out the recipients of her organs and gruesomely removing what he needs. Driven by the need to give her a second chance at life, Barrett nevertheless is horrified when he succeeds. His creation looks like Amanda, but there is something missing. The person he brought to life is not the same person who died. Though she has the same brain, the same eyes, and the same heart, her "soul" has moved on and cannot be regenerated with science. What is it that made Amanda so uniquely Amanda? If her memories and ideas are stored in the brain, then where did her collection of thoughts go? How else can we identify ourselves, scientifically, if not as a bundle of our thoughts and experiences?

All of these questions lead to the larger ethical implications of resurrecting the dead. Who has the right to restore life? Even a mother, the essential creator of life if there ever was one, does not control the workings of life and death. She can decide to bring forth life through her own body, but if her child dies, she does not have this same life-giving power to reanimate him, just as Walter could not bring young Peter back to life.

According to the science of *Fringe* it does seem that the "life essence" is preserved for those with the scientific means to access it, if only for a few hours after death. John Scott, for instance, was "questioned" by officials at Massive Dynamic after he died. What did they access? It couldn't have been brainwaves if he was clinically dead. Some sort of imprinting on the brain tissue?

The nature of the human spirit is addressed in "Of Human Action": Massive Dynamic has been dabbling in cloning, exploring the feasibility of mind control. The experiment's long-term results question the notion of individual identity. If each human being has a unique human essence, what about clones? Do they share the same soul?

If these characters can be given new life (resurrected) through scientific procedures and mechanized parts, then who's to say that semi-organic matter, organized into a structure that resembles a human being with comparable cognitive and emotive capabilities, can't constitute human life too?

Shapeshifters: Technology as a Substitute for Humanity

The Enemy From Within

The shapeshifters reflect the fear that we have of the imposter. In an era in which many people are filled with anxiety about terrorist activities and new strategies of warfare, the idea of one's neighbor as a covert enemy is relevant. Some of *Fringe's* shapeshifters have been living in the guise of the same human being for years. Their spouses, friends, and colleagues are unaware of the change within the person they know, that the real person has died and been replaced by a shapeshifter. In some cases the shapeshifters seem to forget that they aren't human, that they aren't the bundle of emotions and memories with which they have come to identify themselves.

In "Momentum Deferred" Peter tells Olivia that the film *Invasion of the Body Snatchers* terrified him so much when he was young that he couldn't sleep for several nights. Considering that this is a monumental episode for the shapeshifters, "mechano-organic hybrids" that are quietly infiltrating the human race by killing people and taking on their forms, it is no accident that Peter drops this reference. *Invasion of the Body Snatchers* is a classic alien-as-imposter narrative, one that reflects the fear that the enemy lies within — and could be any one of us.

From the Oklahoma City bombing to the 2011 politically motivated Arizona shooting, domestic acts of terrorism unhinge our faith in our fellow citizens. They can unravel the trust that is necessary to thrive in a free society, sometimes turning neighbor against neighbor in a downward spiral of paranoia and fear. The so-called Times Square Bomber, Faisal Shahzad, whose failed car bomb was

INTO THE
LOOKING GLASS

discovered in May 2010, is a classic case of the enemy from within. To his neighbors in a Connecticut suburb, Shahzad appeared to be a typical young father, working hard to support his wife and two small children. By many accounts he was quiet and somewhat reclusive but pleasant and friendly enough. He was born in Pakistan and became a naturalized American citizen, living the typical immigrant story of a man looking for a better life for himself and his family. But it turns out that he merely "shapeshifted" into this role, effortlessly deceiving his neighbors and colleagues. Even more shocking than Shahzad's act was the Fort Hood, Texas, shooting, in which Major Nadal Hasan, a psychiatrist serving in the U.S. Army, shot and killed thirteen military personnel and wounded many more. His "enemy within" status was at a whole different level than Shahzad's: a man born in America working within a highly specialized band of soldiers, an organization designed to defend *against* "the enemy," was secretly its adversary.

Events like these expose our underlying fears: how do we identify "the bad guys" if they live among us, look like us, speak like us, and act like us? How can we tell when they begin to change inside, becoming radicalized and embittered or motivated by a poisonous ideology? How can we distinguish a Jared Lee Loughner, the alleged shooter in the Arizona massacre, from any other angry young college student who behaves strangely from time to time?

The *Fringe* writers use shapeshifters to explore this fear. The shapeshifters infiltrate almost invisibly, taking the shape of an "insider" so that they can destroy a society slowly and quietly from the inside out. They might be in one body for years before moving on to their next victim, to carry out another mission. In the case of some shapeshifters they are in one position so long that they grow emotionally attached to friends and family, compromising the strategy. When this happens they must be "disabled," as Newton puts it ("Do Shapeshifters Dream of Electric Sheep?").

Comparisons

"Do Shapeshifters Dream of Electric Sheep?" — one of the more significant shapeshifter episodes — pays homage to Philip K. Dick's novel *Do Androids Dream of Electric Sheep?* on which the classic futurist film *Blade Runner* is based. The novel actively explores what it means to be human, a strong theme running through the shape-shifters' storyline. In season 2 Thomas Newton, a shapeshifter leader, was nicknamed the "Omega man" because of the Greek letter tat-tooed on his head, a reference to yet another popular narrative.

I Am Legend is the story of the only man on Earth immune to the effects of a worldwide pandemic, one that seems to turn humans into vampires. The novel, written by Richard Matheson and published in 1954, emphasizes the humanity of those living hosts of the disease, who act like vampires (and seem very zombie-like to the modern-day reader), but may be able to adapt to the germ and recover from it. The antagonist, however, lives in a state of paranoia, never knowing if he can trust them. The combination of references — Dick's novel and Matheson's story — suggests that this new breed of "person," the shapeshifter, may possess human qualities, even if they *are* more machine than man.

In "Do Shapeshifters Dream of Electric Sheep?" Newton says that humans' major weaknesses are emotion and ethical responsibility. He tells Olivia that she is susceptible to emotional weakness, even if she doesn't want to admit it: "Every night when your head hits the pillow, in the last moments before you go to sleep, your emotions betray you, and you question your ability to pull this off. Words like *integrity, self-respect* — they haunt you. They form a line that you're unwilling to cross and that will lead to your undoing." The down-side of being human, from this shapeshifter's perspective at least, is precisely what makes human life unique: not only empathy, but also the ability to distinguish between what is right and what is expected (duty).

Though our external shape doesn't shift we play different roles for different people in our lifetimes — the teacher, the rebel, the laborer, the skeptic, the believer, the parent, the child — modifying our behavior in relation to those around us. Is a shapeshifter an embodiment of the famous Shakespeare line, "One man in his time plays many parts"? Walter quotes part of this *As You Like It* soliloquy in "Over There": "'All the world is a stage,'" he tells Olivia, "or, in this case, both worlds." The life cycle of the shapeshifter demon-strates the superficial performances that are required of everyone. Our external selves will continue to change throughout life.

The "life cycle" of the shapeshifters is one of reincarnation and seeming immortality. Like the Cylons of *Battlestar Galactica*, they can have many lives. In fact it is their job to take different human forms, to kill in order to stay alive. If in the same body for too long, a shapeshifter could start to decompose. In "Momentum Deferred" the shapeshifter that replicates Charlie has to take copious amounts of mercury in order to reverse his deterioration since he's been in that one form for too long. But in "Do Shapeshifters Dream of Electric Sheep?" some shapeshifters have been at the same "position" for years, possibly as a result of a different design.

In either case the shapeshifters resemble Cylons in more than just their life cycles. First of all they are organic-synthetic hybrids who can "download" into new bodies in order to prolong their "lives." When they find a new body they take their essential data with them, much like a spirit would be reborn into a new life form in the religious notion of reincarnation. (The venue for the downloading of new Cylon bodies is called the Resurrection Ship.) This is where the lives of shapeshifters and Cylons diverge: Cylons come back as the same person again and again. Shapeshifters don't have an original form or "self"; they rely on the death of humans in order to take a human shape.

Underneath their human skins, shapeshifters are monstrous, amorphous-looking creatures. They appear fully organic as they shift from one body to another, but hideously lizard-like. What does this say about what is lurking beneath the surface of human skin in reality? Are we all shapeshifters to one degree or another? Are we all programmed by some higher (or lower) being?

The Technological Singularity

In *Battlestar Galactica* the Cylons evolve past their original "toaster" status to become higher beings. In "Momentum Deferred" we see that, like Cylons, shapeshifters are fully capable of designing and constructing a model of their own kind. It is interesting that Newton, the only shapeshifter shown assembled in a way that a machine is put together, seems to lack the more human qualities that the other shapeshifters can at least simulate. (In contrast, the other shapeshifters arrive in the prime universe as embryonic forms.) Walter reveals their machine-like parts when he does an autopsy on one in "Momentum Deferred," identifying them as "mechano-organic" hybrids, at least partially human though genetically engineered. Like in the case of a clone, the genetic replication of a human, a hybrid raises the question of whether it constitutes a separate human being with a unique spiritual energy. Certainly when the mechanized parts of the shapeshifters are hidden from view, it's much easier to accept them as human, as when we are first introduced to the developmental stage of the hybrid in "The Man From the Other Side."

In this episode an embryonic shapeshifter is found in an abandoned building and brought to Walter's lab. Walter believes that he can help it continue to develop by reanimating it with electricity. It resembles a giant human embryo and, though we know that it is partly mechanical, it appears completely organic at this stage. As a result its brief moment of life is quite compelling. It is in obvious pain. Walter is able to breathe life into it, essentially resurrecting it, but only momentarily. Walter inadvertently damages it in the process of examination and it "dies" within minutes. This brief awakening of the hybrid simulates birth and death rather than the switching on and off of a machine. Just before its death the shapeshifter shares essential information with Olivia, indicating that something bad will happen. Most significant is its expression of remorse: its last words are "I'm sorry." It is unclear whether it is apologizing to the Fringe team, to Walter, or to Walternate for not fully carrying out its mission. Though some of its words sound as though they emanate from a failing computer, the shapeshifter also seems to be operating at some very human level. Its death is a solemn moment in the lab, as if those present empathize with the hybrid's pain and feel loss because of its "disabled" state — death.

However beastly the shapeshifters appear without the guise of human skin, they resemble animals much more than machines, and because of this they seem to originate from a natural biological development rather than a man-made material. Therein lies the problem: the shapeshifters' ability to replicate the appearance of humans is their best weapon. Is it possible they could be planning to take over? Are they imposters of both worlds, acting as enemy from within this universe and the alternate universe? Would they turn against

Walternate? If that was their plan, the resulting battle would be the ultimate war prophesied in the ZFT Manifesto — the destruction of humanity by technology, a war between humans and the robots they created. This is the technological singularity scenario so well dramatized in *Battlestar Galactica*. And considering all of the anxiety about advances in technology and science throughout the series, this kind of conflict would serve as a fitting culmination of this theme.

In the real world, the technological singularity is an imagined point in time when humans create such a sophisticated and intelligent computer that we will no longer need to create any new technology — the technology will reproduce, design, and upgrade itself. But how would the incorporation of organic robot-soldiers change humanity in our own world? How could it affect the most sacred spaces, such as family?

One of the most important projects of human life — having a family — could be made foolproof with new innovations in reproductive science. Further it could be argued that with such an abysmal rate of successful marriages in the U.S., it would be more practical to choose a shapeshifter as a spouse when it's time to raise a family, someone reliable enough to carry out the most important of all jobs, raising the next generation.

In "Do Shapeshifters Dream of Electric Sheep?" two different shapeshifters pose as men with families. Unlike the hypothetical scenario proposed above, the families have not invited the hybrid into their homes; they have no idea that a shapeshifter replaced the human they knew, even after several years. One of the shapeshifters, Ray Duffy, has grown emotionally attached to the wife and son of the man he replaced, and he begs Newton to let him remain in his position. But are his feelings valid? Are they "real"? The final time that shapeshifter-as-Ray sees Nate, the seven-year-old boy he considers his son, he's supposedly leaving for a night shift at work. Some kind of conflict equivalent to guilt must be roiling around in his shapeshifter mind. As he comforts Nate, assuring him that he's safe from monsters, he adds, "You know . . . sometimes . . . monsters aren't all that bad. Sometimes . . . if you get to spend some time with them, they can be very surprising. They can be incredibly sweet and pure and capable of great, great love. And then, one of them might actually become your very, very best friend." Nate, who considers his "father" his best friend, is clearly quite capable of forming an emotional bond with a partially mechanical being and to Nate, the shapeshifter is a lovable being. But does "Ray" have the same capacity to love that a human does? It would seem so. He chooses to protect his family from a fellow shapeshifter, abandoning his duty and, more significantly, overriding his own programming. Somehow he rejects his basic computer program for the sake of something that is valuable only to humans — love.

Battlestar Galactica explored this same territory with Six, a genetically engineered cyborg who desperately wants to be loved by a human (Gaius Balter) and seems more capable of love than many of the human characters. With a propensity for romantic passion, jealousy, and love, as well as ethical responsibility, Six's human essence supersedes her software commands, like Ray Duffy's does.

This idea of a robot with human feeling brings us back to the original question of this chapter: what are the identifying characteristics of a soul? What is the essence of a person? Both Ray Duffy and Six appear to have the capacity to reciprocate human affection, but are their responses only simulations of human affection? If the actions or emotions are spontaneous responses that exceed the limits of their programming, a combination of feelings that has never been assembled in the same exact sequence, it seems reasonable to acknowledge that these machines, human or not, do have their own essence of life. Despite their mechanized parts shapeshifters could emulate human emotion to such an extent that they are, for all intents and purposes, fully participating in a human relationship. Perhaps this is what it means to have a soul: a person or entity that has the ability to form emotional attachments, at both a physical and an intellectual level, can be said to have some sort of spiritual essence of its own.

In a History Channel special, "The Science of the Soul," Hiroshi Ishiguro, a developer of androids at Osaka University, explains the traditional Japanese belief that objects, as well as humans, have souls — we imbue our creations with souls in the process of creating them. He and other researchers in the robotics department are working at the cutting edge of artificial intelligence; he envisions a day when androids will be able to replace their human counterparts for certain tasks. The Osaka University robotics team has developed some of the most life-like, emotionally "intelligent" robots to date. Ishiguro believes his android has a soul: one doesn't have to be human (or even alive) to be spiritually endowed. He does not equate the term "soul" with the notion of consciousness. Under this belief system, shapeshifters — who are undoubtedly conscious — would be considered on par with humans in terms of spiritual, intellectual, and emotional value.

But Peter does not appreciate the shapeshifters' ability to form human attachments at all. Like Newton he sees the "death" of a shapeshifter as the simple disabling of a computer. Neither Walter nor Olivia approve of Peter "killing" the shapeshifters, but what value do they see, if any, in the shapeshifters? Is there something Peter is missing in his belief that they are "just shapeshifters"? Is it possible that his opinion of them has more to do with his own status as something "more than human"? Or *other* than human? When Walter first finds out about the Peter's destruction of the shapeshifters in "Reciprocity," he tells him, "Every relationship is reciprocal, Peter. When you touch something, it touches you. You're changing, son. When you touched the machine, it changed you. It weaponized you." The shapeshifters are "weaponized" too — indeed, they *are* weapons. Does Peter find their presence threatening or does he find the similarities between himself and the shapeshifters too close for comfort? Perhaps he has some sort of relationship with them, and with Walternate's regime, that motivates him to disable the hybrids. In any case there is a sense that the shapeshifters' status as "Others" is akin to Peter's Otherness.

It is clear that Peter has been "touched" by the machine in some irreversible way. Could this relationship between man and machine symbolize how we have been altered by technology? Perhaps there is no going back now. Like Peter, we are all partially weaponized in order to survive the possible technological singularity.

Technology as an Extension of Humanity

At the end of "Of Human Action" Nina reveals that Tyler Carson, the boy responsible for his own abduction, is one of many Tylers. Part of a Massive Dynamic cloning experiment, he and other boys like him were created for the sole purpose of finding out whether or not mind control was possible. He reaches out to find his real mother, a very human thing to do, only to discover he was a product of the lab rather than the offspring of a loving couple. His mother was only a surrogate and her relationship to Tyler ended when she was no longer needed for the experiment. Essentially Tyler never had a mother. His experience illustrates a post-human world, one in which the biological requisites of the past are no longer relevant.

When we rely on technology for the creation and maintenance of life, we incorporate the synthetic into the organic, which is not necessarily a bad thing. Science has progressed to such an extent that if someone loses the use of a limb or organ, they can continue functioning with the aid of prosthetics. But what happens to our natural powers of cognition when we begin to rely on synthetic parts of the brain or man-made nerve cells? Further what is the difference between a "real" human idea and one that's been generated with the help of an electronic device? It could be argued that we are already connected to electronics in a profound way: even if they are not implanted into our heads, computers are more entangled with human identity than ever before. Many of us *do* use computers for tasks that until recently we did on our own: to generate ideas and problem-solve. In a recently published paper, Inside Digital Media Inc. senior analyst Phil Leigh argues that "smartphones and tablets are becoming cognitive prosthetics. Owners increasingly use them as intelligent aids as routinely as amputees use mechanical limbs for body extensions." Our mobile devices commonly serve as "cognitive prosthetics" to such an extent that we could compare some of our cognitive processes to the shape-shifters' programmed human intelligence.

In his work on the technological singularity, Ray Kurzweil argues that beyond a certain point there will no longer be a distinction between biological organisms and machines, and the division between our physical selves and our virtual experiences will become invisible. "The singularity will represent the culmination of the merger of our biological thinking and existence with our thinking." He asserts that our world will still be a very human one, but that humanity will be completely redefined as we reach beyond the limits of biology.

By strict definition many people are already cyborgs. A cybernetic organism is just a biological life form enhanced with synthetic aids such as contacts or prosthetic limbs. Even a watch or a pair of glasses could be classified as a mechanized aid because the object is integrated into our physical identity, unlike something like a calculator, a tool that is separate from the body. We should also consider plastic surgery; the incorporation of synthetic breasts could "aid" by enhancing appearance. What about synthetically concocted moods and personalities through antidepressants and anti-anxiety medication? These man-made devices and substances could alter our personality, and thus are synthetic aids. But do things such as wigs and high heels change us? What about cars, cell phones, and laptops? All of these items are, to some degree, extensions of our selves, enhancing, obscuring, or detracting from our identities. They influence the way we think, the way we think about ourselves, and the way others perceive us. But does the integration of these objects erase our humanity or does our humanity further evolve as a result of new technology?

In *Fringe* we see how new technology alters characters, sometimes changing them at a fundamental level. Many times a character is described as having been made "special" through science, usually meaning that a scientist who is playing God somehow enhanced them. Walter and William Bell consider Olivia to be their creation, as well as the other cortexiphan children. In "Momentum Deferred" Rebecca Kibner, a former test subject, tells Walter that he made her special by helping her see things no one else could. In "Power Hungry" Dr. Fischer tells Joseph Meegar that science has made him special. Nina has been re-created in part through the power of technology. She is a cyborg: part machine, part woman. Though only her arm is affected does having a synthetic body part make her less human?

Olivia's experience in Walter's drug trials changes her nature forever. The alternate world provides a "control group" for the characters, making it that much easier to see the effects of scientific advances on humanity. Without cortexiphan Fauxlivia is a different kind of person — a happier, more likable person, according to Olivia — due, at least in part, to the fact that she was not subject to experiments.

And yet cortexiphan was originally created to preserve the great potential that children possess against the limitations that develop in adulthood. Walter and Bell wanted to explore that potential to create superhuman beings; the ramifications of such a process, if successful, would change the future of humanity. Is it right for this dormant quality to be cultivated through synthetic methods? How human is a superhuman? Should a species distinction be drawn between the two, if superhumans became markedly different in intellect or sensory power?

For a long time we have distinguished our place in the biological world from that of other living creatures by our sense of self-awareness. However it is not as widely accepted anymore that humans are the only animals with this capability. Other higher primates display this behavior, and recently scientists have proven that magpies might also be self-aware. However self-aware, they likely do not have the capacity to retain memories for long, and they certainly can't make a record of their thoughts and memories. The same can be said of all other non-human animals. Some primates use tools and even seem to create unique cultures, but none can record their history, whether in memory or on paper. We can and do contemplate our origin, puzzle out the purpose of existence, and consider our mortality. Being human means we have a special capacity for empathy and a tendency to create moral boundaries and social institutions.

So it seems fairly simple to distinguish ourselves from other biological creatures, but the line between human intelligence and artificial human intelligence is not clear. Is it necessary to value one over the other if they both seem to operate in the same manner? At a 2008 summit on the question of humanity, sociologist Nikolas Rose acknowledged the close proximity that we have with man-made machines. He told *Wired*, "I think we're more than biological creatures."

In "The Man From the Other Side," a human embryonic stem cell is reflected, enlarged, and developed in the shapeshifter embryo that Walter pokes and prods in his lab. This image reflects a real-life controversy about the beginning of human life. Does stem cell research devalue humanity by creating life (a human blastocyst) only to destroy it for the sake of further research? Is Walter's engineering and destruction of this "robot" all that different from the creation and destruction of fully organic material?

Is enhancing the mechanism and software of a shapeshifter any different, from a moral standpoint, than enhancing humans through cortexiphan? Consider too those individuals whose genetic code was altered, likely by a ZFT figure. The goal of Walter and Bell's experiments was to create super soldiers for a new kind of army, precisely the same goal that drove the development of shapeshifters. The line between humanity and post-humanity seems awfully thin when we examine these two scenarios.

Walter himself has acted as a guinea pig, usually in his own experiments. But one experiment he will never remember — and for good reason. At Walter's request Bell removed certain parts of his brain, presumably because they contained both painful memories and dangerous ideas. Did Walter compromise his own humanity in doing this? As humans we are all called upon to bear our memories and control our ideas. *Eternal Sunshine of the Spotless Mind* (2004), a film that dramatizes the dangers of "wiping the slate clean," warns against unraveling one's unique bundle of memories. After all what is the essence of a human if not his or her collection of ideas, emotional attachments, and memories — both good and bad? The fact that Walter had forgotten something so important as the existence of an alternate universe has far-reaching consequences. While Walter pined away for years on end at St. Claire's, Walternate was making plans to infiltrate and destroy the entire universe.

CHAPTER 10

Looking-Glass Worlds
The Alternate Universe

> "Two roads diverged in a yellow wood,
> And sorry I could not travel both
> And be one traveler, long I stood"
>
> — Robert Frost, "The Road Not Taken"

The parallel universe is the most significant (and central) concept of *Fringe* thus far, serving not only to explore an important scientific potentiality but as a meaningful allegory. It opens up a broad philosophical discussion about identity and the nature of the self.

Like time travel the alternate universe in *Fringe* has some grounding in real scientific theories; the two ideas are closely "entangled," so to speak. In the last several decades new theories about the nature of reality and the possibility of other universes (or "many worlds") have emerged. This chapter primarily explores the science fiction tradition of alternate worlds, but there is theoretical physics behind the fictional ideas. In the 1950s Hugh Everett III proposed what would become known as the many worlds theory.

The famous "double slit" experiment, which some argue is central to quantum physics, demonstrated that particles sometimes behave like waves. When a subatomic particle — let's say an electron — passes through what we can imagine as a board with two small openings, it must "choose" one slit or the other. But quantum physicists discovered that the particles seemed to pass through both at the same time, creating interference with one another, like a wave. But how could a particle, a small bit of matter, be like a wave or be in two places at once? One possibility was that the measurement or observation of each individual particle affected its behavior. The "Copenhagen Interpretation," established in 1935, explains that the electron behaves as a waveform until it is observed, at which time it becomes a particle again. Another possibility, Everett's idea, suggested that a second reality was momentarily created based on the two options. The particle passed through one slit in our world and the other slit in another world and then reunited as one particle. Further there are multiple outcomes of the particle's trajectory: it might miss the slits altogether in another reality.

Physicists have discovered that subatomic particles, in fact, do not travel in the same manner as larger objects in the visible world. On close inspection electrons actually jump around in an unpredictable manner; they disappear and appear without moving through the space in between. Where do they exist during these quantum jumps? Subatomic particles' bizarre movement suggests that for every opportunity in which there is more than one option — or, from a human perspective, for every new decision we are required to make — new realities emerge.

Another way to approach the idea of parallel universes is to ponder the other spectrum of the physical world — the farthest reaches of space. In his 2005 book *Parallel Worlds*, string theorist and theoretical physicist Michio Kaku suggests that parallel worlds *do* interact with one another, perhaps creating new universes as they collide. According to string theory, alternate universes possibly exist in "parallel dimensional membranes." Another string theorist, Brian Greene, reveals the implications of an infinite universe and how the notion of a never-ending world *requires* that there be parallel universes to our own. In an interview on National Public Radio's program *Fresh Air*, Greene considered the possibility that the universe is infinite. In this context the "universe" simply means everything that exists. If it is true that our universe goes on forever, then "there are only so many ways matter can arrange itself within that infinite universe. Eventually matter has to repeat itself and arrange itself in similar ways. So if the universe is infinitely large, it is also home to infinite parallel universes." He compares the universe to a deck of cards that are shuffled an infinite number of times: "If you shuffle that deck enough times, the orders will have to repeat." The composition of matter can only be arranged in so many ways; the exact arrangement of matter will be duplicated at some point, and an infinite number of times too. If true, then there is another Earth out there just like ours and other human beings who are our exact doubles. And, like in *Fringe*'s alternate universe, there would be universes with slight variations on ours.

Parallel universe theories are much more complex than that, of course, but the scientific possibilities are extraordinary. The existence of "many worlds" is purely theoretical at this point, but the mathematical constructs of today could very well turn into hard data in years to come. In a recent interview Dr. Sean Carroll of the California Institute of Technology said that it might even be possible for someone to "devise a machine that lets one universe communicate with another."

The Narrative Tradition of the AU

In Lewis Carroll's story *Through the Looking-Glass* (1871), Alice discovers that on the other side of the mirror, things aren't just opposite; they are completely nonsensical. At first the differences reflect a simple inversion: it is summer on one side and winter on the other. One side is messy and the other is clean and organized. But beyond the reaches of the mirror reflection, the "reality" of Wonderland turns out to be very different from Alice's world. When she looks down at the chess pieces she sees that they move and speak, and she finds that flowers have faces and voices.

Olivia's experience is similar. When she and the team cross over to the other side, initially things seem similar to the world back home, but she soon learns there are gaping holes in the universe plugged with a resin-like material, tenuously holding existence together. There are no talking flowers, but the advanced technology, such as instantaneous travel, appears magical. Some characters who are dead on the original side, like Charlie and Olivia's mother, are living, and Walter's counterpart, Walternate, behaves like a textbook villain with a plan to wipe out Olivia's entire universe.

Many classic tales employ alternate reality storylines to illustrate the possibilities of what could have been; the concept of "the road not taken" is not confined to the realm of science fiction. Besides fantastical children's tales like *Through the Looking-Glass* and *The Wonderful Wizard of Oz*, other more realistic narratives (relatively speaking) such as Charles Dickens' *A Christmas Carol* (1843) use the parallel world idea, when the Ghost of Christmas Yet to Come reveals a future in which Ebenezer Scrooge is still an unreformed selfish old man. *It's a Wonderful Life* (1946) explores an alternate universe, one in which George Bailey was never born. These are both redemption stories; they provide the central character a fresh perspective and a second chance. They are also strongly grounded in Christian imagery of angels, sin, forgiveness, and rebirth. In these stories the characters are completely transformed as a result of glimpsing another possible reality. The alternate reality is depicted as a nightmarish scenario, something to be feared. It serves as a warning about what might happen if the course of destiny slips off balance and also illustrates the web of connections and influences one individual can have on his or her community.

All three of the aforementioned narratives focus on a single character's history (and alternate history). Science fiction stories, however, tend to consider a broader perspective of the what-could-have-been storyline by showing the grander repercussions of one small change. Sweeping historical shifts are portrayed in science fiction alternate universe tales, although the general concept is very similar to that in the more conventional works of fiction. In most cases the other reality, or the imagined reality, reflects the deepest desires and the greatest fears of the central characters.

Stargate SG-1 and *Doctor Who* have utilized the alternate universe mode extensively. Numerous comic book narratives, as well as the stories in video games, use the alternate timeline scheme too. There are few television shows that base their entire narrative on alternate universes, but one of the longest-running franchises within this medium has explored the AU narrative mode to a great extent: *Star Trek*. In an original series' episode, "Mirror, Mirror," a "mirror universe" storyline was employed and, later, the same idea was explored more deeply in the *Deep Space Nine* series. *Star Trek: Enterprise* revisited the theme in "In a Mirror Darkly," a two-part episode that features the crew's mirror universe selves. The recent J.J. Abrams *Star Trek* movie (2009) used an alternate universe to resolve any continuity errors with previous Star Trek narratives. In a review from the *Boston Globe* Ty Burr argues, "Conceptually, this is a genius move: it establishes the entire movie as an alternate, parallel *Star Trek* universe in which Abrams and his screenwriters Roberto Orci and Alex Kurtzman can do as they wish, fanboys and the canon be damned." (Incidentally Alex Kurtzman and Roberto Orci are two of the original creators of *Fringe*, and Abrams is the show's executive producer.)

Other films use this mode too, with the alternate reality scheme not necessarily defined in scientific terms. Many times the technical specifications of the alternate universe are ignored altogether. *Sliding Doors*, the 1998 feature film starring Gwyneth Paltrow, demonstrates a split in reality by showing two different outcomes of a single incident. When the main character, Helen, gets caught in the sliding doors of the train, her timeline diverges. Two different courses follow, one in which she misses the train and the other in which she successfully catches it. The movie follows both storylines, revealing some major differences but also some striking similarities, sometimes leaving Helen facing similar circumstances in both timelines.

Similarly *Donnie Darko* (2001) features a "Tangent Universe" where all of existence is threatened by an impending black hole. The premise is that if Donnie does not take action, the tangent universe will collapse on itself in twenty-eight days. According to the tenets of the film's fictional *Philosophy of Time Travel*, the collapsed Tangent Universe will create a black hole, taking the Primary Universe with it. Might this same thing happen in *Fringe*, where a black hole will result from the crashing together of the two universes? Walter describes the "soft spot" as a small hole that will grow into a vortex and suck everything into it ("6B"). (This spot was described in the alternate universe as a micro black hole.) In *Donnie Darko* Donnie is the "Living Receiver," responsible for saving the primary universe by sacrificing himself. Like Peter, he has a fateful relationship with the workings of the universe. His own existence is threatened in order to save the existence of everyone else.

"Catch That Zeppelin!" (1975), an alternate-history short story by

Fritz Leiber, also employs the parallel universe trope. Though much of the action is set in a timeline with a history very different from our own, there are revealing glimpses into our world, where cars are still powered by gasoline, "blackamoors" are still suffering the aftereffects of American slavery, and planes, rather than Zeppelins, are used for air travel. The story is narrated by Adolf Hitler, but an Adolf with a much more redeeming history. What makes this story significant to *Fringe* are the alternate universe's distinguishing characteristics, especially the use of airships, a common image in alternate universe stories. When Walter showcases the window to the alternate universe at a meeting with military leaders, a dirigible airship is seen near the Empire State Building ("Peter"), the same building where Leiber's narrator is planning to catch his Zeppelin flight. We see the Empire docking station again in "Immortality" when Fauxlivia is waiting for Frank's airship to arrive. Like in "Catch That Zeppelin!" technology seems smoother and more efficient in the alternate world of *Fringe*, and social problems seem more under control, though not solved.

As mentioned in chapter 4, "All the Myriad Ways" by Larry Niven is an exemplary parallel universe story and especially comparable to *Fringe*. It posits the multiverse theory in which there are an infinite number of universes, all variations on our own. The idea that each individual has made every conceivable choice for every different set of circumstances leads many people to despair. In other words, it doesn't matter what choice you make; there are an infinite number of selves who will make the "wrong" or unethical choice. In this story the people feel a close connection to their other-universe counterparts. They understand that they are only one part of the whole. It might do Olivia some good to realize that Fauxlivia is just another part of her, that they share the same emotions and tendencies.

This concept is something that Walter begins to acknowledge in "6B." He understands why Walternate has made certain choices, realizing that he is more like Walternate than he would like to be. He understands that they are essentially the same person. Olivia acknowledges this fact out loud when she first meets Fauxlivia: "You've got to trust me. I'm you" ("Over There, Part II"). Later in the same scene Fauxlivia says, "You are nothing like me" to Olivia, something Olivia has tried to believe ever since, essentially fighting against herself.

Fringe's Alternate Universe

The first voyage into the alternate universe happens in the season 2 two-part finale ("Over There"), but the existence of it is mentioned much earlier. In a season 1 episode, aptly titled "The Road Not Taken," Walter explains to Olivia that her visions are probably not hallucinations but glimpses into another reality in which things are slightly different. He describes this in terms of branches, where the diverging universes are shaped by human decisions. His understanding is that each decision will create a different outcome and thus another reality. He says that the idea of life as linear is only an illusion, that in reality every choice we make "leads to a new path. To go to work. To stay home. And each choice we take creates a new reality."

When Olivia glimpses a subtly altered world, one in which Broyles' desk is situated differently and there are two victims of the pyrokinesis incident rather than one, she feels like she is going crazy. But Walter explains that she is actually glimpsing the other side, which might mean that she is physically here but seeing through Fauxlivia's eyes. At one point Charlie — from over there — interacts with Olivia. Does he see her or Fauxlivia? Perhaps this example of glimpsing the other side is more like a hallucination compared to the actually crossing over that she experiences at the end of season 2.

In "White Tulip" Olivia's consciousness undergoes a similar, if more common, alteration. She experiences déjà vu as the Fringe team investigates the train passengers' deaths. Walter suggests that déjà vu could be a glimpse into the other world (and a reassurance that one is on the right track). Another interesting aspect of this episode is that we see a microcosm of the branching universe phenomenon, all in one episode. Dr. Peck makes different decisions on each trip he takes back in time, and in doing so he creates new realities for everyone. In one reality he inadvertently kills a carload of train passengers, but in another he prevents this tragedy. To extrapolate from that, within each of the parallel universes, is there an infinite number of new realities being created every second? If so, this complicates the idea of the two parallel universes. Does the term "parallel" indicate that these universes are equally authentic and that they can stand alone? Or should we assume that an infinite number of universes exist? For the purpose of this chapter, I will assume that there are only two universes, and that they have the potential to meld into one, possibly creating a third universe and erasing the first two.

Crossing Over

The rules of the parallel universes seem fairly clear. Though the two universes operate independently of one another, there are cracks in each that may result in the destruction of one or both worlds. The technology and history of the worlds are slightly different, but most people hold the same jobs as their counterparts, live in the same places, and are married to the same people. The one thing that seems inconsistent is the mode of travel when crossing from one world to the other. The following is a list of different ways things and people move from one universe to the other:

- An old typewriter and a mirror: Moving data from one universe to the other is a simple, if fantastical, process that's reminiscent of the Alice stories, both with its low-tech, old-fashioned style and the use of a mirror.
- The glass window: In the 1980s Walter and William Bell created a window that allows images of the other side to become visible.
- Body surfing and drug use: The cortexiphan kids worked together using their superhuman abilities to cross over.
- Walter's device: Walter's initial mode of crossing over included a special machine and a soft spot in the universe, which was located on an iced-over patch of Reiden Lake.
- The mystery of William Bell's travels: It is possible that Nina and William Bell were somehow involved in the creation of Walter's machine, although they both discouraged Walter from crossing over. Apparently Bell began traveling after this first breach. But how he did it remains a mystery, as Brandon says in "Over There, Part 1."
- Alternate universe technology: Olivia momentarily crossed over when she was submerged in the tank of water ("Amber 31422"). Later she used Walternate's old lab to cross over

permanently ("Entrada").

- The shapeshifters: They seem to cross over in embryonic form, but how do they return to the alternate universe?
- Love: The couple in apartment 6B communicates across universes, which Walter describes as some sort of "quantum emotional entanglement."

The Allegory of the AU: Duality and Balance

The two universes represent the duality within each character. Peter has a dark past and a potential for destructive acts, but he is also a good person who cares deeply for his father. At times Olivia seems emotionally broken and self-destructive, but she also serves as a beacon of strength and idealism. Walter's dual nature is the most explicit. As a mad scientist he has created his share of monsters, but he tries to balance these transgressions by helping to undo the damage he caused. Like Peter he has a latent destructive side that he must keep at bay.

The construct of the two universes also symbolizes the duality of the show's overarching themes: fate and free will, destruction and creation, mind and body, reason and faith. In this way we can look at the parallel universes as two sides of the same coin. For instance in one world Olivia is sensual, and in the other she operates almost solely by rational logic. But she needs both mind and body to function as a whole person, just as the universes seem dependent on one another for the other side of their "coin."

Drawing from Eastern religious traditions we find excellent models of balance, whereas notions of opposition and duality predominate many Western matters of faith and philosophy. Christianity, for instance, draws sharp lines between heaven and hell and good and evil. In faiths such as Buddhism and Hinduism, symbolic images — a balancing of stones and myths about gods of creation and destruction — promote wholeness. Consider the image of the yin and the yang, a picture of inclusiveness that maintains a balanced tension between black and white. It can be difficult to manage a marriage of two opposing sides when we think of them as disconnected rather than two parts of a whole. But in many schools of thought, opposites are complementary; both sides must be present for either to thrive. Peter's reference to the popular self-help book *If You Meet the Buddha on the Road, Kill Him!* in "The Firefly" may signify his need for balance, not only through Eastern philosophy but through embracing life's ambiguity. Accepting the tension of contradictory ideas and feelings is one way to achieve balance.

Passion Versus Reason

Western thought traditionally creates a disconnect between the mind and the body or passion and reason. The advances in science and psychiatry in the twentieth century has only exacerbated this construct. Many passionate emotions can be attributed to hormonal surges and dismissed as less "real" than the cold hard facts. And if anyone is a fan of cold hard facts, it's Olivia.

Olivia struggles with her inability to engage in intimate relationships. She suppresses her emotions and does not allow herself to be vulnerable around others. Because of her past she is always on guard, ready to protect her interior life from any intruders. She does not share much information about her personal life, leaving others to guess at her true character. Even in play she's uncomfortable revealing anything intimate about herself. In "The Road Not Taken" Walter guesses that Olivia is a "Corn Flakes gal," the description a reflection of Olivia's plain, pragmatic approach to life. But she's not interested in sharing; instead she just changes the subject. When passionate emotions come into play, emotions that are influenced by adrenaline or other hormonal responses, Olivia has a problem. She seems to think that anger, jealousy, love, or lust will leave her irreparably vulnerable.

Fauxlivia, on the other hand, embraces both the sensual and emotional qualities of life. She is outspoken and gregarious, always joking around with her colleagues. Her sense of levity stands in stark contrast to Olivia's grave demeanor. Fauxlivia is a more colorful version of Olivia, both figuratively and literally. She laughs easily and often, wears makeup, and is in a passionate romantic relationship. The color of her hair is a bone of contention for some viewers who think an exact replica should have the same hair color, but the hue actually reflects her sensual nature. Red symbolizes passion. It also happens to be the representative color for the alternate universe. Olivia, on the other hand, lives in the blue universe and her nature reflects its cooler tone.

Creation and Destruction

One of the most important themes in *Fringe*, the creation/destruction dichotomy, is a fundamental theological concept common to many world religions. The teachings of Hinduism tells us that everything with a beginning must have an ending. There is a god of creation (Brahma) and gods of destruction (Shiva and the goddess Kali). Shiva stands not only for change and destruction, but also for letting go. There are other religions, especially polytheistic ones, which have gods of destruction, sometimes better known as gods of war, natural disasters, or death. They are usually viewed as representatives of a very important part of the life cycle.

Although religious themes are not nearly as prominent in *Fringe* as in *Battlestar Galactica* or *Lost*, the prophetic vision of Peter's involvement with the end of the world echoes mythological traditions in its prediction of an apocalypse and Peter as a figure of religious sacrifice. The machine will destroy one of the universes, according to the prophecy, but it is a machine that also creates. Though the drawing of the machine resembles a Leonardo da Vinci sketch, with Peter's body comparable to the Vitruvian man, his pose is also Christ-like, an image of a sacrificial son-of-god on the cross. Peter is the son of a god-like figure, a modern-day scientist who has manipulated the world to such an extent that he has "created" the world in which they live. Will Peter be able to save one or more worlds by activating the machine at the cost of his own life?

Fate and Free Will

"Fate is a tricky thing," says Nick Lane in "Over There, Part 1," explaining why he's now decided to help Walter and the others cross into the other universe. Just moments before, Walter quotes Shakespeare — "all the world's a stage" — perhaps unwittingly suggesting that life is like a play, mapped out from the very beginning.

Although the Observers seem to know the fate of human history, they cannot always predict how people will respond or what choice they will make. A strong case is made for both destiny and the individual's freedom to create his or her own path.

Consider how fate is introduced in "6B" — as a matter of probability. The coin is used as a device for Walter to determine if the apartment is in a soft spot, but it is also the tool that appears to control destiny. The flipping of a coin determines the fate of the couple that has been together for several decades. The husband, Derrick, loses the coin toss and as a result is electrocuted when he goes to fix the breaker. Though flipping the coin was an act of free will, they left it up to chance (or fate, perhaps) to see who would be chosen to carry out the task at hand. In the other universe the opposite happens: the wife loses the coin toss and ends up dead.

Similarly fate and free will function together to orchestrate Olivia and Peter's relationship. The season 3 episode "Subject 13" suggests that Peter and Olivia's relationship was meant to be. But we know that Olivia's involvement with Walter was not exactly an act of destiny. Though after his release from the institution Walter claims not to remember important events from the past, there were other forces at play when Olivia was brought into the Fringe Division. Either Nina, whose relationship with Broyles is a bit of a mystery, or William Bell must have had a hand in it. (In chapter 11, the tension between fate and free will is explored in greater depth.)

Balance

The structure of two opposing ideas is mirrored in the two universes, also at odds with one another. As Peter suggests, there may be a way to reconcile them and keep both intact.

When Walternate explains that "nature only recognizes balance and imbalance" and that he will unilaterally restore balance by destroying one of the universes ("Amber 31422"), he seems to miss the point. If we view the two worlds of *Fringe* as two halves, then restoring balance requires that they both remain intact. From Walternate's perspective the destruction caused by the holes in the "fabric of reality" warrants some sort of extermination of this side, since he does not assume that the two "worlds" are of one piece. But from the viewer's perspective (outside of both worlds) it seems to make the most sense that the two are halves of a whole, especially if these universes are fated to merge.

Neither world is perfect; neither side is completely right or absolutely wrong about the way it perceives reality. Accordingly neither world is complete. It seems that the two worlds need one another and that neither can function on its own. Each of the characters is missing something that his or her counterpart possesses, whether it's a personality trait or a skill or a loved one. They would be complete (or at least closer to complete) if they could somehow merge.

The Doppelgänger Effect: Reflection and the Double

The Lab Notes that correspond with "The Dreamscape" address the nature of one's identity as a recurring reflection: "Herein lies the danger of a strange loop, an endless spiral of meta-realities, each self gazing into yet a deeper self. The experience could lead to the destruction of identity. Or perhaps its affirmation — for what is self but an endless recursion, looking at oneself in a mirror within a mirror within a mirror." In the introduction to *The Hidden Reality: Parallel Universes and the Deep Laws of the Cosmos*, an accessible text about the possibility of parallel universes, renowned physicist Brian Greene reminisces about the double mirrors of his childhood bedroom. He says that contemplating the infinite reflections may have enhanced his own creative perspective of the world. "I delighted in seeing image after image populating the parallel glass planes, extending back as far as the eye could discern"(3). Although he acknowledges that mirror reflections, of course, do *not* signify alternate worlds, Greene opens the book with this image to clearly illustrate the notion of parallel selves. As a child he would stand between the two mirrors and watch the line of reflections follow his own movements. "Sometimes I would imagine an irreverent me way down the line who refused to fall into place, disrupting the steady progression and creating a new reality that informed the ones that followed." In *Fringe*, like in many other altverse stories, the mirror serves as a portal to the next world over. Consider the shapeshifters' mode of communication: they use a special mirror to reflect their typewritten messages. This process has absolutely no scientific grounding, but it reveals the narrative's preoccupation with the double — the replica that is slightly off, something similar to Greene's "irreverent me."

The warring of the alternate universes represents the self fighting itself — aggression and repression directed inward. In fiction the double dramatizes the contradictory nature of the self, reflecting the potential that normally lies dormant in each person. *Fringe* employs the archetype of the double in various modes, but one clear instance of it is the incorporation of twin siblings into an episode's central plot. In "The Road Not Taken" twin sisters endowed with pyrokinetic abilities become the subject of the Fringe team's investigation. Their presence, which precedes the appearance of the alternate *Fringe* universe, foreshadows the far-reaching doppelgänger effect that occurs once the other universe emerges. In season 3 twins are again the subject of an investigation, this time for the alt–Fringe team. In "Amber 31422" one twin is trapped in amber for several years while his twin brother takes his place, pretending to be the husband of his brother's wife and acting as father to his kids. This scenario stands as a clear parallel narrative to Fauxlivia hijacking Olivia's life.

In another entry of his Lab Notes Walter writes, "I read my old notes and I see myself through a glass darkly." This frequently quoted line, "through a glass darkly," from the first book of Corinthians, conveys the inability to see oneself clearly and fully in a "face-to-face" meeting with the self. Walter sees a distorted shadow of himself, an unrecognizable copy. This idea of seeing the self "darkly" is brought to the forefront in the alternate universe where Walternate is an even more distorted version of the self Walter knows.

That jarring moment when one recognizes his or her reflection in a store window after initially seeing the self as a stranger creates an "evil twin" effect. Viewing the self as Other, even for a split second, is a fitting metaphor for recognizing the "shadow," the Jungian image of the hidden personality. This phenomenon is described well in Robert Heinlein's classic time travel and multiverse story "By His Bootstraps" (1941). Bob Wilson sees a duplicate of himself from the future, but does not recognize him: "Still, there was something familiar about the face; he felt that he should have recognized it, that he had seen it many times before under different circumstances." Perhaps those "different circumstances," perceiving the self from within the physical body, make all the difference.

Indeed seeing a clear reflection of the self is uncommon. This is what "the double" can provide: a "glass" that reveals unseen parts of one's self. From a narrative perspective it's a way to reveal new dimensions of the characters, which make a story richer and more compelling. In Fyodor Dostoevsky's novella *The Double* (1846)

Nikolay Mikhaylovsky spots a doppelgänger of himself. He becomes increasingly anxious to the point of mental instability when the imposter seems poised to destroy his life. The double takes over his professional life and his social standing, making him completely obsolete. Perhaps these are the fears that the *Fringe* characters develop, especially Olivia whose life was temporarily usurped by Fauxlivia.

The trope of the double is as old as storytelling itself. Sometimes the double is a ghost, a shadow, or a spirit; in other instances it is more subtle, perhaps a case of mistaken identity. But what does it mean to have a shadow or reflection of one's self come to life? The presence of a doppelgänger usually compels a character to explore his or her dual nature through the alter-ego who is perhaps less rational, more creative, or more courageous. Olivia, for instance, learns from Fauxlivia's example that she is capable of intimacy, and Olivia finds a balance between her own personality and her double's. Let's examine a few of the characters and their doubles more closely.

Olivia/Fauxlivia: Like Bob Wilson, Olivia is forced to confront her doppelgänger; when Olivia holds Fauxlivia at gunpoint, Olivia explains, "You gotta trust me. I'm you." ("Over There, Part 2"). After Olivia returns from "over there" she complains that Fauxlivia took over everything when she came to this side, pretending to be Olivia. She feels that an imposter has tarnished her home, her clothes, and her love life, and she is outraged that Peter could mistake her double for her. She tries to keep Fauxlivia's haunting presence at arm's length, completely separating herself from her counterpart, when in fact Fauxlivia is Olivia. Fauxlivia is what Olivia fears, what Olivia hates, what Olivia denies. She is Olivia's shadow self, what Sigmund Freud called the Id. To borrow Freudian language Fauxlivia, like the Id, responds to the "pleasure principle," while Olivia seems to fear it.

Walter/Walternate: The major difference between the two Walters is that Walter has engaged in painful soul-searching for years, trying to atone for his wrongdoings, while Walternate has turned his own suffering into a powerful desire for vengeance. Walter's guilt has turned him into a fragile but compassionate human being while Walternate's rage has made him cold and dogmatic. Walter lost both his freedom and his mental stability; Walternate continues his work as he rises in the ranks of power. In one universe Walter is able to form meaningful bonds with others; in the other Walternate is dictatorial and unreflective, and people fear him rather than love him.

Charlie/Scarlie: Charlie's death in season 2 affects Olivia deeply. We can see how his absence has compounded Olivia's reserved nature by contrasting it with Fauxlivia's close relationship with "Scarlie." The lighthearted banter that Olivia once shared with Charlie is lost. But Charlie is more reflective than Scarlie. Although they share the same sense of humor, Charlie is less animated than his alternate self, as well as more nurturing.

Broyles/Colonel Broyles: Broyles and his alt-world counterpart, Colonel Broyles, are very similar. On this side Broyles is no longer married or living with his family. Colonel Broyles, however, has suffered through the abduction and abuse of his son, who was eventually returned but was never the same again. Essentially the two Broyles share the same sense of duty and honor. As Olivia tells Broyles, "He wasn't that unlike you. He was honorable, committed. He feared for his family, for their future" ("Marionette"). Colonel Broyles proves to be a hero in "Entrada," not for just one universe but for both. He confirmed what we had already suspected: that the people from the other side are just like us — they have their weaknesses, but they can also perform very noble deeds.

Astrid/Altstrid: Astrid's alternate universe counterpart is a strange choice for the character, if an interesting one. Altstrid, like Olivia's alternate self, is something of an examination between nature and nurture. It appears that something traumatic happened at some point in this other Astrid's past. Unlike Astrid, she is stiff and robotic, a brilliant but emotionally challenged human being. She is so connected to her computer, always coming up with the probability of one set of data or another, that she often seems like she's turned into one herself. Though Astrid is quite brainy too, she is much more socially competent than Altstrid.

The Nature of Reality: Illusions, Visions, and the Imagination

Fringe effectively incorporates psychological thrills and fantastic potentialities by manipulating the mysteries of the human mind. It is only when Olivia is experiencing intense fear, coupled with love, that she can see through to the other side. At first the viewer interprets her visions as only hallucinations or déjà vu, but soon enough it becomes clear that there is another reality, one that is always "right in front of our eyes. We just can't see it," as Walter explains in "Peter." Nonetheless there always lurks a sense that none of this is "real," that, perhaps, much of the story's action is happening only in Walter's head (or Walternate's).

That narrative trick, however, might not go over well with audiences. But if it were to turn out that the story was "just in someone's head," William Bell's elusive existence suggests it is actually *his* story. Bell always knows what to do, what *must* happen, and what's going to happen. But his omniscience is matched if not exceeded by the Observers. Is the whole story some sort of collective dream of the Observers?

In some narratives, especially those that are not explicitly fantastic, alternate realities are illustrated through dream sequences to explore other dimensions of a character or to show how things would work out if a crucial decision had been different — like in Charles Dickens' *A Christmas Carol* (as previously mentioned). The Observers as dreamers would be a science fiction twist on this idea: if it turns out it was all a dream, it was an *alien's* dream.

Though the dream explanation is an unlikely resolution for the series, it points to a very important narrative component to *Fringe*: perspective. Perhaps this is not a crazy man's hallucination or a dream at all but instead a compilation of the data that the Observers have collected. Like the it-was-all-a-dream resolution, this idea would turn our perspective of the show's reality on its head. What if they are simply gathering information for a report on humans, something they can share with their own people?

This is all speculation of course, but it is just one example of how the creators of the show could easily change the viewers' understanding of *Fringe* simply by playing with perspective. We have been led to think the show is mainly about Olivia, Peter, and Walter, but what if we "zoom out," so to speak, and it is revealed that the humans are only one subject of interest in the Observers' vast laboratory? In an odd way this would bring us full circle, back to the question of the mad scientist and the ethical implications of science and engineering.

There are some episodes in which the question of reality is scrutinized in a different way. In an intriguing scene in "Concentrate and Ask Again" Sam Weiss makes us question what is real. He seems to be above all of the other drama, just watching to see what happens. But how does he, a bowling alley manager, know so much about Peter, Olivia, and the other universe? Obviously things are not what they seem within the realm of Sam Weiss. Is all of this happening in Sam Weiss's fantasy world?

In "Olivia. In the Lab. With the Revolver" Sam tells us that he is "older and taller" than he looks. The "older" description suggests the possibility that he is something akin to *Lost*'s Richard Alpert, a character granted immortality, though this is completely downplayed in "The Last Sam Weiss." But how do we explain the "taller" part? Going back to the possibility that all of humankind is part of a much larger experiment in an unfathomably enormous lab, perhaps Sam is only a visitor who has altered his physical dimensions so that he can interact with humans. Is it possible that Broyles' assessment of the Pattern in the pilot episode was more accurate than he could have known? His explanation would serve as the perfect foreshadowing for this theory: it's "as if someone out there is experimenting; only the whole world is their lab."

The Power of Imagination

In "Subject 13" the significance of the human imagination is explored. Walter Bishop is well aware that we can create something extraordinary out of ordinary working materials: he uses his most distinguishing feature — his mind — to change the world, or to create new worlds altogether, new "futures" as the Observer says.

The idea that we can manipulate our realities is one of the more inspiring themes of *Fringe*, even though the manipulation can turn destructive. As horrified as we are by the making of monsters through hybridization or rewriting of genetic codes, we are awed by the scientific possibilities of such an act. Though Walter jeopardizes the fate of two (or more) universes by saving a single life, that act changes the direction of his life entirely. He has singlehandedly altered his reality.

In "Subject 13" Elizabeth tells Peter that although we don't always like our reality, we "have our hearts and our imaginations to make the best of it." Indeed Walter has used his imagination to "make the best of it" as he sees fit, and Elizabeth encourages Peter to do the same. By manipulating the machine, is Peter undoing his father's mistakes? Would he redefine reality according to his own ideals or take into consideration what is best for the greater good?

Elizabeth's message in "Subject 13," which emphasizes the power of the human spirit, is a compelling one, not only for great minds like Peter and Walter, but for humanity in general. As she points out the simple act of reengineering a tulip so that it will grow in a warm climate is one way to "make the best of" what we have and change reality to suit our tastes. Tulips in Florida are much like snow in Florida — rare and short-lived. Nonetheless, as Elizabeth says, the professor who made a new kind of warm weather tulip "used his brain and his imagination to turn the world into what he wanted it to be." Peter, in turn, encourages young Olivia to imagine things "the way you want them" and then to turn them into reality. With this newfound power Olivia makes it snow right then and there on a field of white Florida tulips.

As it would happen another creation of Olivia's, the drawing of Peter and herself, sets off a change of events in the next world. Inadvertently Olivia informs Walternate that Peter is in another universe. Her drawing initiates a string of events that alter an entire universe. In effect this small act of artistry serves as an illustration of karma. Our words, deeds, and imaginative creations will have unforeseen repercussions far beyond our reach, and one day they will ripple back to us again. Young Olivia's crossing over and mistaken meeting with Walternate is an interesting example of this. How could she know that one day she would be at the center of a trans-universal war, initiated by Walternate? It all began innocently enough, in a field of white tulips and snow. Olivia chose to alter her world. She answered the question that Elizabeth posed to Peter, which the audience also considers: "How would you change the world if you could?"

* This particular flower has become a recurring image in the series, signifying forgiveness, worth, and spiritual grace.

CHAPTER 11

FAITH AND SCIENCE
WHITE TULIPS AND SOUL MAGNETS

"Unless you believe, you won't understand"
— Isaiah 7:9 (Quoted in "Unearthed")

Fringe does not frequently grapple with tenets of the major religions, nor does it regularly incorporate explicit symbols of faith. We rarely see characters in sacred temples or practicing any kind of religious ritual. Walter occasionally mentions his own belief in a higher being, but Peter and Olivia make it clear that they are persuaded more by reason than by faith. Even so, the faith versus reason dichotomy arises time and again.

In "Unearthed," for instance, when Peter pulls out Walter's copy of the *Tibetan Book of the Dead*, he and Olivia contemplate belief in an afterlife. According to Tibetan thought, Peter explains, "the near-death experience can often converse with those who have already died." In this episode a young girl returns to life after a momentary death, and Walter is apparently doing some research on the possibility of the afterlife. In regard to its existence Peter tells Olivia, "I'm gonna put my money on healthy skepticism." Peter wants Olivia to divulge her own outlook on the spiritual, but as usual she's not very forthcoming about her feelings, saying only, "My mother believed in God, but all the praying in the world didn't stop my stepfather from terrorizing her." Though she doesn't come right out and say it, Olivia's traumatic experiences damaged more than her faith in people; it dispelled any faith she might have had in a higher power. If there is a god, he certainly wasn't paying any attention to her mother. It is understandable that Olivia would also put her money on skepticism. To her anything else would just be too risky. Her mother's "faith just seemed to put her in harm's way," so why would Olivia make the same mistake?

In the novel *Cat's Cradle* (1963), which addresses the human desire for religion and myth while cautioning against the promises of advanced technology, Kurt Vonnegut presents his reader with the perfectly amoral scientist Dr. Felix Hoenikker, a man who has no use for "rules that other people made up," little interest in other people, and no patience for religion. He dismisses the necessity for moral guidelines and ethical boundaries that one shouldn't cross. His son explains to the narrator that "after it was a sure thing that America could wipe out a city with just one [atomic] bomb, a scientist turned to Father and said, 'Science has now known sin,'" a slightly paraphrased version of a quote from J. Robert Oppenheimer, the Manhattan Project director. Dr. Hoenikker's response to that was "What is sin?" On another occasion, when Hoenikker's secretary tells him, "God is love," Hoenniker immediately challenges the underlying assumptions of such a statement — that both God and love actually exist.

This characterization of the scientist as a coldly curious researcher, seeking facts but not necessarily truth, is typical of traditional science fiction and illustrates the danger of science without humanity. Walter was once this kind of man, rejecting the notion that "knowledge cannot be pursued without morality," a cautionary statement uttered by his lab partner, Carla Warren. Presumably he has changed over the years; he has learned from his own ethical breaches and paid a high personal price for his scientific endeavors. Unlike Dr. Hoenikker, Walter has an enlarged capacity for emotional engagement. He also possesses a sense of spirituality and a respect for the sacred. He repeatedly atones for the sin of crossing into the other universe, an act that should have been beyond the reach of man, or at least Walter thinks so. It appears that his penance is endless; he continues to make reparations for the fact that he put both universes at risk and kidnapped his son's double. These transgressions and Walter's escalating guilt — mounting each time he remembers something new — inspire in him a belief in God. Although he doesn't practice a religion or even share his beliefs with his own son, Walter is a believer.

He finds a great deal of inspiration in sacred texts. His allusions to Greek mythology, the *Tibetan Book of the Dead*, and the Christian bible illustrate his acceptance of diversity in religion and a respect for the truths that mythology can provide. They spark his imagination and seem to aid in his scientific creativity. When Astrid reads from *The First People*, a book that seems sacred in its own way, Walter immediately makes a connection from technological advances to a spiritual life. The book describes the First People as "a people of great technological prowess who made the ultimate discovery. A mechanism known to them as The Vacuum, containing at once both the power to Create, and to Destroy." Walter explains, "Many religions speak of such a power. And science, the Big Bang. And it's counterpart, the Big Crunch. The universe expanding and contracting. And expanding . . . an endless cycle of creation and destruction" ("6955 kHz").

Walter's god and Walter as God

Walter acknowledges his belief in God in "White Tulip," but it's hard to say what Walter means by "God." What is his conception of a grand design or a higher power? As viewers we know that the white tulip was sent from a time traveling scientist (not from a god), the same man who told Walter that science *is* God. But the tulip's place of origin seems irrelevant. It serves its purpose, a comfort that religion frequently provides its believers: forgiveness. It is widely recognized that white tulips symbolize forgiveness and mercy. The notion that there is hope for redemption is central to many faiths. Spiritual remorse and penance can help people forgive themselves.

The faith in a higher power that Walter exhibits in "White Tulip" stands in stark contrast to his attitude when he was making his first attempt to cross over to the other universe. Carla Warren strongly cautions against it and refuses to collaborate on this project. Walter accuses her of being weak-minded: "I always considered you as a scientist, Doctor Warren . . . despite your personal needs for religious claptrap. I see I was wrong." When she tells him that some things should be left to God's will, he makes explicit what he thinks about a higher power: "There's only room for one god in this lab and it's not yours." The only god in whom Walter is interested is *Walter*.

At this point in his personal history Walter sees himself as the great creator and destroyer. The products of his genius have made him arrogant; he believes that because he has the power to manipulate and change things, he is entitled to do so at will. And if he leaves behind a path of destruction, so be it. He has after all designed theories for hybridizing super-creatures, built a time travel device, and developed a window to another universe. It's no wonder he feels like a god.

Like this younger version of Walter, Walternate is not concerned with the ethics of manipulating the universe for his own purposes. In "Amber 31422" he tells Colonel Broyles, "Nature doesn't recognize good and evil, Phillip. Nature only recognizes balance and imbalance. I intend to restore balance to our world. Whatever it takes."

In "Peter" Carla Warren reminds Walter that "knowledge should not be pursued without morality," but Walter immediately rejects this sentiment. He seems under the influence of some sort of scientific possession, wherein he can only see himself as the creator and a merciless creator at that, only taking into consideration his own interests.

Once he becomes responsible for the possible destruction of the entire universe, he finally realizes that he's in over his head. He has messed up something that he can't fix and he calls on a higher power to, at the very least, forgive him. In the Lab Notes from "Unleashed" Walter admonishes himself for his past research: "I didn't seek medical cures or better food or safer energy. I sought only to prove that I could, to find the limits of the possible." By the time we are introduced to him in the pilot episode, Walter's identity as a scientist has undergone a drastic change: he now "knows sin," he knows love (especially for his son), and he knows God.

The Spirit and the Universe(s)

Many viewers were upset that Peter failed to recognize Fauxlivia for who she really was. Peter could not distinguish between the two Olivias' "essential energies," as Bell might put it. If we assume that each individual has its own unique soul, then how does the spirit life differ, if at all, between universes? Do Olivia and Fauxlivia share the same spirit (or soul or "essence")? They behave differently, but characteristics in personality often emerge from one's environment and are not necessarily innate. If the parallel universes have branched, one from the other, wouldn't they originate with only one spirit shared by all of the versions of the self? In this sense does it matter that Peter acted on his feelings for Olivia with Fauxlivia, impregnating the over-there Olivia instead of the over-here Olivia? They are essentially the same person. In fact, even though Olivia feels that her life has been hijacked by a stranger, she also acknowledges that Fauxlivia is a happier version of her, one who has lots of friends and laughs easily. Though she's envious of this person, Fauxlivia *is* her. She is Olivia without the cortexiphan trials and the death of her mother. Like Walter explains in "The Road Not Taken," branching universes create versions of ourselves that we may never know, but they still reflect an inner essence that is ever present in the "original" self.

It is possible that Peter could not tell the two Olivias apart because they are both of the same spirit. Certainly Olivia won't get pregnant just by sharing a soul with Fauxlivia, but her potential for mothering Peter's child is ever present. Fauxlivia, despite her underhanded espionage and trickery, is a fairly likable person, and it is easy to imagine that she and Olivia are two sides of the same coin.

Walternate initially appears evil compared to Walter. Yet they still share the same essence and possess equal capacities to make the same decisions. In many ways Walter has committed breaches of ethics that exceed Walternate's cold deeds.

Sam Weiss

In contrast to the more practical and scientifically technical ideas that usually arise in *Fringe*, Sam Weiss offers a much more mystical faith-based approach to life. He requires his "clients" to trust him and to maintain a sense of hope in life. With Olivia he tries to develop her patience, and he tests her faith in herself.

Little is known about Sam Weiss, and his connections to the main characters thus far consist only of a longstanding relationship with Nina and a mentorship with Olivia. He is something of a sage. Once when Olivia is growing impatient with Sam's cryptic instructions she tells him to "quit the Yoda crap." But in "Concentrate and Ask Again" Sam is revealed to be even more than a mentor and therapist. He seems to have more insight, if not power, than we first thought and may be operating outside (or above) the physical realm. His bowling alley serves as a metaphysical space, a place where spiritual matters are re-examined.

Sam tells Olivia that she is one of the only good people he knows. Does he have any authority on good and evil? Viewers know that Olivia is extremely ethical in both her personal and professional life. She seems to be a decent yardstick by which to measure goodness, but how does Sam know her so well?

Olivia originally goes to Sam in search of physical rehabilitation, and Sam, or perhaps the bowling alley itself, cures her injuries from the car accident. Like in a biblical healing story her recovery is sudden and unexpected. One moment she's walking with a cane, and the next she is standing straight and tall, adroitly pointing a gun at Sam's head. While there's a possibility that Olivia somehow healed herself, there's something mystical about Sam's place that suggests his involvement. Or did her belief in herself work in concert with his seemingly magical powers? Later Sam helps Olivia recover from an emotional wound: the death of her partner. In a very roundabout way, he brings comfort to Olivia by allowing Charlie to "speak" to her from beyond the grave, knowing that Olivia will find the message that she needs to hear. She discovers that Sam is right: Charlie's message — "You're gonna be fine" — helps her overcome her grief. In this way Sam Weiss serves as an intermediary between the living and the dead.

The Afterlife and Immortality

William Bell has succeeded in pulling off the ultimate science experiment: life after death. With a simple cup of tea, and Olivia's unwitting aid, Bell is able to extend his life.

For William Bell an afterlife was always a scientific possibility. After all energy cannot be destroyed and so the consciousness must go *somewhere*. So says the science of *Fringe*, at least. Walter tells Peter that he and "Belly" used to argue about where the soul's energy goes after death: "William theorized we should be able to capture that energy using what he called soul magnets." If his theory was right then Bell would be sure to contact Walter from the Great Beyond ("6B").

In "Stowaway" when Agent Lincoln Lee and Peter are looking through Dana Gray's belongings as part of their investigation, the one book they find that is "not clinical" provides the clue for understanding what Dana is doing — trying to die. The book is titled *The Afterlife of the Soul*. In this episode a particularly Catholic narrative is given some attention: the Ascension of Azrael. Azrael is an archangel, sometimes considered an angel of death. One of Dana's crazier suicide victims utters the words "like Azrael, let his angels carry my damn soul to heaven," right before he shoots himself in the head. Azrael was a soul who could not move on from purgatory without the aid of a host of angels, whose purity equalized his own sin. In some faiths he is a figure to whom grieving families can pray for their deceased loved ones. He helps souls cross over to the afterlife, something Dana needs, but he's also considered something of a grief counselor, just like Dana. It is interesting that she is described both as a "compassionate soul vampire" and a "stowaway to heaven." Both terms could also be used to describe Azrael.

Though not necessarily true in Bell's case, the belief that the soul or consciousness has energy is usually a matter of faith. Walter first acknowledges the existence of the soul in "Unearthed," when he proposes that Andrew Rusk's spirit has unfinished business and, as a result, is taking possession of another person's body. In this episode Walter reveals his own particular brand of faith. He tells Maureen Donovan, the devout Catholic mother, that he too must rely on faith. Indeed he shows us that he *does* need faith in order to see his scientific experiments. In the lab he must have faith in his own intellect and imagination, in scientific theories, and in the work of other scientists. He even asks others to have faith in seemingly wild theories, even ones grounded in religious tradition.

In this same episode, in fact, Walter uses the term "resurrection" to describe Lisa Donovan returning from the dead, but the priest seems to disapprove of the word. When Walter suggests that there is such a thing as demonic possession, the priest, in an interesting twist of roles, is the one "of little faith." He says that believing in demonic possession is superstitious, but Walter reveals the priest to be dogmatic, simply following what the church tells him is outdated. He, the "man of science," references the Bible to uphold a faith in something scientific: "there are examples of casting out spirits right through the Bible, Father." Walter believes he can save Lisa by performing a good old-fashioned exorcism on her. There is no question that Walter's objective is to do something traditionally religious: cast out the spirit, not of a demon, but of a dead man. Walter is clearly acknowledging the existence of an afterlife. The spirit of Andrew Rusk is haunting the living in order to avenge his killer.

In "Os" the idea of soul magnets is explained. William Bell is dead, but Walter needs him more than ever. He believes that going through Bell's old files could help him "remember how to think the way I used to, the way we used to." He feels like an incomplete person, not only because parts of his brain are missing but also because his longtime partner in science is gone forever. Or so we are led to believe. When the clanging of the bell in Nina's office summons Bell's consciousness, he returns, choosing an odd choice for his so-called vessel: Olivia Dunham.

Walter's Lab Notes from season 1 are significant here; they include an excerpt of Edgar Allan Poe's poem "The Bells," a work that emphasizes the inevitability and the indiscriminate nature of death. The speaker of the poem points out that after death we are not men or women, human or animal. We are just "ghouls," a frightening sentiment. Throughout the poem the repetition of the term "bells" seems to march the reader quickly through the four stages of life toward a merciless death. But for William Bell it is the bell that gently escorts the spirit back to the living.

The implications of the soul magnet are quite interesting. Coupled with the innovation of the shapeshifters, the trapping of the consciousness could mean immortality. Indeed the episode ends in Peter's shapeshifter chop shop with Bell/Olivia telling him that the decoder key is in Bell's office at Massive Dynamic. Does this mean that Bell is truly the inventor of the shapeshifters? If so, it would seem that the soul magnet and shapeshifter technologies go hand in hand, creating endless life for the souls of humans. Science and engineering are fulfilling the promises of religion.

To get to this point, of course, innovators like Walter and Bell must open their minds to the possibility and have faith in their own human intellect. This is the faith that emerged from the twentieth century as believers shed their superstitions one by one and embraced the observable world. Science has cured the sick, given sight to the blind, and made food more abundant, available to "the masses."

Predestination

In "Stowaway" when Peter says that he does not believe in fate, Bell, who is using Olivia's body as a host, reveals a less scientific side of himself. He says, "Sometimes when one walks away from his fate, it leads one directly to fate's doorstep." Now that William Bell believes in a literal human spirit, the evidence of which he can see in the work of his soul magnets, has he also become a believer in predetermination?

Later in the same episode Bell dismisses science altogether, "What if, Peter, this isn't about biology or physics?" Is *Fringe* losing its grasp on scientific explanations, even those far-fetched ones that most scientists would claim are based in pure fantasy? The writers do not even attempt to simulate any solid scientific theory. Bell suggests that perhaps Dana Gray, the woman who couldn't die, had been spared for such a long time because she was meant to save those people from the train bombing. She took a job with a crisis help line to connect with people who were dying; she was trying to stow away on the souls of others, hoping to use them as a transport system to the afterlife. Instead, as Bell suggests, her true purpose was to prevent the deaths of an entire train full of passengers. He explains to Peter that it doesn't matter what you call it: "Destiny, fate. Jung called it synchronicity. The interconnectedness of apparently unrelated events." Bell puts a different twist on his ideas by adding "as a scientist, I like to believe," an interesting way to juxtapose the opposing worlds of faith and reason. He says, "I like to believe that nothing just happens, that every event has some meaning. Some sort of message. You just have to be able to listen closely enough to hear it."

At this point Bell sounds more like a spiritual guru than a scientist. (He also sounds markedly similar to John Locke, the castaway in *Lost* known particularly for his fatalist outlook on life: "We were brought here for a purpose, for a reason, all of us.") And why shouldn't he? Here he is floating around in the world of spirits, stowing away as a passenger in a living body, trying to hold on to life. Why shouldn't he feel that there is a very important reason for his presence, among the only group of people in the world who might be able to save the universe from destruction?

The character of Dana Gray is also used as a means to address the notions of fate and meaning. She tells her clients that each raindrop has a purpose to nourish and support life, and that they should see themselves as individual raindrops. "Every drop of rain holds the promise of re-growth." Although her metaphor is a bit hokey, even to the distressed client ("What does that even mean?" he asks), it does support two important motivating factors in the lives of humans: hope and meaning. What both Dana and her client need and, more generally speaking, what many people seek in religion is the faith that there *is* purpose in life. Dana, whether she realizes it or not, eventually illustrates that there is a meaning to her extended life.

There is no doubt that she served a noble purpose in the end, but was it fated, as Bell suggests to Peter? Like all people, Dana Gray's life served many purposes. In a short span of time we learned that she was a mother, a wife, a grief counselor, and a hero. Were all these roles, and everything else she did in life, predestined?

When Nina visits Sam in "Concentrate and Ask Again" he further reveals his powers of omniscience. He knows what's going on in both universes even though he hasn't had any involvement in these events. When he tells Nina that the fate of the universe depends on whether Peter chooses Olivia or Fauxlivia, we know that his reach is far greater than we initially thought. As the bowling balls crash together, the nature of Sam's reality takes on a more epic significance. The balls represent the different universes, and Sam might very well be a manager of something far greater than a sixteen-lane bowling alley. Perhaps he oversees the entire cosmic plan, while allowing his "clients" the free will to choose as they wish. Sam doesn't seem to care who Peter chooses or which universe triumphs. Perhaps he has a lot more to worry about than one little universe. Further, are the Observers, those movers and shakers in the realm of fate, working in conjunction with Sam? Or, conversely, are they working against his wishes? The Observers seem intent on keeping the course of events in line, while Sam appears to be cheering on the powers of free will.

Religious Moments in Fringe

- The confessional, the devil, prophecy, and an impression of stigmata in "The Ghost Network."
- Resurrection in "Marionette" and exorcism in "Unearthed."
- The Tree of Knowledge and the Fall of Man: Walter eats the fruit of the tree of knowledge by pushing man's knowledge beyond its limitations; like Adam and Eve in the story of Genesis, a change takes place in him, from innocent curiosity to the possession of "the knowledge" to guilt-ridden suffering as an outcast. In one of season 1's promotional videos Walter is shown with a very red, very shiny apple, the same apple used for the glyph images.
- Carla Warren, Walter's lab assistant in the 1980s, attends church every Sunday ("Peter").
- Bell's soul magnets explore the religious notions of reincarnation, resurrection, and immortality.
- The Ascension of Azrael is referenced in "Stowaway."
- Religious texts: the Christian Bible, *The Tibetan Book of the Dead*, *The Afterlife of the Soul*

CHAPTER 12

Unsub

The Observers

"You have changed the future. You have created a new set of probabilities."

— August, "Peter"

All evidence seems to suggest that the Observers are time travelers from an earlier (or later), more technologically advanced race of beings. It's difficult to say why they are all white, hairless, and male. Perhaps the side effects of temporal displacement include the loss of both hair and pigmentation. In "Bad Dreams" Olivia explains the term "unsub," short for unidentified subject. Unsub has been used in other fictional narratives about criminal investigation, including a short-lived television series simply titled *Unsub* (1989) that featured an elite FBI forensic team that investigates violent crimes.

But in the context of *Fringe* the term "unsub" is more comparable to UFO, something extraordinary and unlike any other observable life on this planet. With *Fringe*'s tone being more similar to *The X-Files* than to a police procedural, the unidentified bald men are more akin to aliens than to common subjects of investigation. But considering *Fringe*'s dearth of references to extraterrestrial life, could these guys be even *more* terrestrial than humans? Are they from underground where their cylinder originated? Amid all of the man-made monsters and strange disfiguring diseases, the Observers are the only subjects of curiosity that resemble alien life. Though it is more likely that they are from another time and not another place, they are still alien to our human culture. Further Walter definitively tells us in "The Firefly" that the Observers are *not* human.

It is reasonable to assume that there are twelve Observers, each one named after a month of the year, though we have yet to meet them all. We know of four: September, August, December, and July. September has a special connection to Walter and Peter Bishop. August has also been prominently featured, most notably in "August" when it becomes clear that he is emotionally motivated to protect a young woman and seems to alter fate in order to save her. December is the oldest of the known Observers, suggesting that the month indicates the maturity of the Observer (although the actor who plays August appears older than September). Does this mean that January might be the child found in the basement of a condemned building ("Inner Child")? Or is there someone even younger?

The child who was found underground (without hair and extremely pale) supports the theory that the Observers are some sort of underground people. The hole in which he was found (under a building) was said to have been sealed for seventy years. Since these beings age so slowly perhaps he is a seventy-year-old child, a human who won't be fully mature for hundreds of years. (Every ten years is equal to a year to the Observers, in which case an Observer who looks about eighty is actually 800.) Like the adult Observers this child possesses powers of telepathy, seeming to call back the construction worker and to communicate with Olivia in silence.

The term "rogue Observer" has been mentioned but, thus far, that story has not been told. Perhaps the antagonist in "The Arrival," the one who used a mind-reading patient on his victims, is one of these rogue operators.

Demeanor

The Observers have a strange, halting style of speech, as if they are not fully comfortable with human interaction. September's gaze is strange, and the animalistic way he turns his head back and forth when he is concentrating suggests there is something more going on in his brain than in a human's. His stiff posture, formal suit, and hat give him a robotic demeanor. The Observers appear to be peaceful men but when violence is necessary, they don't shy away from it. September, for instance, has exhibited super powers: he can catch bullets and read minds. Perhaps it is his ESP that makes him such a good fighter; he always knows the next move his opponent will make. The Observers do not possess a keen sense of taste; they use very spicy condiments to flavor their food. This characteristic seems to have been borrowed from the WB's *Roswell*, in which the alien teens can taste very little flavor in human food. Similar to the Observers they coat their food with hot sauce in order to taste *something*. Should we take this as a sign that the Observers are from another planet? Is the mythology of *Roswell* strong enough to transcend the confines of its own narrative?

Technology and Codes

The Observers' technology is simple in structure but extremely technologically advanced. The gun that September uses on Peter, for instance, can be used as a defense mechanism without inflicting any permanent damage. In this way their technology is culturally advanced: one can disarm his or her enemies without actually committing a destructive act of violence. In "August" when the Fringe team gets a hold of one of these guns, Broyles notes, "Our techs had never seen anything like it." They aren't even able to fire it. Similarly the digital binoculars seem quite sophisticated, though their purpose is unknown. Are they for seeing far distances or are they for seeing the world more precisely through the human lens? They seem to serve as a computer, recording important data. This suggests that they are multi-tasking machines, at once translator, recording device, and vision-enhancer. Another contraption attributed to the Observers is the capsule that emerges from the ground in "The Arrival." September makes it his mission to keep this capsule, the "Beacon," safe and send it back underground. The underground nature of the capsule links it to another mysterious technological device that originates from under the earth: the enigmatic machine, with parts that had been buried at significant coordinates around the world. The machine may have originated with the Observers, although is not nearly as simple in structure as their known inventions. The Observers are concerned with both of these anomalies — the beacon and the machine — but why?

The symbols from the Observer's journal in "The Arrival" appear both ancient and futuristic. They don't reflect any known human language — if the writing can be called a language at all — but some of the shapes do resemble certain hieroglyphs from ancient cultures. When September writes he doesn't look at the journal, yet the text is straight and even. This makes him appear robotic, but it's probably just a sign that the Observers sense things differently from humans.

When Astrid, who majored in linguistics, studies the Observer's journal, she is shocked at the lack of a pattern in his writing. "So far," she explains, "I have counted twelve hundred and forty-six distinct characters, and not a single one of them repeats." If a series of characters contains no repeated symbols, then what he is writing is not a language at all. And if it's a code, it's a very complicated one, one that could not fit in the relatively small capacity of human calculation. Brandon divulges his own research on the Observers' writings when he makes a clear connection to cuneiform and the earliest written languages of humankind.

Telepathic Abilities

The Observers have the ability to vocalize the thoughts of humans. Like one of the cortexiphan test subjects ("Concentrate and Ask Again") they are mind-readers. "It was as if he knew my thoughts before I did. As if he were inside of my head," Walter tells Peter in "The Arrival." They also can predict or foresee events to come, probably because of their ability to travel through time, but they don't know which set of circumstances will develop into history. In "The Firefly" September tells Walter, "There are things that I know. But there are things that I do not. Various possible futures are happening simultaneously. I can tell you all of them, but I cannot tell you which one of them will come to pass."

Some Influences: Isaac Asimov, Kurt Vonnegut, and Arthur C. Clarke

To understand the Observers we should look at their fictional predecessors. What can the weird-guys-with-clairvoyant-powers archetype in science fiction reveal about the telepathic baldies of *Fringe*?

In the world of *Fringe* the famous science fiction author Isaac Asimov is an old chum of William Bell. In the reading of Bell's will in "The Box" he says, "My great friend Isaac once said, 'Life is joy, death is peace. It's transition that's difficult,'" which paraphrases Asimov's original quotation. We know that the writers are familiar with Asimov's wise adages, but are they so familiar with his writing that they might borrow a very particular group of characters, an organization of men who travel through time, keeping tabs on all of humanity? As noted in the chapter on time travel, in Asimov's novel *The End of Eternity* "Eternals" are able to travel "upwhen" and "downwhen" through history making small changes to events with the purpose of improving the human condition.

The End of Eternity is not the only source of inspiration for *Fringe*'s Observers. Many other narratives deal with the theme of a time adventurer, a single pioneer with a moral reason for slightly altering history. There is the TV series *Quantum Leap,* though Sam, unlike the Observers, is called upon to really "get involved," not just to watch. Or consider Marvel Comics' "Watcher," Uatu, a bald guy from a highly advanced civilization; he is immortal, omniscient, and has the ability to change shape. His job is to observe other civilizations, with the stipulation that he is never to interfere in their conflicts. But, like the Observers in *Fringe*, he sometimes bends the rules in order to diminish human suffering.

In "Johari Window" Walter suggests that he is friends with another legendary science fiction writer, Arthur C. Clarke, who wrote the screenplay for Stanley Kubrick's *2001: A Space Odyssey.* In the film the alien life is unseen, a spirit of "limitless capabilities and ungraspable intelligence," as Kubrick described it. Is this, perhaps, what the Observers are? Some sort of force that humans cannot perceive with their limited senses? The Observers do seem quite uncomfortable in human skin; maybe their real form is so dissimilar from anything in the realm of human perception that they take on human form in order to interact with people.

The Tralfamadorians of Kurt Vonnegut's *Slaughterhouse-Five* (also mentioned in chapter 7) are fatalists, and they know how the universe ends. They see time all at once "like a mountain range," just as the Observers seem to. Both life forms seem to be present at all points in time. As Brandon explains to Olivia in "August," rather than moving in a linear pattern from point A to point B, they can move back and forth, like through a closed tube.

The Observers are also similar to the Martians from *The War of the Worlds*, if only in that they are very cerebral, sexless, utilitarian forms of life.

These older stories may help us determine what kind of control the Observers have over the history of mankind, especially the past and future of the Bishop men. Some of these other characters are so eerily similar to the Observers that it makes speculation about *Fringe* all the more interesting. If the Observers have as much power as the "Eternals," then why can't they go back in time and prevent Walter from crossing over in the first place? Maybe that's what September "has set into motion," a series of events that will do away with *both* Peters and set things back to the way they were "supposed to be," with both little boys, on either side of the universe line, dying from illness. It appears that this is what happened in "The Day We Died," when Peter unexpectedly disappears and, according to the Observers, is wiped out of existence completely.

Their Plan for the Universe(s)

September and the other Observers seem to believe that there is such a thing as the right path and the wrong one. He indicates in "The Firefly" that there is a natural course of events, insinuating that it should not be altered; it is the correct path. "We have upset the balance in ways I could not have predicted," he tells Walter. Apparently Walter's actions have ripped apart the fabric of reality. But if the Observers intentionally show up at certain times in history to push things in a certain direction, then why did September show up in the alternate universe just as Walternate was going to discover the cure for Peter's fatal illness? He distracted Walternate from his work, and as a result Walter was compelled to save Peter. If the Observers can predict the course of events to such a subtle degree (as he does in "The Firefly"), September should be able to predict (or literally foresee) that Walter will see the positive results of Walternate's trial and that Walternate, being distracted by the Observer, will miss it. He should also know that Walter will respond by traversing the universes and abducting Peter. Is September also culpable for the "upset" in the balance of the universes?

When September saved Peter and Walter from the icy lake, why didn't he follow them home to make sure that Peter would be returned to the other universe? Why didn't September foresee that Walter would keep Peter or how Walternate would respond? September has made it clear that he cannot definitively predict the exact outcome; he has visions of several different future scenarios but does not know which one will come to pass. But one doesn't have to be omniscient to know that a father would seek justice, if not revenge, in a situation like this. Is it the Observers' lack of humanity that makes it difficult for them to predict or understand how a person will respond to set of circumstances?

Choice

Walter and Peter have both demonstrated a strong sense of faith in free will. Peter is determined to create a solution to the impending war, one that does not involve destroying either universe. It seems impossible to the others, but Peter believes that something can be done, and Olivia is ready to help. As he approaches the machine in the finale of season 3 he is fearless in the face of imminent danger, clearly demonstrating that he is determined to change the fate of his world. Even when destruction seems inevitable Peter believes in his ability to control his destiny.

Walter's faith in Peter's ability to choose his own path has wavered. Nina exposes Walter's dwindling sense of free will in "6955 kHz," as they discuss Peter's future and his seemingly fated relationship with the machine. "It's a drawing, not destiny," she tells Walter, serving as the high priestess of free will to remind Walter of his own power and his responsibility to choose his own destiny. He must take control of his life for his own sake as well as his son's. She tells him, "Don't become a fatalist now."

Similarly Peter is no pessimistic fatalist. In the same episode Fauxlivia suggests that Peter would have "no choice" but to defend his own universe if it came down to a face-off between the two universes. She insinuates that they might be forced to make some otherwise unethical decisions in this situation, to defend the world "no matter the cost." But Peter is hesitant to make an assertion, reminding Fauxlivia of the humanity of the Other: "There are billions of innocent people over there . . . just like here . . . people with jobs, families, lives. I got to believe there's another way. And whatever my part in all of this is . . . I got to believe there's another way. There's always hope, right?" Peter will make the most difficult decision of all, and in doing so he demonstrates the defining characteristic of humanity: the ability to choose one's own destiny.

Trapped on the other side Olivia makes the same choice — to find another way. She promises Colonel Broyles that she will do whatever she can to establish peace between the two worlds. Throughout the series Olivia has demonstrated her capacity to stand up for a "third option" and to find the creative way out of a nasty problem. Both she and Peter are similar in this regard; against all odds they continue to follow a path based on the most ethical choices available.

Determinism

Rather than a religious concept of destiny or predetermination, September's theory is in line with the philosophical notion of determinism, which holds that most events are causally determined by a set of factors; everything that is going to happen has already been determined by the events and conditions that are already in place. We cannot change what has already been set into motion. The *Stanford Encyclopedia of Philosophy*'s definition differentiates this fatalist perspective with the mystical notion of destiny, saying that it "first became subject to clarification and mathematical analysis in the eighteenth century" and that "determinism is deeply connected with our understanding of the physical sciences and their explanatory ambitions." Essentially this is a description of predetermination for the man of science (and the fans of science fiction).

September illustrates this theory in "The Firefly" when one act sets an entire chain of events into motion, and he traces and controls this chain. Further one seemingly innocuous act, like catching a firefly, can create an imbalance in the universe. From the Observers' perspective there is a particular chain of events that keeps the precariously balanced universe together in working order. In "The Firefly" September sends Roscoe's son through time, which in turn leads Roscoe to Walter. When Walter discovers that his own actions led to the death of Roscoe's son, he feels guilty for preserving the life of his own son at the cost of Bobby's life. Because of his regret Walter allows Peter to involve himself in a dangerous situation. He lets Peter go, despite his fear of losing his only child. Walter must stay and "save the girl" whose inhaler was intentionally taken by September, who knew the course of events would depend on the girl's asthmatic distress.

The success of this plan supports the notion that the Observers can determine what will happen based on a single action. In an earlier episode in season 3 ("The Plateau") a man with an extremely low IQ is given a serum to increase his intelligence, echoing Charlie's story in Daniel Keyes' novel *Flowers for Algernon* (1966). On *Fringe* the man becomes so gifted that he uses mathematical calculations to maintain a determinist outlook and predict what will happen next. When he balances a pen on a mailbox, he knows it will fall and attract the attention of a bystander who will pick it up and inadvertently distract a cyclist who will almost crash . . . and so on. He can map the chain reaction in advance and foresee each outcome at an extraordinarily accurate rate. Are the Observers, like the man in "The Plateau," just extraordinarily intelligent, a race of superhumans who can predict the future based on statistical data?

Their Entrances

Thus far there is no sweeping conclusion to be made about *when* the Observers show up. They always appear at the scene of disasters or key moments of conflict, usually to make an objective record of the situation, much like a journalist. After all they are there just to observe, not to get involved. They have been seen at the site of important, game-changing moments in history such as the Boston Massacre, the execution of Marie Antoinette, and the assassination of Franz Ferdinand, which triggered World War I.

In contemporary sightings the Observers are usually in urban settings; most of the time it is just September who shows up. They have been included in every single episode of *Fringe*, providing viewers with an ongoing Easter egg hunt — seen on the sidewalk by the Massive Dynamic building, at train stations, in hospitals, inside other public buildings, in diners and cafes, at airports, in Walter's lab, in Walternate's lab, on the street, in news television coverage, at a night club, on a soccer field, in a corn field, at Walter's beach cabin, at the graveyard where the other Peter was buried, in a small town, at a church, at Reiden Lake, near Walter's house, outside a movie theater, on an overpass, and on the greens at Harvard.

September is usually just glimpsed, as a face in the crowd or in the background of an event. However, there have been crucial moments when the Observer feels he must interfere in the course of events.

Season 1

- September plays a key role throughout "The Arrival." He is visibly concerned about the safety of the cylinder and he makes contact with Walter, apparently cashing in the favor that was owed him. But it is not until "The Road Not Taken," near the end of season 1, that he interacts with Walter again, showing up at his lab to speak to him.
- "There's More Than One of Everything" features one of Walter's transformative moments. September brings him to the beach house and Walter begins to remember the past that he had long forgotten. Rather than telling Walter what he should remember, September *shows* him. In accompanying Walter to the other Peter's gravesite, the Observer demonstrates his empathic sensibilities. His connection to Walter's experiences is deeper than we first expected.

Season 2

- A non-Observer messenger mysteriously hands September photographs of Walter in "Fracture." These photos appear to have been taken with the high-tech viewing device that the Observers use. This conspicuous meeting reveals that September and the others are actively engaging in the human world, recruiting people to carry out acts of espionage for them. Tracking the lives of particular humans has become something much more than simple passive observation, as we see in the next Observer-centric episode, "August," in which they review photos in CIA-like fashion.

- In "August" the Observers meet at a restaurant where they slather hot sauce on their food and share information about a person of interest: Christine Hollis. The topic of their meeting is the "irregularity" that August has created by preventing Christine from boarding a plane doomed to crash.
- In "Peter" September makes a "mistake" by distracting Walternate from the cure for Peter's illness. Coming out of a movie in the alternate universe, the other Observers meet September and are unhappy about this mistake. August tells September, "You have changed the future. You have created a new set of probabilities." December commands that September must "take action to restore balance": the Observers will continue to manipulate the course of events.
- At a bar in "Over There, Part 1" Olivia receives a file directly from September.

Season 3

- September plays an active role in manipulating the course of events in "The Firefly." He tests Walter to see if he is ready to let his son go, to prepare Walter for Peter's vanishing act in "The Day We Died." When he tells the other Observer "everything has been set into motion," it's as if they are playing a game of dominoes, applying the rules of causal determinism and using their extraordinary intelligence to consider the "new set of probabilities" ("Peter"). Once September has taken the inhaler of the girl whom Walter is supposed to later save, September concludes that a very particular series of events will proceed. However at the end of this episode he admits to the other Observers, "I feared my experiment would fail." Is everything an experiment to the Observers? Is it all just a game that they are playing to see if their theories are correct? Are they scientists, using the "whole world as their lab" ("The Pilot")?
- In "The Day We Died," although there is still no explanation of the Observers' exact purpose, their power of omniscience

becomes quite plain. As they stand in a semi-circle near the Statue of Liberty and December says, "They don't remember Peter," it is apparent that the Observers have a strong connection to the order of the universe.

Other Questions and Theories

Are the Observers guardian angels in a sense? Are they supernatural beings required by some higher design to manipulate the human world, but also to remain detached? They take the form of mortal beings so they can see the universe through human sensibilities, but we know they are *not* human. Whether their intentions are "good" or not, their omniscience and wisdom make them god-like. Perhaps they are messengers of something more transcendent. Through the lens of mythology their characters are quite reminiscent of demigods, but still their identification lies squarely in the realm of futuristic science fiction. But where did they originate? Are they extraterrestrials like Uatu, "The Watcher"? Their pasty complexions and hairlessness suggest they are from a place without sunlight. Why are they named after the months of the year? Do they each represent one of twelve eras in human history? If so, maybe the *Fringe* mythology is hinting that all time is circular — that after the December period, time will be reset all over again.

PART III

AUDIENCE

THE SMALL SCREEN AS LOOKING GLASS

CHAPTER 13

Transmedia Storytelling
Comics, Games, and Marketing

"Explore alternate realities. Uncover scientific mysteries. Don't
just imagine the impossibilities. Be part of them."
> — Fringe Now, Fox.com

Like Walter we are continually being observed. The Observers
signify the technology that is "watching over us" all the time, the
various programs that track our locations, our internet behavior, and
our shopping habits. September is quite the techno-savvy watcher,
always seen holding sleek gadgets and writing equations that predict future events with precision. Corporate observers of television
viewers also have plenty of devices for prediction: the Nielsen rating
system, digital video recording readings, Facebook, alternate reality
game participation, and even discussion board contributions. Just
the act of viewing a show or visiting a site might elicit attention
by an official "watcher," but actively participating in digital fandom
will undoubtedly put a viewer in the network's field of vision. Fox
encourages this participatory culture; they facilitate activities for fans
as part of an integrated marketing strategy. Through their comics,
games, Facebook page, and community boards, we, the viewers, can
be observed, measured, and recorded. None of this is surprising,
nor is it necessarily a bad thing. Fans have the chance to actively

participate in their favorite pop culture narratives more easily than ever before. The following section serves to explore *Fringe*'s transmedia landscape and examines the opportunities for both fans and Fox's marketing team.

The Comic Books

At the 2008 Comic-Con in San Diego, *Fringe*'s marketing team distributed a promotional prequel comic book not only to generate interest in the show itself, but also to plug their six-issue *Fringe* comic book series (DC Comics and Wildstorm), which at the time of this writing consists of two six-issue volumes. The publication of such materials is nothing new in the world of transmedia television storytelling. Joss Whedon's *Buffy* season 8 comic books and graphic novels continue to be wildly popular among fans, long after the conclusion of the TV series. *The Walking Dead* originated from the comics medium and in its first season enjoyed success as AMC's flagship genre drama.

Fringe's comics, though not deemed part of the canon, are sanctioned by the show's executives, and snippets of them can be found in video format on Fox's official *Fringe* site and Facebook page. One was even packaged with the season 1 DVD collection. They serve as prequels to many of the characters' storylines, filling in the narrative gaps.

The first issues offer backstories about Walter Bishop as a prodigious graduate student and his lab "assistant" (according to issue 1), William Bell. Walter is characterized as extremely serious in contrast to Bell's impulsive, fun-loving nature. Bell is also supposed to be a few years younger than Walter in the comic-verse. These characterizations are surprising given that Bell is consistently depicted in the show as the older, wiser, and more cautious of the two scientists. Thus the comic suggests that, over time, Bell and Walter switched personas and that in their college and postgraduate years they were very different men.

For instance in "Like Minds," from the first issue, Bell is working late hours in a classroom, attempting to solve the Morianz equation and listening to "Thank You" by Sly Stone. Walter, who has been working in an adjacent office, enters in a huff and turns off the blaring radio (which must have been highly advanced technology in the early '70s — it appears to be a handheld "boom box") to Bell's great annoyance.

In the show Walter is the one imposing music on others. His passion for music in the workplace is clearly demonstrated by his extensive vinyl record collection, shown many times, as well as his request for a piano in the lab. We've seen him grooving to music from Al Green and Robert Johnson to the fictional band Violet Sedan Chair. It's as if music is an essential part of his creative process. But according to the comics this was not always the case. To interpret this discrepancy through the lens of the comic book, perhaps Walter adopted this practice after he and Bell went their separate ways.

After switching off Bell's music Walter quickly solves the equation on the chalkboard. Considering that only five other people in the entire world had ever solved it before, Bell is quite impressed. But Walter doesn't want to chat about it — he snubs Bell's attempts at a formal introduction and slams the door behind him. This brief interaction illustrates that, in this world at least, Walter is the more focused of the two, by far, and virtually a misanthrope, a very different person from the warm and friendly, scatterbrained man we've come to know. If we use the non-canon material to interpret the series, this backstory would suggest that Walter's institutionalization and brain surgery were far more transformative than viewers initially imagined. In issue 2 Walter once again demonstrates a certain detachment. His approach to science is extremely studious and "by-the-book," a perspective that older Walter would detest. Young Walter demands that Bell stop distracting him from an experiment, while Bell rattles off a story about Albert Einstein's socks. Once again this seems the kind of thing that Walter would be interested in, a silly anecdote that he might mention to Peter in the middle of an important procedure.

In issue 4, however, comic-book Walter appears more amiable. He now owns a dog, for which he seems to have great affection. The dog stays at Walter's side as he works. Bell however wants Walter to remove it from the lab while they are trying to fix a mysterious device. But Walter objects, saying, "But these are his formative years. I can't leave him at home . . . look at that face. He's adorable." In contrast to this, in the first issue Walter has no empathy for animals. He is completely unable to understand that the lab mice could experience fear. It is Bell who suggests that the experiment was unsuccessful only because "Jimmy," the mouse, was terrified. "His soul is in torment," says Bell, to which Walter replies, "That's complete nonsense." But as we know from his relationship with Gene the cow, TV Walter has a great capacity to empathize with animals, probably even more so than with humans. By connecting the comic narrative to the television story, we can trace an unbroken line of character development in which Walter took a dynamic turn: he changed dramatically sometime after he and "Belly" became friends.

The other stories in this first series such as "From the Fringe: Space Cowboy" and "The Prisoner" are unrelated to the main characters' storylines; they are standalone freak-of-the-week episodes that don't incorporate Walter or Bell. However they do offer some extremely terrifying fringe science events such as bioengineering catastrophes, unending time loops, and neural transference. In many cases the stories have a parallel connection to the science that young Bell and Walter are developing within the comic book narrative.

The other issues, also published as a graphic novel in 2011, offer prequel stories for Peter, Broyles, Astrid, Nina, and Olivia. Once again the characters are not consistent with what we see on television. One issue tells the story of how Olivia first became a special investigator. She must pass a rigorous test in a virtual war game, but someone tampers with it, and so she has to find and expose the offender.* In "Tomorrow" the reader gets a glimpse of Peter's life as a jack-of-all-trades in Baghdad. It explores the internal conflicts with which Peter grapples in season 1: the tension he feels between doing the right thing and taking the path of least resistance. The illustrations, however, make it difficult to discern which character is Peter, as the illustrator has failed to incorporate any distinguishing characteristics: no defining worry line between the eyebrows, no round face, no blue eyes. Broyles' story spells out what viewers essentially

* In an episode in *Tales From the Fringe* one detail suggests that the Olivia story is actually a Fauxlivia story. Fauxlivia is an award-winning sharp shooter, and in "War Games," the Olivia-centric comic episode, she takes an almost impossible shot and succeeds, blowing the gun out of a perpetrator's hand without touching him.

already know: that his wife got fed up with the demands of his job and she left, kids and all. The comic book unveils another character, perhaps an old partner of Broyles, but this detail appears to be purely non-canonical.

The graphic novel also features some backstory for William and Nina's relationship, a welcome explanation for such a significant gap in the show's narrative. By using a different medium to tell this part of the story, *Fringe* overcomes the confines of television. It is not believable to use the same actor to play a character who is supposed to be 60 years old in one scene and 30 in another, and computer generated touch-ups often make for very strange-looking facial features. But the graphic novel allows the story to be told without the limitations of using live actors.

Astrid has her own story too, a glimpse of her life as a college student living in New York. The depiction of Astrid — her dialogue, actions, and appearance — is closer to the character we know from the show than any of the others offered in this collection of comics. She is portrayed as sweet but tough, intelligent but humble. The other characters don't seem to shine through as clearly.*

Regardless of their association with the show, the comic books have their own unique appeal. The stories that do not feature the TV show characters are more dynamic, perhaps because they are not forced to work within what has already been established. They are just as creepy, if not more so, than what we see on television. Like the show they feature fringe science phenomena like rapid aging, time travel, genetic manipulation, and reanimation. It's no coincidence that the title of the second series is *Tales From the Fringe,* a nod to the famously spine-chilling *Tales From the Crypt* series. One particularly sinister premise can be found in "Non-Fiction," a story that features Observer-like men in suits. The mood is as dark and dreary as it is strange and horrific, while exploring one of the most dominant themes of *Fringe*: the question of free will.

There are certain devices that the comic format adopts from the

---

* The actress who plays Astrid, Jasika Nicole, is a comic artist in her own right. Most of her work is autobiographical and can be found at her personal website, JasikaNicole.com. The site itself is also an interesting glimpse into the actress who brings Astrid's wonderfully complex personality to life.

show, such as announcing the scene's location using three-dimensional letters suspended in the air. For the first series the cover of each comic book features an official glyph from the show. The covers of the second series show photos of the television characters, even though their likenesses are not used in the illustrations inside the book.

Comic books have also been used *within* the show to signify the subtle differences between the popular culture of the two universes. The Green Lantern and Arrow are red instead of green, and Superman's adventures are attributed to Batman. In *Tales From the Fringe*, these alternate universe comic images are included: Supergirl cradles a dying Superman, and the famous lightning bolt *Batman Returns* cover image is changed to a Superman cover.

On its *Fringe* site Fox also features online video comics as special promotional devices. The brief comic-book style stories serve to illustrate a certain scene or character in greater detail. For instance one episode explores the plot of "The Firefly," showing exactly what happened to Roscoe Joyce's son, Bobby.

More Transmedia Storytelling: Games, Puzzles, and Audience Participation

Alternate reality games (herein referred to as ARGs) tend to blur the lines between television narratives and their promotional marketing schemes. Usually the viral marketing *is* the game, but it is sometimes difficult to discern where the playing of that game begins and ends. The distinctions between the material described in this chapter and the next are based on what is interactive and likely sanctioned by Fox and what is generated by fans or unofficial producers. Not all of the games included below can definitively be attributed to official *Fringe* promotional schemes, but they all appear to be initiated by "top down," rather than grassroots, marketing.

It seems that the producers of *Fringe* took their cue from the success of *Lost*'s viral mystery-puzzles. The Lost Experience, an interactive digital scavenger hunt, was unprecedented in its broad appeal to fans. Never before had such a large component of a television audience participated in a venture such as this. *Lost*'s audience was highly participatory with its ravenous appetite for hard-to-crack codes. However deliberately on the part of the show's creators, *Fringe* shares key ingredients of *Lost*'s successful recipe: mysterious numbers, creepy visual motifs, obscure symbols, and an amorphous global threat.

All of these attributes make excellent fodder for the fast-moving world of fan boards where the collective sleuthing of clever viewers can unravel narrative puzzles thoroughly and quickly. Television shows have developed more sophisticated storylines in response to the ability of viewers to keep pace with the most enigmatic plot twists thrown at them. Fans jump online for a kind of communal code-breaking post-episode. By the time *Fringe* premiered, this digital culture was well established, and creators of the show took full advantage of the ARG precedents created for shows like *Lost* and *Heroes*.

Search For the Pattern

At the same Comic-Con where the comic book teasers were distributed, the marketing team initiated a real-life scavenger hunt to get fans excited about the show's mysteries in advance of the premiere in September. It was an official Fox ARG and participants were required to register at the now-defunct site SearchForThePattern .com. They could sign up for a chance to win a trip to *Fringe*'s premiere party in New York, but the actual scavenger hunt itself took place near the convention center in San Diego. According to one fan there was a phone number included in the hunt instructions. When the participants called they could hear Lance Reddick's voice; it was Lieutenant Philip Broyles providing the next clue. Many of the glyphs were incorporated into the game too. For details of the hunt, visit Fringepedia.net.

Imagine the Impossibilities

Imagine the Impossibilities is a website filled with mysterious messages that offer a deeper understanding of the show, but, like any TV show's ARG, it does not form part of the *Fringe* canon. Each of the site's pages is marked as a piece of evidence for "Case 0091," and each features the Fibonacci equation (Walter's favorite set of proportions) in one way or another.

The first page plays a video loop that is like a blend of *Lost*'s "Room 23" brainwashing images and a conspiracy theory documentary. It flashes images of herds of sheep and a ram's horn as a Fibonacci spiral. There is a voiceover newscast announcement detailing the strange "sheep pattern" spotted in Iowa. Another page shows a bumpy, hand-held camera video clip of a computer screen on which another video plays (with fuzzy sound and picture). The next page uses the perspective of an office security camera to show a man printing or shredding a document — it's not clear which. The video plays forward and backward as the lights fade and brighten. For a moment a drawing of the Fibonacci spiral has a spotlight on it.

The site is intentionally mysterious and appears, at first, to be a bunch of misdirected, yet highly confidential, government files that the visitor has accidentally stumbled upon. The idea is that viewers will solve cases on their own, trying to figure out the meaning of the pattern, although no new cases have appeared on the site since season 1.

There Is More

Fox launched this ARG on its official *Fringe* site in the spring of 2009. A yellow dot on the site served as a portal to the game. (The URL, which is no longer active, was Fox.com/Fringe/ThereIsMore.) On the site was a video montage over which the voices of William Bell and another man could be heard: "Is the incident contained?" "Yes, Dr. Bell." "How bad?" "Bad!" By clicking on another image (of the Walking Liberty half dollar) the voice of Dr. Nicholas Boone (from the season 1 episode "Midnight") was heard saying, "How far would you go for someone you love?"

At this time fans were actively searching for a way to break the glyph code. In this ARG participants could see the apple with the Fibonacci sequence swirling around it, and when they clicked on the 89 (a Fibonacci number), a strange voice uttered a string of sounds. Played backward it said, "Expand your consciousness."

Complete the Pattern

In Complete the Pattern, a game that Fox initiated during season 1, fans could test their knowledge of the Greek alphabet and complete what looked to be a string of chemical bonds. The "sneak peek" posted there previewed "The Ghost Network," the third episode of the first season. Also available were screen savers or, as the site describes them, "exclusive digital content." This site is no longer active.

GetGlue Contest

More promotion than game, a more recent interactive program offers participants the opportunity to obtain some of the show's official props. GetGlue, a social networking site for pop culture, has been linked to *Fringe* since 2009, but their big campaign push came in the spring of 2011.

GetGlue offers participants prizes, usually in the form of stickers, for answering questions about their favorite television shows, recording artists, films, and books. Each Friday, starting on April 22, 2011, when "6:02 AM EST" aired, GetGlue featured a special code that users could use to enter the giveaway contest. Eligibility required that the participants register with the GetGlue website and "check in" at certain times. As of May 8, 2011, the *Fringe* page had generated 196,000 check-ins compared to *Supernatural*'s 43,000 check-ins and *American Idol*'s 85,000, indicating that the prop giveaway had generated a good deal of viewer participation, especially considering that these other shows far exceed *Fringe* in the ratings and general popularity.

MassiveDynamic.com

Launched in conjunction with the premiere of season 1 in 2008, this site appears to be the official website of Massive Dynamic is the creation of Fox's *Fringe* marketing team. Some of the website's pages were featured in "The Dreamscape"; they popped up on Olivia's computer when she was researching the company. The site mimics the mysterious aura surrounding the fictional corporation that we see in the show, but much of the information provided on the site is not necessarily part of the official canon. Instead the site illustrates the potential characteristics of such a shadowy corporate conglomerate. There is nothing that identifies the company as a fictional one; it poses as a thriving company specializing in products that range from computing and business to health and video games. Most of the products that Massive Dynamic offers *do* appear possible at first glance;

the descriptions seem more scientific than science-fictional . . . until fans read the claim that Massive Dynamic might be able to make "near instantaneous travel a possibility in your lifetime."

The fields in which Massive Dynamic has expertise include everything that is important to the human race including computing, communication, personal health, environmental health, energy, biology, and leisure. And the motto that we see in the show — "What do we do? What don't we do?" — is prominently displayed on the site.

To create a very authentic feel, the Massive Dynamic website incorporates all of the characteristics expected for a technologically advanced super company of the twenty-first century, save for a Twitter feed. It has a page for employment, press releases, and even "employee access." Some of the links on the news and updates page lead to real articles in *New Scientist Magazine*, adding yet another layer of authenticity.

Where's Baldo?

As we've already discussed, the appearances of the Observers are significant. At least one Observer is hidden in every episode, usually in a crowd scene, and finding him is itself a game, a good, old-fashioned seek-and-find challenge. Many fans refer to this game as "Where's Baldo?" playing it as each new episode of *Fringe* airs and, as we will discuss in the next chapter, share their findings online.

Fringe Now

While the Fringe Now interactive games and video comics are undeniably huge promotional spots for Sprint, one of *Fringe*'s strongest advertisers, the content was still fairly entertaining. The Tales From the *Fringe* page offered additional episodes from the *Fringe* comicverse, like the one mentioned above about Bobby Joyce's fate. The Alt Universe Articles promised to reveal secret messages after a participant enters a code based on the glyphs provided. The most interactive feature was a Facebook-linked game that required the participant to respond to directives from the show's leading characters. These are not scenes taken from regular episodes, but clips filmed specifically for this game, in which Walter, Astrid, and Broyles speak directly to viewers. There is an option to play the game without linking to information from Facebook (as "Jane" or "John Doe"), but it's more engaging — and amusing — to have Astrid call you by your name and to access random bits of information from Facebook to illustrate what the "AU you" would be like. The objective of the game, which is divided into five "chapters," is to identify an intruder to the lab and track him or her down. This game incorporates the devices and lab equipment that the characters use in the show, showing viewers how to manipulate the DNA identification simulations and FBI-style tracking systems.

The final feature on Sprint's Fringe Now page was the "Quick Response" icon that allows fans to "gain instant access to content for Fox shows." By scanning the code with a QR scanner on their smartphones fans received "insider content, videos, first-look photos, show secrets, behind-the-scenes footage, or exclusive cast interviews."

The Science of *Fringe*

Fox's official *Fringe* website also offers science lessons corresponding to episodes from seasons 2 and 3 of the show. The lessons, designed using a K-12 teaching model, were developed for Fox by Science Olympiad, a non-profit educational organization that serves as a consultant for schools, parents, and, apparently, television production agencies. They promote science education through workshops, research, and competitions, and the lesson plans they have designed for *Fringe* are quite similar to their regular curriculum. The Science Olympiad website encourages teachers in grades 9 through 12 to use the *Fringe* lessons in the classroom. Teachers who use them and complete a survey are also eligible to win "Science of *Fringe* Prize Packages."

This odd mix of traditional learning and TV marketing is reminiscent of Lost University, an official ARG for *Lost* fans who wanted to delve deeper into the science, psychology, sociology, and philosophy of *Lost*. The program was offered as a combination of online activities and interactive lessons through Blu-ray. Participants even received diplomas in the mail when they had completed the courses. Like Lost University participants, fans of *Fringe* can choose to learn more about real-life applications of the scenarios they watch unfold on television.

Written with teachers in mind, each Science of *Fringe* plan includes learning objectives, online resources, procedures, additional discussion ideas, extensions to other subjects, national science standards alignment, and episode relevance. For "The Day We Died" the lesson covers reverse engineering. The topic connects to the episode's "electrillights" that the End of Day–ers use to tear holes in the fabric of the universe, hoping to bring about the apocalypse. Reverse engineering is vital to a case like this one: in order to defend themselves against a force with such advanced technology, the Fringe team must understand how the technology operates.

Like a high school science experiment, this particular lesson includes instructions on taking apart common household electronic devices to determine their functionality. The discussion questions provide real-life examples of reverse engineering practices, such as "the allied cracking of the German Enigma machines in World War." The theme of changing history through the manipulation of technology is a driving force in *Fringe*'s narrative, and it's incorporated into this science lesson.

Other lesson topics include weather forecasting ("6:02 AM EST"), gestation ("Bloodline"), magnetism ("Stowaway"), protein modeling ("Marionette"), scientific intuition ("Entrada"), and wind turbines ("Lysergic Acid Diethylamide"). This last one, inspired by one of *Fringe*'s most innovative episodes, is disappointing considering that the entire episode pointedly initiates a discussion of the nature of human consciousness, and the lesson instead explores . . . wind turbines. This oversight did not go unnoticed by fans. One commenter on Fox's Science of *Fringe* page, "Sali," indicated that he (or she) "loves the show" but is disappointed with its increasing depiction of casual drug use. "Creating a lesson on wind turbines out of a show that revolves around the use of LSD? What a farce! Why don't you show scientific data of the damage that LSD causes to the brain?"

Though the lessons include shameless promotions for the show, something not exactly appropriate in a classroom, they do explore real-life science and technology and dispel some of the misinformation and pseudo-science featured in the show.

Glyphs, the Code, and Other Easter Eggs

The mysterious glyphs that flash on screen during the opening credits feature everyday objects of scientific interest — an X-ray, a seahorse, a flower — but with abnormal genetic alterations. An apple sliced in half reveals its core — two human embryos facing one another. A tree frog sports the Greek letter phi amid the spotted pattern on its back. An X-ray of a butterfly has phalanges (finger bones) as wings. A hand with six fingers. A silhouette of a seahorse with a Fibonacci spiral incorporated into its shape. Blue smoke forms the shape of a woman's face and what appears to be part of an animal skull on the far side. A daisy has dragonfly wing petals. And a curled ram horn has the number phi (also known as the Golden Ratio) imprinted along its spiral.

The visual shock of these images serves to usher the viewer into the realm of freaky fringe science, but how do the glyphs function within the larger context of the show? From the beginning the producers had an intention for these curious pictures. Before the show ever aired they had a code planned out for their future viewers. The commercial break glyph configurations was yet another game for audiences to enjoy.

As co-producer Jeff Pinkner confirmed early in 2009 at New York Comic Con, they were indeed implementing a code that would be difficult to decipher. It took a while, but by the end of season 1, fans had cracked it, revealing the solution to be a simple substitution process. Before each commercial break one glyph is shown with a glowing yellow dot placed in a particular spot: above or below or to either side of the image. Each picture and dot configuration represents a certain letter. When the dot is placed at the upper right hand corner of the leaf, for instance, the letter A is signified. When the dot is at the upper left hand of the leaf, it represents a B. The letters C, D, E, and F are different versions of the apple glyph, whereas I, J, K, and L use the daisy with dragonfly wings. And so on. At the end of every episode the viewer should be able to spell out a word, although there has been at least one incident in which the pattern was inadvertently broken, creating a nonsensical string of letters. Typically the words foreshadow the next episode. But is there an overarching message that these words will communicate by the end of the entire series?

In an interview with Marissa Roffman of GiveMeMyRemote.com, executive producer J.W. Wyman said, "We just want [the fans] to realize if you look back at season 1 when there was amber on a bus [in "The Ghost Network"] and . . . [you] didn't really know what the amber was, now you realize what [the] amber is. If you look at that in retrospect, you're like, 'Oh my gosh. Oh, I see. This whole thing has a novel-like quality and these guys are going from here to there to take us through this journey.'" Do Wyman's comments apply to the glyph code too? What will the final message be, if there is one? What is the significance of these words beyond their reflection of the show's themes?

Other Easter Eggs include the clues that lead into subsequent episodes. Viewers are expected to find an object on screen to help predict what will happen in the next episode. In most cases it can be recognized and appreciated only after the next episode has aired. For instance in "The Equation" a butterfly appears on screen, and the central conflict of the following episode involves hallucinations of killer Monarch butterflies. Some fans have even noted the significance of recurring rectangular patterns — in the configuration of high-rise windows and on the machine — possibly a reference to the Fibonacci spiral. The Fibonacci sequence is closely connected to the Golden Ratio, mentioned above.*

* This ratio is the number used to create the Golden Rectangle, which in turn can create the Fibonacci spiral. When several Golden Rectangles are connected to one another in a certain way, the Fibonacci spiral appears within the configuration of boxes. This pattern is found in the natural world, including in the structure of a daisy and the horn of a ram.

Each episode features several glyph letters, which spell out one or two words. The following are the decoded commercial break glyphs from every episode in backward order, starting with "The Day We Died": No more, multi, agent, fears, fated, erode, earth, switch, hearts, romad, hatch, alter, unites, adapt, cross, escape, decay, event, shift, breach, alert, amber, repatterned, Weiss, weapon, return, heart, bridge, secret, energy, peters, reveal, father, window, mutate, avenge, portal, hidden, blight, arrive, déjà vu, betray, memory, burial, mirror, tower, grave, vision, eight, belly, Peter, Walter, Olivia, avian, Bishop, saved, trade, voice, taken, codes, cells, surge, rogue, aeger, child, observer. The formulation of these terms into a revealing message might someday be the final game of the entire series.

Other significant clues include on-screen patterns, such as light configurations and symbols. The pattern of green and red lights is one of season 1's noteworthy recurring images, in which they are frequently ordered as follows: green, green, green, red. These lights appear on the Observer's binoculars as part of the computer graphics. The same pattern appears in season 1's "The Equation" as a hypnotic flashing-light sequence that lulls its victim into a trance for a short period of time. At the end of season 2, the colors blue and red become significant. Blue represents the prime universe and red indicates the alternate universe. When an episode operates primarily in the alternate universe, the opening credits will feature a red shading as the background color, but the original sequence, for episodes featured in the first universe, use a blue-tinted opening splash. *Fringe* fans also enjoy discovering the hidden glyphs within the diegesis, such as when a seahorse can be seen on one of the books in Markhum's bookstore in "6955 kHz" or when the leaf appears on a lamp behind Olivia in "The Plateau."

Marketing and Promotion

Product Placement

According to BrandSpotter.com a variety of products were featured in *Fringe*'s first season including Audi, Bosch, Cisco, Dell, Epson,

Ford, Motorola, Panasonic, and Stryker Instruments, some of them intentional product promotion, and some not. The product placement campaigns within later season episodes are more evident than ever before. Since the show's Nielsen ratings are quite low and DVR viewers make up quite a significant portion of overall viewers, it's possible that Fox agreed to make product placement more obvious — and more lucrative — to make up for *Fringe*'s less-than-stellar traditional advertising draw. For instance the opening of "The Last Sam Weiss" appeared to be more car commercial than television episode. An automobile cruised down a highway — a fairly typical image for a car ad — and most striking was that the characters featured in this scene were unconnected to the rest of the episode. We never saw them again, and yet it appeared that the man who was driving the Ford Focus knew something about the sudden, violent lightning storms. Save for the lightning phenomena, this opening sequence, in which the Ford emblem is clearly featured three times in two minutes, is completely disconnected from the rest of the story and plays out merely as a car advertisement with a cool soundtrack (The Doors' "Riders on the Storm"). It seems silly that such careful attention is given to the car's rear-view camera, as if it's a technological device significant to the world of *Fringe*. As "onemadscientist" commented on an article discussing Sky 1's choice to cut all product placement scenes, "Everyone is going to miss the entire first scene of 'The Last Sam Weiss,' since it was one giant Ford commercial." Andrew Hanson of the *L.A. Times* also points out that this episode began with a car commercial, but not as an indictment of Fox or *Fringe*. This is an expensive show, he contends, and with DVRs being more widely used, maybe product placement is our future.

Sprint's product placement in *Fringe* has been obvious for a long time. The cell phone's special features, such as video conferencing, are routinely employed by the characters, and the Sprint logo is always in full view. At one point Astrid offers to download episodes of the children's science show *Zoom* on her Sprint device to cheer up Walter, and she makes a very promotional display of it as she offers it to him. The Sprint logo is also well positioned on the Fox *Fringe* website, and especially made itself known on the Fringe Now page.

In one of the interactive games a Sprint phone was used to play a live video feed of a Fringe Division raid.

So is this what television advertising is becoming, at least for low-rated, expensive shows? Will our favorite long-term mythologies be littered with logos and mottos, promotions for real companies in our fictional worlds? More specifically, is this the price we're paying to get another season of *Fringe*? Although it feels cheap and underhanded, maybe it's one way to keep quality broadcast television on the air. Fans seem to have mixed reactions to the blatant product placement, some saying it is "shameful" and others saying it serves its purpose as a source of funding. One fan on the *Fringe* Forum made an interesting note about the direction of this trend: "How do you think *Gossip Girl* stays on the air (or anything on the cw for that matter)? It's not because of ratings, or its advertising commercials. It's because of product placement, specifically clothes and accessories, seen because teens don't watch commercials." The key word here is "teens," the generation that will be watching (and buying) programming and products far into the future, those who have grown up in an age when viewers can easily opt out of traditional television commercials.

Promoting *Fringe*

The promotions leading up to season 1 were largely incorporated into the aforementioned ARGs; with fans' voracious appetite for participatory activities, traditional commercial advertising pales in comparison to online games and Facebook promotions. Nonetheless there are at least a few noteworthy corporate productions that served to catch the eyes of future viewers. In 2008 Fox released a full-length music video featuring Ror-shak's cover of "A Forest" by The Cure. It is a vivid promotional montage with spine-tingling images of Olivia, Peter, and Walter in Fringy settings. The glyphs are given special attention in this video as they come to life in the characters' hands. The most chilling scene shows Walter slicing open a very red apple to reveal two twin embryos where the core should be. His expression in this particular circumstance is disturbingly Walternate-like. But even more visually and aurally stunning is the commercial that incorporates a Nine Inch Nails' tune. It's difficult to describe exactly what is happening in this video; some kind of organic substance appears to be growing and moving in unnatural ways, while Trent Reznor whispers, "I have seen history" and "A war is coming" in the background.

Between seasons 2 and 3 Fox released a series of brief videos featuring comments by the cast and crew called "*Fringe:* Just the Facts." It was a collection of ten webisodes, each one focusing on an essential component of the storyline: Walternate, the Observers, the "activation" of Olivia, and so on. Several months later when Fox moved *Fringe* from Thursday to Friday nights, an act that upset much of the *Fringe*dom, the marketing team geared up to move the viewership over too.

Fans and their efforts are the centerpiece of the following chapter, which examines *Fringe*'s promotional push at a more grassroots level. It addresses the rollercoaster that was season 3: the shift to Fridays and the show's tenuous chance for renewal strengthened by its fandom.

CHAPTER 14

THE *FRINGEDOM*
FANS, CRITICS, AND SOCIAL MEDIA

"Thank you for making yourselves just obnoxious enough that
the bosses had to keep us on the air."

— Joshua Jackson, "*Fringe*: Fan Thank You"

More than one clever fan-critic has speculated that the Observers represent the show's viewers. Fox community discussion board contributor "Zeppelin" initiated a conversation using the assertion that the Observers represent the "millions and millions" of fans: "We also are always observing everything . . . writing down, thinking about, looking at intently, making choices . . . determining the importance of the facts, observing, detail by detail, all the important events in the universes of *Fringe* and foreseeing moments with historical relevance." Fans, like the Observers, transcend time and space in relation to the series, seeing everything, just like the Observers, and remembering even when the main characters may have forgotten, for instance, that Peter ever existed.

So if the Observer is a proxy for the viewer, what does this say about the function of the audience? Certainly *Fringe* does not draw attention to itself as a fictional work to the extent that other popular shows do (consider *Supernatural*'s meta-text), but is it possible that there is more to the Observer than his diegetic context? Consider

September's role in Walter's life story. He tries to stay detached and silent. There is a set of guidelines that requires him (and the rest of the Observers) to avoid getting involved. But in Walter's later years September does interact in the Bishops' lives and he does participate in human life, as a person with a distinct identity. He continues to observe but he also counsels, engages in conflict, and discusses the fate of the characters with his fellow Observers.

This pattern of behavior is akin to the modern-day television viewer. Not long ago most television audiences passively watched the story, with very little interaction with the production community. Now through technology and social media audiences "get involved" with the storytelling process. Perhaps we "say too much," like September, because we have multiple venues in which to speak our minds. It's true that no single fan "counsels" the writers, but as a group they collectively make suggestions for the plot and the fate of the show's production. As demonstrated by the season 4 renewal campaign, cheered on by Joshua Jackson (Peter Bishop), there is a line of communication between the viewer and the viewed. As John Noble says in the cast's thank-you video, we, the observers, had something of an influence on the show's destiny.

It's hard to know whether or not the writers pay close attention to the theories posted on fan boards or the suggestions that viewers make. How much do they listen to the complaints and the speculation? Should they listen at all? In an article published shortly after the season 4 renewal announcement, Ken Tucker of *Entertainment Weekly* made the point that when we listen to new songs by our favorite bands or read a good novel, we don't stop in the middle and suggest that the creator go in a different direction: "I don't sit around with my finger hovering over my latest iPod song download or fretting in the midst of reading a long piece of fiction, pondering what *I* want the musician or the author to do, trying to second-guess the creators — I just *get on* with it, and enjoy the critical thinking afterward, not measuring whether the show/music/book has lived up to my predictions/wishes/dreams for it." This is a reasonable comparison — and a good point for those who seem to incessantly "second-guess" the writers and producers — but it's important to note that television is a different medium with its own set of conventions and limitations.

For starters, we *do* have to wait a considerable amount of time between "chapters," time that can be spent "fretting" about what the showrunner is thinking. Whether or not we view episodes when they air or later on a DVR, the format of television scheduling lends itself to mid-story discussion and critical analysis. This schedule creates a completely different kind of audience, one that "observes" many different levels of the creative process.

This format also happens to fit nicely with the newest forms of communication. Rather than passively consuming the show, viewers have an opportunity to interpret, reframe, and even re-imagine the television narrative. So if the Observer is the television viewer and the act of viewing has an effect on the writers, and subsequently the characters, then what are the creators of *Fringe* trying to say about us, the audience? Like September we can predict possible futures for the show's plot, but we can never know for certain which will play out. In "The Firefly" September explains to Walter that although he can foresee some things, he cannot control them; every action causes "unforeseen ripples." Studious fans are very good at laying out plausible predictions or "theories" about the show, but they do so with no certainty regarding how things will turn out. Even the writers who can plan exactly how events will ensue are subject to uncertainty; there are forces outside their control like ratings, renewals, and actors' contracts.

FringeBlogger.com writer Roco says it best when he explains, "Both the Observer and his 'colleagues' are watching mankind experiment with fringe science, and we, the viewing audience, are also observing events from an almost 'unseen' position (or dimension, if you will) — indeed, we are also *observers*, and we are also *here*." There is no doubt that, despite Olivia's status as hero or Peter's willingness to sacrifice himself, the Observers play one of the most crucial roles in *Fringe*. Though their name signifies a fairly passive task, they have a tremendous responsibility in the universes of *Fringe*. Those viewers who are still *here* — the dedicated fans, in other words — also have a responsibility to the show, one that involves careful watching and critical interpretation. The effect that critical "readers" can have on a television narrative is more profound than one might think. It seems that the closer we scrutinize a TV story, the more we keep the creators accountable for their quality of storytelling. In an interview Blair Brown (Nina Sharp) explained the effect that fans' commentary has on the production of the show: "It makes us better, it makes the show better, it makes us smarter." She emphasized how it holds the creators and actors responsible for keeping the show "surprising" and thought-provoking.

Fans and the Renewal Campaign

In the spring of 2011, after *Fringe* was relegated to the Friday night "death slot," the fan base launched a massive campaign to save the show. In an interview with *Entertainment Weekly* Joshua Jackson inspired fans with his own entreaty: "It is going to take the people that like the show to watch the show and start the campaign and show their support if they want to see us stick around for another season." This plea to fans was later followed up with a thank-you video after the official announcement of the renewal in which each star of the show acknowledged the fan base as a major contributor to the show's success. John Noble and Blair Brown both noted the fans' online presence as significantly influencing the renewal process. But Lance Reddick's comment was probably the most compelling and sincere: "I know so often fans think that they need us . . . but I would be digging ditches or doing something else if it wasn't for you. So — thank you. Really."

On his television blog TVOvermind.com, Jon Lachonis published a letter to fans explaining specifically how they could help keep the show on the air. He urged fans to talk about the show "where Fox would see it," by joining message boards and supporting the big *Fringe* blogs such as FringeBloggers.com and FringeTelevision.com. He suggested that by using social media bookmarking tools the fans could create the buzz necessary for executives to take notice. His theory on how to save *Fringe* was based on the premise that "*Fringe* fans are *Lost* fans." He contended that "*Lost* fans did more grassroots promotion for that show than any other show in history — they can do it again. In order to save *Fringe* fans need to talk about the show. The *Lost* fans that remain need to exercise their veteran fandom skills to create the kind of grassroots marketing *Lost* enjoyed for so long."

Lachonis's article is a perfect example of viewers teaching other viewers how to be "good" fans. It is also indicative of the power of online collaborative rallying. Lachonis acted as leader, attempting to organize the passion of viewers and help them focus their enthusiasm in productive ways. Ken Tucker of *EW* wrote a similar article. In his unambiguously titled appeal to viewers and potential viewers, "*Fringe*: Save This Show! A Guide (and a Plea) for New Fans," Tucker explains why *Fringe* is so important. He catalogs the compelling qualities that *Fringe* brings to television audiences: "the bonds of family, the ecstasy of romance, the exhilaration of intellectual inquiry, and a secret government agency working to protect you from all kinds of crazy, weird stuff." He asserts that *Fringe* is "the best portrait of a fractious family since *Frasier*, or perhaps even *M*A*S*H*," and he ends his persuasive essay with a strong, *Fringe*-themed point: fans should watch "because right now, *Fringe* is promising you nothing less than the world — two of 'em, in fact."

The same type of campaign that Tucker and Lachonis were waging ensued over at FringeBloggers.com, FringeTelevision.com, and TheFringeNetwork.com. Serious fans at these sites were instructing their readers and telling them how to handle the "crisis" of an impending cancellation.

Ratings and the Digital Video Recorder

Several factors contributed to *Fringe*'s renewal for season 4, and one of those is the large percentage of DVR viewers, which boosted the overall numbers. Though the traditional Nielsen rating system would indicate that viewership was quite low in the latter half of season 3, especially after the show moved to Fridays, the DVR numbers tell a different story.

Fringe viewers are DVR users; they tend to utilize DVRs to a greater degree than fans of other shows. Shortly after *Fringe*'s first Friday airing in January 2011, the ratings looked grim, at a measly 1.9 adult demo rating. But a few days later, that viewership number rose to 2.7, a 42 percent increase thanks to the DVR numbers. In a *New York Times* article, "DVRs Give More Shows Lifelines," Bill Carter contends that Kevin Reilly, Fox's top programming executive, "would have been considered borderline delusional" if he "renewed the show based only on the ratings that arrive the morning after each *Fringe* episode." Carter explains that "for its broadcast on Friday nights, *Fringe* manages only about a 1.7 rating (about 2.24 million viewers)," putting it in cancellation range. But when the DVR viewers are factored in, the rating swells to at least 2.5 and, fortunately for *Fringe*, the "official" number for advertisers includes up to three days after the show is first broadcast. (In the industry it is referred to as "C3.") There is no doubt that the inclusion of the DVR numbers helped *Fringe* get renewed.

Social Media

The season 4 renewal campaign would have looked very different without social networking giants Twitter and Facebook, which have become central agents for the promotion of pretty much everything and for up-to-the-minute entertainment news.

In March 2011 Twitter-friendly fans kept in close touch with executive producer Joel Wyman as he tweeted about the show's renewal prospects. Prior to the official announcement he appeared to be as in the dark as anyone else, but his (Twitter) attitude was always upbeat. He continued to remind fans that Fox executive Kevin Reilly considered *Fringe* to be one of his personal favorites. Wyman also urged fans to ignore rumors of cancellation until an official announcement was made. Just a few days before the renewal he responded to a flurry of tweets about cancellation rumors. Wyman tweeted, "Hi. I just hopped on and saw all this. Some people love bad news SO much they make it up." Not long after this comment he reassured his followers, "We will come here first with the news of a pickup." And he kept that promise. On March 24, he tweeted, "*Fringe* was picked up!!!! Thanks *Fringe*dom!"

This special access that fans, those who visit Twitter at least, can have to an executive television producer is only a recent phenomenon. To be able to join the producers in real time and celebrate a season renewal is groundbreaking. Viewers can communicate directly with a creator, and a producer can instantaneously address his or her audience in a way not possible before Twitter. The day after the show's renewal was confirmed, Wyman took the opportunity to directly address his fans again: "Jeff [Pinkner] and I just heard that *Fringe* fans sent 'buckets of Red Vines' to Fox. Awesome!"

A recent predecessor of this Twitter fandom — fans having close digital access to celebrated TV writers and actors — can be found in the discussion forums of large fan sites. Producers and actors can address the participants in real time in these forums, but the format is more exclusive than that of Twitter, requiring the user to log in to a certain site at a specified time. Twitter allows messages from a wider spectrum of celebrity personalities to be available for any internet user to see.

Of course we can't be sure that Wyman or Jeff Pinkner are tweeting for themselves or if their marketing teams are assigned that duty, but Wyman's good-natured tone seems fairly consistent throughout his comments. His Twitter voice reflects the same warm and soft-spoken, yet slightly awkward personality we see in his interviews. And the spotty timing of his commentary would reflect the very hectic schedule of an entertainment executive.

In the thank-you video mentioned earlier, John Noble revealed, "We see the blogs and we see the arguments . . . the defenses and the attacks — it's a very lovely debate." The specific online venues are not mentioned here, but it's probably safe to assume that they have found many of these comments on either Facebook or Twitter.

In an interview with Daniel Fienberg of Hitfix.com, Jeff Pinkner expressed his enthusiasm for interacting with fans and listening to their input: "We've said it before: we care very much what our fans and what the audience thinks. We also know that's not representative of the entire audience. We strive to take what the audience thinks into consideration, while at the same time not allowing it to, in and of itself, drive the ship." For the season 3 finale, Pinkner answered tweets during the Eastern time zone broadcast of "The Day We Died," and Wyman was available while it aired on the West Coast. Fox promoted these rapid-fire discussions, instructing fans to use the hashtag #FringeTweetLive.

With or without the chummy connection between creator and fan, Twitter provides a venue for fan communities to flourish and to share the viewing experience with one another in real time. Using certain hashtags, most notably #Fringe, in their comments, viewers can watch the show together. This is the modern day version of sitting in a theater together, witnessing the story unfold as a group.

Fans can "turn" to each other to exclaim their shock and disgust, or they can demonstrate their amusement with an LOL. With social media, audiences have the freedom to express their immediate reactions to the narrative.

Blogger Sam McPherson contends that the most active *Fringe* communities are on Twitter: "We find each other through hashtags like #Fringe and #TheDayWeDied, and often we live-chat during the shows. Mostly though our tweets express shock or (when Walternate does something dastardly) outrage. Twitter's probably the best place to gauge just how shocking *Fringe* is. . . . There's generally a communal sense of awe after a spectacular episode." Twitter allows viewers who would otherwise watch in isolation to develop into full-fledged participants of the viewing event. This sense of call-and-response community is reflected in Twitter usernames like @theViewingParty, which conjures an image of a group sitting around the flickering light of the TV, invigorated by lively discourse.

Among the dozens of Facebook pages fans have created in support of *Fringe*, there is the #FringeMovement, using the Twitter hashtag in their title and encouraging viewers to follow *Fringe* to Fridays; Save *Fringe*, which has been "liked" by almost 5,000 users; *Fringe* France with a surprising 12,000 "likes"; and many more with fewer followers, such as Seeing Patterns and Fringe Olivia. The *Fringe* Movement was created by a grassroots organization that describes itself as "a group of fans that provide fellow cortexifans resources to promote the hit TV show *Fringe*." Their website is sleek and professional, but it also has a strong grassroots sensibility, using phrases like "get involved" and "get trending!" They have clear objectives that employ language modeled on popular social movements: "(1) To spread the word about *Fringe*'s new night and to encourage U.S. fans to watch LIVE (2) To keep the international *Fringe* community informed and united about the show (3) To welcome new fans to the worlds of *Fringe*!" This single example of a fandom hub, which incorporates Facebook, Twitter, websites, videos, Tumblrs, and traditional TV viewing, demonstrates just how inextricable these different sources are. Online activity has become so interconnected, and fans of cult TV shows have a variety of venues to voice their fandom.

From a corporate perspective Facebook is a significant part of fan interaction and audience feedback. As popular as some fan-made social media gathering spots are, Fox's official Facebook page has the largest following by far and the strongest presence among the *Fringe*dom. The page offers quite a few resources for *Fringe* fans, including samples from the *Tales From the Fringe* graphic novel, behind the scenes photos, links to full episodes, dozens of short videos, special discussion boards, and quizzes. The benefit of an official Facebook page is that it provides reliable, up-to-date information about the show. With all of the official promotions fans can be sure that they are getting the correct times and dates, if not a critical examination of the show's content. This page is also a venue for fans to express their gratitude, annoyance, or admiration in the hopes that executive folks might be listening. But on Fox's official *Fringe* Facebook wall each comment prompts hundreds or even thousands of responses, and individual sentiments are often lost in the cacophony of voices.

A revolutionary idea only a few years ago, Facebook has settled into its role as an institution in most users' lives, especially in the lives of cult TV fans. It is standard for any television show to establish a Facebook page, and for broadcast television to boast the highest numbers of "likes." Facebook certainly served to promote the *Fringe* renewal campaign, reaching users who might not otherwise be exposed to Fox and WB promotions. Posting videos is one of the more effective means to hook viewers, and so the official *Fringe* Facebook page often employs video clips. The sneak peeks and trailers were consistently posted there during season 3. Although these videos were available on the Fox website and countless other online venues, the convenience of Facebook ensured that more fans would see them. The kinds of viewers who might not search for the latest sneak peek or episode trailer on their own but *do* spend a lot of time on Facebook would get their daily dose of promotion right in their newsfeed.

Critics: Blogs and Discussion Boards

According to Sam McPherson, a contributor to TVOvermind.com and a blogger deeply invested in *Fringe* from the very beginning, the fandom of *Fringe* is a smaller but more condensed community than the audiences of other comparable science fiction fantasy shows: "*Fringe* hasn't spawned the amount of websites that *Lost* has, but the few sites that do exist are really highly trafficked." McPherson identifies those venues as FringeBloggers.com and FringeNetwork.com. Continuing the contrast to the hugely popular island show he says, "With *Lost*, fans were usually grouped into two categories: they loved the characters, or they loved the mythology. In general there seem to be more *Fringe* fans toward the middle of that spectrum. Most discussions I've seen are both about the mythology and the characters. Of course that could be because the show ties the two aspects together so integrally."

Other major blogs include FollowingThePattern.com, a podcast site that also features "Terry the Fringe Rock Star" blog; TheFringeReport.com; TheFringePodcast.com; and Spanish sites Fringelatino.blogspot.com and ZonaFringe.blogspot.com. One of the more bizarre fan sites depicts *Fringe*-inspired singing chipmunks. David Wu, a music artist and fan of the show, creates a musical parody to recap each episode, chipmunk-style. He calls his project "Fringemunks" (DavidWuMusic.com/FringeMunks).

FringeBloggers.com provides extensive coverage of *Fringe*-related news and in-depth analysis of the show's narrative. One of the more noteworthy items on this site is its timeline, a resource that organizes the *Fringe*'s rather temporally messy narrative. Attributed to blog contributor LizW65, it is comprehensive and well maintained. It distinguishes between the prequel events, those that occurred before the Glatterflug incident of the pilot episode, and those that occurred in 2008 or after. Prequel components are categorized by the approximate year they happened, and later events are listed both under a season and a year. It even includes the documented sightings of the Observer that began in 1770.

Interview with Roco, administrator of Fringe Bloggers

Q. When did you begin writing about *Fringe*?

A. I began writing about *Fringe* quite a while before the show actually aired [in September 2008]. It was probably around January or February 2008. One of my goals (along with the other team members who have been a part of the process) was to help support the show through the creation of an online community, where fans could gather, share, and experience *Fringe* together.

Q. To what extent have you connected with other *Fringe* fans through your online presence? Do you feel that there is a tight community in *Fringe*dom?

A. The *Fringe* community is indeed tight — though of course, that doesn't mean we always agree! Fans have different opinions and are passionate about their point of view, but at the end of the day the fanbase rallies around the show and there are many great discussions taking place between fans from all over the world. Particularly at FringeBloggers.com and Fringe-Forum.com.

I've had many great interactions with other *Fringe* fans, whether on the blog, forum, by email, or via various social media channels such as Twitter and Facebook. Working with the staff team at Fringe-Forum.com, for example, has also been a great experience. Since we cover *Fringe* at Seriable.com, we also have a growing *Fringe* community there too.

Q. Compared to other fandoms, how would you describe *Fringe* fans?

A. *Fringe* fans are extremely passionate about their show; they're probably one of the most dedicated TV series fan bases currently out there.

The Observers have their own dedicated resource on this site too. "The Observer Files" features every single Observer sighting on the show and even some outside of the show. There are "sightings" of an Observer in the real world, which are mostly photographic manipulations of his image, making it appear that he attended high profile events such as a NASCAR race and an *American Idol* taping. This site also has a page that maps out the major (and some minor) differences between the two universes, a list of the books that appear in the show, and a glyphs code translation spot.

TheFringeReport.com offers dynamic insight into the world of *Fringe*, especially in the pages "The Notebook" and "The Theory Scoreboard." Regarding the latter, administrators invite readers to propose their own theories and fans get a chance to keep track of who can make the best predictions about plot resolution with sections for confirmed, unconfirmed, and disproved ideas.

FringeTelevision.com, another major blog serving the *Fringe*dom, offers a page dedicated to all things Easter Egg–ish and provides a direct link to the best screen caps of the show. Other items include links to the full episodes on Hulu, a wiki, and reviews. Following the season 3 finale the editors of this blog posted their own list of some popular *Fringe*-related web sources featuring "The Day We Died" reviews and, interestingly, made no distinction between professional review and amateur blog entry. This blurring of the lines between journalist and blogger is quite evident in the world of television recaps and reviews. The "official" voices seem to matter less and less, as support for fellow fanboys and fangirls grows in strength. However, Geoff Boucher is one professional journalist who covers *Fringe* and seems to identify with the common fan. His *L.A. Times* blog boasts the subtitle, "Get in Touch With Your Inner Fanboy."

Most of the *Fringe* discussion boards operate in conjunction with the multiplatform blogs and websites mentioned above. Claiming more than 8,000 participants, there is Fringe-Forum.com, administered by Roco of Fringe Bloggers. Another active discussion board is situated as part of the official Fox *Fringe* site and is dubbed the "community forum" (fringe.community.fox.com). Twitter and Facebook are not traditional discussion boards, but they are certainly home to countless discussions, and in a less exclusive way than on some of the dedicated fan sites.

Role-playing games, in which each participant chooses a particular character and contributes to a collaborative story, are another type of online venue for fans of *Fringe*, although currently there have only been a few RPGs active since the series first aired. As far as wikis go, for *Fringe* the main one is Fringepedia.net, a site administered by FringeTelevision.com. This wiki is reliable in its archiving of episodes and episode transcripts, but the homepage announcements are not quite up-to-date. There is also the FringeFanWiki.com, self-identified as "the Alternate *Fringe* Wiki Site."

Fan Production

Like most other science fiction shows with cult followings, *Fringe* has spawned a number of communities for fan vidding and fan fiction. FringeFiction.com is a dedicated site for stories about the show. Archive of Our Own (or AO3), a multi-fandom archive, houses hundreds of text-only narratives that incorporate the mythology and characters of *Fringe*. Contributors to *Fringe*'s FanFiction.net group are quite prolific too. LiveJournal supports several "*Fringe*fic" communities as well, featuring writers exploring and re-imagining the Olivia-Peter ship, the most obvious pairing in *Fringe*. Less obvious pairings include Peter and Astrid, Walter and Astrid, Nina and Broyles, and even some slash (same-sex pairings) fiction with Lincoln and Peter. There is also a small audience for the Olivia/Astrid femslash pairing, but generally slash relationships are not as popular in *Fringe*fic as they are in other fandoms. Yuletide, an annual fan fiction challenge, is another online project in which *Fringe* fan-authors have assembled. *Fringe* also has a presence on Dreamwidth, both in fan fiction pages and on the *Fringe* TV vidding site.

The majority of *Fringe* fanvids, viewer-made video productions that accentuate or re-imagine a specific aspect of the narrative, are promotional in nature, using series of images that don't change the canon much, but simply make the show more appealing to certain audiences. Some of the most dynamic *Fringe* fanvids are the ones that offer crossovers with other shows and films. One such fan video, posted by ImaginetheUnknown on YouTube, incorporates elements of *Inception*, *Supernatural*, *Fringe*, *Lost*, and even one brief shot from *Flashforward*. Most of the dialogue that this fan-producer uses originates from *Supernatural* and *Inception*, and yet, viewing it through the lens of a *Fringe* fan, it appears to support the "Lysergic Acid Diethylamide" storyline, which did not air until a month after this YouTube post. Another interesting crossover, which promotes the Fauxlivia/Lincoln pairing, reveals an interesting parallel between Claire's baby from *Lost*, Aaron, and Fauxlivia's child, Henry. It is titled "This Baby Is All of Us" and was posted by Kirwani90 on YouTube.

One of the most stunning works by *Fringe* fans is hollywoodgrrl's "Boom Boom Pow" *Fringe*-centric video, which premiered at Club Vivid during the 2010 Vividcon, an annual convention celebrating the art of fan production. This well-edited piece highlights some of the most violent and dangerous moments that the *Fringe* team encounters in seasons 1 and 2 and depicts Olivia as the true centerpiece of the show; she comes across as both tough and surprisingly glamorous. This is all accentuated, of course, by the music of the Black Eyed Peas. Another noteworthy vidding project uses the film noir images from Walter's story in season 2's "Brown Betty" to create a more serious depiction of the episode. Again Olivia is the star of the video, depicted as both a Humphrey Bogart–type hero and a vulnerable heroine. *Fringe* fan-producers are also quite inspired by Walter's antics, as demonstrated by the high number of "top Walter Bishop moments" videos on YouTube. One of the more amusing *Fringe* fan productions is a montage of Walter's illicit drug moments set to the tune "Because I Got High" by Afroman created by a fan-producer by the username of dacharmedone. Another popular Walter-centric vid theme is the many names of Astrid; yell4help's piece, simply titled "What Walter Calls Astrid," offers a string of comical clips featuring Walter's struggle to remember her name. Re-imaginings of the Peter/Olivia ship are also popular in fan production, as in fan fiction.

The world of fan production and creative interpretation presents an interesting profile of *Fringe*'s audience. With the growing availability of editing tools and the presence of so many fan fiction communities, viewers continue to creatively interpret what they find in the canon of the show, highlighting what is most important to them and leaving out what doesn't serve their purposes. These re-imaginings of *Fringe* are as significant to understanding the show as are the interpretive blogs and critical reviews. But more than pro-viding a greater appreciation of the show itself, vidding and fan fiction offer a good deal of knowledge about the viewers and what they find valuable in a television narrative. Their creative works are undoubt-edly a reflection of the show, but the fan-produced narratives also transform the mirror image into something new. Fan-creators unveil new layers of meaning and unforeseen dimensions of the original narrative; they stretch the canon and shape it into a reflection of themselves. In the next chapter I will use the looking-glass metaphor as a symbol of the television screen and explore how the larger social context is reflected in *Fringe*. This final chapter will also address how *Fringe* is a refracted image of our world; as fanvids are filtered narra-tives of *Fringe*, the television show itself is a creative interpretation of society's current state of affairs.

CHAPTER 15

Mirror and Lens
Reflection and Refraction
Through the Screen

"The books are something like our books, only the words go the
wrong way; I know that, because I've held up one of our books
to the glass, and then they hold up one in the other room."
— Alice, *Through the Looking Glass, and What Alice Found There*

The metaphor of the television as a mirror, or "looking glass," suggests the small screen is something that precisely imitates the world
of its audience, yet television narratives are not exact simulations of
the real world. The symbol of the mirror, also used in this book to
represent the two worlds within *Fringe*, is not a strict representation
of the viewers' relationship to the show. In fact the television "glass" is
more often used as a lens through which the image of the real world
passes for closer examination. Technically speaking refraction occurs
"when a wave passes from one medium into the second, deviating
from the straight path it otherwise would have taken." Metaphorically
this "deviation" offers a fresh way to view our own social constructs,
exploring how things *should* be or, in the case of science fiction, how
things *might* be, if only we had the lens with which to see them. The
following section identifies the current social climate from which this
particular television scenario draws its content and tone.

Like any work of fiction *Fringe* is situated within a certain social
and historical context, one that is somewhat difficult to illustrate

without the temporal distance that we have with a completed text. Nevertheless this final chapter offers a few of the current influential factors on the *Fringe*-verse and explores how the show reflects the world of its viewers. This examination of the show's context assumes that the audience is predominantly a Western one and that, given its setting, *Fringe*'s depictions of "real life" are predominantly American. The connections between fact and fiction accounted here do not require that the reflections and/or refractions are intentional on the creator's part. Societal influence is not necessarily a conscious component in the creative process, but acknowledging it *does* reveal the larger force at work in the development of the narrative. In the same way that the spectacularly terrifying plane crash scene from *Lost*'s pilot episode underscored the horrific, televised airline wreckage of the 2001 terrorist attacks, *Fringe* provokes similar visual associations with the world from which it emerges.

Both Sides of the Glass
Cosmic Order and the Nature of Existence

When *Lost* fans discovered that Damon Lindelof and Carlton Cuse did not necessarily have the entire maze of the show figured out "all along," there was widespread disappointment. After the series finale aired, some viewers felt that many of the show's enigmas were void of meaning. Fans of long-term mythology-driven dramas are quite preoccupied with the existence of an overarching scheme or plan. Like *Lost*, *Fringe* offers the promise of a purposeful plan, and the producers' careful attention to the enigmatic details indicates that they have a well-mapped overarching scheme.

The audience's demand for a meaningful show reflects the common need for some kind of higher order in the universe. The deep-seated longing to find a reason for our existence, this quest for "the truth," is at the heart of most religions. This sentiment echoes throughout many popular culture stories ("the truth is out there"). Many faiths offer entire maps of the cosmic plan, from creation to the incarnation of a god to judgment day. It's much easier to accept these social institutions and to know there is a happy ending somewhere than to accept the random, accidental nature of the universe.

In her speech "Absolute Nothingness," theologian Sheila Harty challenges her listeners to embrace the vast, immeasurable nothingness that is our universe, rather than protecting themselves with a flimsy construct of faith. She points out that most people simply cannot accept the meaninglessness of life and so they defend themselves by building a vast narrative to explain everything. "This socially constructed faith offers a shield against the howling hyenas of the night — for to reject the Master Story is to exile oneself." Not only does the story comfort the individual; it allows him or her to establish a role in the larger community.

Perhaps this is where fiction, and television shows specifically, can fill a certain void in modern day secular life. Many popular culture experts have argued that serialized television can serve as something of a religious text or a substitute for the sacred experience. The story itself becomes a code of beliefs interpreted by different viewer-believers who passionately defend their own ideas about the narrative, a television show rather than a sacred text. We may never solve the puzzle of the universe, or even prove that a puzzle exists in the first place, but in a constructed fantasy world, one that imitates our own world, we can "find the patterns" and piece them together. We enjoy knowing that the universe, at least the fictional one(s), can be understood and solved. It is rewarding to predict what's going to happen based on the clues that the *creator* provides.

The process of deciphering fiction may not help us understand the purpose of our own existence, but it gives us hope that there is an intentional cosmic design. By understanding the worlds of *Fringe* or *Lost* or *Buffy*, maybe we can understand our world a little better. On National Public Radio's talk show *Speaking of Faith*, Diane Winston, editor of the book *Small Screen, Big Picture*, said, "I'm not saying that TV is going to . . . replace scripture, but it is a site where people are asking very basic questions about the meaning of life and where they fit in and how to behave as good people." Of course finding meaning is not restricted to religious perspective, or the "why" of life.

How things work is just as important to discovering the truths of the universe. Scientists continue to search for some sort of theory that explains everything, some kind of complete unified explanation of the universe, one that marries classic physics and quantum physics, two opposing camps that explain the puzzle of life at two very different levels. Indeed some physicists would argue that the answer is within our reach and that it lies in string theory, but there is no consensus on this yet. The desire for an overarching hypothesis that explains everything is reflected in Walter's enthusiasm when he first discovers the definition of the Vacuum, as the destroyer and creator of "everything." He says that the device confirms many of his theories and that it is likely the "key to the universe." Quite fittingly then, this would make Walter a god (though, in this episode, he does not yet know it).

But *Fringe*'s cosmic order presents a myriad of other possibilities that might someday be revealed as part of our own reality. Most obvious is the theory of multiple universes. The AU trope is a favorite of many science fiction fans simply because it presents a strange mix of hope and dread. If we fail in this life, whatever that entails, perhaps our double is succeeding in the next universe over, or vice versa. It opens the imagination to new possibilities: am I a rock star in another reality? Who did my alternate self marry? Is my double a city dweller or a suburbanite? A high school dropout? A drug addict?

Alternate universes can also help explain strange occurrences that we encounter in real life. Walter explains déjà vu, for instance, through the construct of multiple realities in "The Road Not Taken." Alternate realities could also explain surprisingly accurate hunches, based solely on intuition. Perhaps the magic of intuitive problem-solving can be attributed to the alternate self sending out warning signals to his or her doppelgängers in parallel universes.

Another component of *Fringe*'s cosmic order is the notion of destiny. For all of their efforts to ground the stories in science, the writers of *Fringe* suggest that existence is more or less predestined. They seem to contend that the characters are fated to do everything they do, even if September claims that there are "many futures." It is no coincidence, for instance, that Walter, Olivia, and Peter come together years after the initial cortexiphan trials. It is not by chance that the machine was built for Peter or that Olivia develops special powers. Even if some of these scenarios are explained in scientific terms, the show nevertheless offers viewers a depiction of life that is guided by predetermination and seemingly fixed paradoxical time loops. Everyone seems to have a predetermined purpose; they do not choose their fate for themselves.

Other elements of *Fringe*'s cosmic order are made clear by the end of the first season. In the *Fringe*-verse, time travel is possible but we can't change the past (apparently with "Peter's consciousness" being the one exception), the fabric of the universe can be destroyed, and mind control is possible. By the end of season 3 the cosmic order of *Fringe* also suggests that the consequences of time travel could threaten the existence of some people altogether.

In the season 3 finale the Observers tell us that Peter never existed for the others; they don't remember him because he was never born. But how can we make sense of this idea? If no one remembers Peter, then what is the purpose of his presence in the show? "The Doctor," the ultimate time travel expert from the *Doctor Who* series, might be able to help us out with this issue. A central theme of *Doctor Who*'s season 5 is that, despite major shifts in the timeline, one can never really be completely erased from history, not if the memory of that individual is "imprinted" strongly enough on another individual. In the season 5 finale of *Doctor Who*, the Doctor asks Amy, "Do you remember what I told you when you were seven?" Amy can't recall, and so she asks him to remind her. "That's not the point," he answers. The point is that she hold on to her memories, so that even if one version of history is erased her memories are not completely lost. "We're all just stories in the end," he tells her.

Is this what Peter will be — "just another story," a vague memory buried in the depths of Olivia's consciousness? But the story, according to the Doctor, is stronger than we might imagine. Walter would likely entertain the Doctor's notion, and he would be the first to propose that Olivia would have the power to bring Peter back into existence.

But what does it mean that he never existed in the first place, according to the rules of *Fringe*? If he was never born then how did Walter and Walternate wind up together on this trans-universal bridge? And why is there a conflict between them if Walter never stole Peter to begin with? More importantly, what does it mean to be wiped out of existence? Does it reflect a fear that destiny's fine balance is tenuous? If one thing changes, then it changes everything and everyone, like the firefly that Peter caught as a young boy. This theme dominates season 3, with episodes like "The Firefly," in which September explains that through a series of seemingly insignificant events, Peter's presence in this universe led to the death of Roscoe Joyce's son.

Environmental Crises

Walternate blames Walter for the widespread damage to the natural world of the alternate universe and its ultimate demise. When we first see Walternate's world, entire forests have disappeared. Holes are appearing in the middle of bodies of water, completely draining them. There are massive fault lines in the fabric of the universe, and the "cure" is just as horrific as the ailment. When a crack is identified, the Fringe team immediately releases amber into the area. The substance captures anyone in the quarantined section, holding them frozen for eternity, conscious but unable to move.

Walternate has published a book about the death of the universe (*ZFT*), but in the text he does not reveal that these events are man-made. They are explained as natural occurrences. When Fauxlivia and her team are informed that the cause involves a person from another universe, they are surprised.

This environmental crisis, and the repercussions of it, mirrors the natural disasters that our world — the real world — has recently withstood. It is interesting that so many natural disasters occurred over the course of the very year that season 3 aired. Because the sheer number of cataclysms occurred in such a short period of time, the zeitgeist was one of collective anxiety. Predictions by religious leaders about the end of the world (see Harold Camping below) were given an inordinate amount of attention in the media and popular discourse. And on *Fringe,* season 3's dramatic plot echoed these sentiments with its continual warnings of a trans-universal meltdown.

The debate about global warming and its effects are echoed in the *ZFT* book and the "half-truths" Walternate has presented as fact to the general populace. Though it is clear that global climate change is also a natural phenomenon, scientists have provided evidence that, like Walter and the cracks in the universe, human beings are to blame for holes in the ozone.

Global warming has been identified as one cause of the increase in violent storms and flooding we've witnessed in the real world. About the 2011 flooding of the Mississippi River, environmentalist

Bill McKibben reported in the *Los Angeles Times*, "What the [army] corps is really fighting is a river swelled not just by the power of nature but by the power of man." The difficult choices that had to be made in response to this flood are paralleled in the decisions that face Walternate when a hole in the universe has been identified. Walternate orders the Fringe Division to immediately seal the breaches, even though human lives are at stake. Hundreds of people are essentially frozen in time so that the universe will survive. Colonel Broyles believes that loss of life is "a tragic but a small price to pay for the greater good" ("Amber 31422"). In "6B" Walter faces a similar decision: to plug the growing vortex with amber, which would kill Peter, Olivia, and others in the process.

On a far less fantastic scale, the tragedy of the 2011 Mississippi flood required the few to pay the price for the "greater good." In the aftermath of a powerful flood in Mississippi in 1927, which claimed hundreds of lives, a system of spillways was built to direct the water away from large cities. Until very recently whole towns were situated on those floodplains, and most of the people who lived there lost their homes in 2011's flooding in order to save the more densely populated areas, the oil refineries, and the chemical plants. Mitch Landrieu, the mayor of New Orleans, said, "The decision to open the gates was a cruel choice. . . . It doesn't make us feel any good that [by] protecting New Orleans, other folks are going to get hurt." However had this tough decision not been made, New Orleans would have had to deal with flooding far worse than that of Hurricane Katrina.

The devastation from tornadoes in the midwestern and southern United States in 2011 also seems to be reflected, though not by design, in the universe-ending events of the end of season 3 where tumultuous environmental changes played out on screen. The winds of the deadly Joplin, Missouri, tornado, which reached almost 200 miles per hour, were so strong that they ripped the bark off the trees and the plants from the ground. The video footage of this storm is comparable to the images of major catastrophes we see in *Fringe*, most notably the severe weather featured in "The Last Sam Weiss" and "6:02 AM EST." More than once this season, Walter prophesies the end of the world. In "The Last Sam Weiss" he turns to God for repentance. Along with films like *2012*, *Fringe* was playing off its audience's fascination with, if not belief in, the end-of-times myth, using images like swarms of locusts as precursors to mass destruction.

Real-life major earthquakes and their aftereffects, tsunamis, have far-reaching consequences and, for some, they are world ending. The shifting plates of the Earth's surface that caused the enormous 2004 Indian Ocean earthquake and devastating tsunami in Indonesia killed thousands and, by some accounts, made the entire planet "vibrate." One of the largest earthquakes on record, its immediate widespread destruction was unprecedented. This catastrophic event seemed pulled from apocalyptic fiction. The devastation of Japan after the 2011 earthquake also seems beyond the scope of reality. The earthquake, the tsunamis, the aftershocks, and the nuclear plant meltdowns: these are all elements of doomsday science fiction, and yet their existence is very real.

Only weeks prior to the disaster in Japan the worlds of *Fringe* were experiencing a similar type of destruction. The "cracks" in the universe and the vortex of "6B" create an effect analogous to the shifting plates of an earthquake. The image of two land masses crashing into one another is comparable to Walter's notion of two universes doing the same thing. Like Walter's theory of everything being sucked into a vortex, the videos from Japan's tsunami show entire villages being swallowed up by the flood of ocean water, recalling the flushing waters of the micro black hole vortex seen in the alternate universe.

Because of its destabilizing character the natural world is often depicted as the antagonist in science fiction and adventure narratives. Some of these recent catastrophes demonstrate how awe-inspiring and horrific nature can be. With the dawn of YouTube and other video posting sites much of this devastation is caught on film and broadcast to the world almost instantaneously and from unprecedented perspectives, making storms and earthquakes even more prevalent in our imaginations and creative works. In *Fringe* the destruction of an entire universe is portrayed in terms with which we can identify — lightning, dark skies, wind, shaking ground, and holes in the universe (perhaps a science fiction re-imagining of holes in the atmosphere). The images of the over-here universe at the end of season 3 — the terrible, cloudless lightning storms — conjure up the genuine fear that we have of our own natural world.

Global Economic Recession

Unlike other crises examined in these pages, economic troubles are not reflected in *Fringe* in any obvious way. The worlds of *Fringe* are similar to our world — Obama is the president and the U.S. is engaged in military conflict — but there is no discussion of the recession. Instead there is a continuous stream of prophetic warnings about how the "fabric of the universe" is deteriorating.

In "The Day We Died" Peter tells Walter and Walternate, "I've seen doomsday and it is worse than anything you could possibly imagine." The images of urban military conflict against the backdrop of Boston's cityscape are quite alarming, but Peter is hopeful that something can be done to prevent this future from happening. However if the holes in the universe continue to grow, chaos will ensue. Similarly, in our own "parallel universe," if the cracks in the global economy continue to worsen, perhaps we are headed down a similar path.

The apocalyptic nature of season 3 was fitting for an audience in the midst of such seemingly world-ending economic turmoil in 2010–2011. The attention given to Harold Camping's prediction that the Rapture would be upon us in May 2011 was a clear demonstration of the general apocalyptic mood. This was not his first end-of-world prophecy, and yet a great number of people sincerely believed him this time around and spent their savings to spread the word, a phenomenon that attests to widespread pessimism about the future of the universe. This very particular anxiety was reflected in *Fringe*. "Our world is starting to come apart at the seams. And the tear is beginning right here!" exclaims Walter in "6B." All of Walter's doomsday exclamations reflect the sentiments of American viewers who were facing job loss and displacement at an unprecedented level. It was not an actual apocalypse, but a major paradigm shift. Like Olivia says later in the same episode, "It's the end of the world as we know it." In the past several years American gas and food prices have soared as the housing market plummeted. Huge banking conglomerates failed. Many Americans were (and still are) unemployed or underemployed, unable to afford their homes. With so much debt and such depressed home values, many homeowners were unable to keep their property. Compared to the economic boom of the early 2000s the general feeling at the end of the decade was that the world decidedly was "coming apart at the seams." Nothing makes sense in this new environment. In "6B" Walter explains that, as the crack in the universe grows, the rules of physics no longer apply. Similarly in our world, the conventions of the free market are suddenly in dispute.

In the face of an economic "doomsday" scenario, stories about the end of the world tend to affirm our greatest fears, even while providing a sense of hope in the face of terror. As the entire universe begins falling apart on screen, audiences can be assured that their own troubles are considerably trivial in comparison. Though we know that even a major economic depression is not the end of the world, we still find apocalypse stories like *Fringe* to be a pronouncement of both our fears and our faith. It is a show in which the heroes are grounded in reality even as their tasks are far beyond the scope of scientific plausibility.

Even in the real world we are always searching for a heroic figure, but political saviors often promise more than they could ever deliver. In contrast *Fringe*'s reluctant hero, Olivia, and unlikely savior, Peter, consistently deliver more than they promise. Olivia is initially uncertain of her capabilities, but others continue to encourage her. In some ways she represents the brokenness and incompetence that viewers may see in themselves. This in fact is what makes her such an extraordinary and inspiring hero. Her past seems insurmountable, and she doesn't have faith in her own capabilities. But Walter believes in Olivia's dormant powers. In "The Last Sam Weiss" he tells her,

I know what it's like to feel unequal to the task required of you. To feel incapable. I'll never be the man I was, but I've come to embrace those parts of my mind that are . . . peculiar and broken. I understand now that's what makes my mind *special*. I wish you could see yourself the way I see you. You have no idea how extraordinary you are. If you would embrace that, there's no end to what you can do.

As Walter pushes Olivia toward her destiny, he also reveals his own heroic abilities. Though he is undoubtedly a genius, his special gifts lie not in conventionally measured intelligence, but in an amalgamation of his experiences, both destructive and creative.

Despite her setbacks and challenges Olivia *does* have special powers and she *is* capable of saving the world. We know that, despite

Walter's memory loss and lack of mental clarity, he too can turn things around and make the universe safe again. In other words these very broken and emotionally battered people can be heroes, and therefore the viewers, with whatever shortcomings they may have, are heartened to know that they could do their own part to save the world from destruction. In short *Fringe*'s scenario invites us to indulge our worst fears, accept our quirks and shortcomings, and to face economic doomsday with a sense of hope and strength.

Divided Families

It is no coincidence that most of the show's characters have endured extremely difficult family issues. Their seriously distraught home lives illustrate the problematic nature of the modern Western family. The social problems that inevitably arise from conflict within parent-child relationships and marital discord are made epic in *Fringe*, where father-son issues are played out across two different universes, and audiences can see characters confront childhood trauma in an *Inception*-like adventure.

Walter, as a young scientist and father, is consumed by his work and driven mad by the decisions he has made "for the family." Elizabeth Bishop, the guilt-ridden mother, eventually commits suicide. Peter leaves his home behind to become a nomadic drifter, cutting all ties with his childhood. By the time Peter returns Walter has been locked away in a mental ward for several years, a stranger to his son. Walter and Peter's set of circumstances reflects the deep divisions present in the modern American family. It's not exactly uncommon for a twenty-something grown-up child to move far away from his parents and start a life of his own, in his own city, with new friends, and new ways of living. In fact it's almost a rite of passage for young adults, at least in contemporary Western culture.

But increased mobility is not the primary issue in family schisms. According to most counts in the United States almost 40% of babies are born to unwed mothers and 50% of first marriages end in divorce. Divided families are hardly the exception in this country. Peter's parents did not get divorced, but Walter's decision to steal Peter from the other universe created long-term family division, one that had far worse consequences than any divorce or domestic dispute.

Olivia's family issues are indicative of society's social problems too. It's not clear what happened to Olivia's biological father but we do know that, from a very young age, she was subjected to a very dysfunctional home life. Her stepfather abused her, her mother, and probably her sister too, until the day that nine-year-old Olivia took matters into her own hands by shooting him. He was not killed, but he never returned to the family. In "Lysergic Acid Diethylamide" Olivia stands up to this looming figure of her stepfather, at least in her own mind. She decides to stop running and hiding, and this confrontation deflates the threat that he poses.

Like Walter, Broyles let his professional life destroy his home life. His wife took the kids and left him when she could no longer stand any more late nights and missed birthday parties. Through the prism of the alternate universe we can see how important Broyles' family was to him, and how much he probably suffered by losing them in the original-verse.

The two universes can also represent that gaping generational divide that so often causes family conflict. Sometimes it seems that the father is from one universe and the son is from another. Walter and Peter's trans-universal relationship is a science-fiction exaggeration of the real-world chasm between parent and child.

War and Conflict

Season 3's fantastic violent scenes illustrate the wartime era in which *Fringe* was created. Bell's season 1 warning — "A war is coming" — continues to permeate the text. In "Lysergic Acid Diethylamide" the conflict is played out inside Olivia's mind, even though to the viewer the scenes are just as big and lifelike as the action in the rest of the *Fringe* narrative. In "The Last Sam Weiss" we learn that Walternate declared a war simply by turning on the machine, and in the final scene, we see that, in a possible future, breaches in the fabric of the universe will bring warfare to the streets of America. Meanwhile Walter continues to remind the others that they don't have much time left: destruction of humankind *by* humankind is close at hand. "Our world is breaking down around us," he tells Peter just before they discover that Walternate plans to destroy their world.

The abstract warnings against the threat of war and the collision of worlds continue to pervade the show's general mood. It is important to remember that the show debuted amid ongoing American turmoil overseas. By 2008 Americans had grown accustomed to long-term international military involvement, and some parallels can be drawn between the conflict in Iraq and the war between the universes. The United States' occupation of Iraq, for instance, has destroyed the world as the Iraqi people knew it before 2003. Because of the ongoing conflict the country's infrastructure has been devastated and whole villages have been deserted, not to mention the thousands of civilian casualties. Though the leadership of Iraq was less than ideal before the United States invaded, the Iraqi government did not instigate the conflict.

Like Iraq the alternate universe was not responsible for the initial "breach." They had done relatively little to invite catastrophic consequences of an invasion from "the other side." The kidnapping of Peter initiated a series of events that undermined the structure of their natural world and the stability of their society. Though Walter had no intention of being an aggressive or destructive force, he was responsible for igniting conflict between the two worlds.

However the same could be said about Walternate, ZFT, the shapeshifters, and the End of Day–ers. In retaliation for Walter's crime they invaded his universe and were responsible for unraveling the fabric of reality, thereby accelerating its destruction and upending the entire world. Primarily *Fringe's* demonstration of war lies in representation, with the clash of universes illustrating the collision of cultures that results from one nation occupying another.

The tragic bombings that ended World War II are used as reference points in *Fringe*, symbols of caution against destructive tendencies. In one episode, World War II takes center stage when a current-day Nazi carries out several bio-terror attacks using a formula that Walter's father had developed. This scenario falls clearly in line with the pervasive theme of enemy as self. Robert Oppenheimer, famous for leading the Manhattan Project and thereby helping to create the atomic bomb, has been mentioned at least three different times throughout the series. Twice he is directly quoted: "I am become death, destroyer of worlds." In PBS's *A Science Odyssey* one biographer explains Oppenheimer's symbolic significance well: "Robert Oppenheimer's name has become almost synonymous with the atomic bomb, and also with the dilemma facing scientists when the interests of the nation and their own conscience collide." This idea nicely summarizes the conflicts that face both Walter and Walternate.

Although there is a strong thread of awareness about the history of the U.S. military, the show also acknowledges the United States' current involvement in international affairs. Though *Fringe* clearly operates in a separate world from ours in certain respects, there is no avoiding the current military conflicts in which the U.S. has been engaged for the last ten years. We know that Peter had been traveling in Iraq before he joined the Fringe team, but it is not clear whether he was motivated by any military interests. Among other languages he speaks Farsi and Arabic, the two predominant languages of the Middle East. He and Olivia first meet in Baghdad and later they return to Iraq to carry out a Fringe mission ("Fracture").

In this episode the Fringe Division has discovered that the U.S. military was experimenting on soldiers and civilian contractors. When they find a suspicious document, Peter's initial comment is "Four words that should never show up in a sentence . . . 'classified-experimental-military-project.'" Olivia notes that the project was terminated and Broyles explains that all of the "U.S. military personnel associated with the project were redacted from the record." Since there is no record of U.S. involvement Peter and Olivia are charged with finding the Iraqi doctors who worked on the experiment. The scenes in Iraq depict a dark, dangerous world, one in which chaos rules the streets and most civilians live in fear, especially in fear of the U.S. government.

The threat of large-scale warfare central to season 3's drama can also be read as a symbolic depiction of the violent uprisings and government changes that recently swept through the Middle East and northern Africa. Technology is playing an increasingly significant role in these revolutions, with instant communication bolstering civilian unity. Like in *Fringe*'s central conflict, technology is both savior and destroyer. New social media and software programs create bonds among citizens but advancements in technology can also be used as tools of repression.

The old mantra that history repeats itself, especially when it comes to destructive war-like events, is pivotal in season 3. It is interesting, and paradoxical, that Walter designed the machine and penned the documents that he has been trying to understand for so long. It's as if a devout follower of a prophetic text discovered that he was the one who wrote the ancient writings in the first place. In a global sense this is history, a story that we wrote but can't decipher. Is the text of *Fringe* urging viewers to consider their own inescapable time loop? Do we really know what will happen based on the past? Are the stories offering a certain hope? Can we fix the "timeline" according to the wisdom of historical texts?

Over the course of its first three seasons, *Fringe* has evolved from an *X-Files*-inspired procedural to an epic drama of mythic proportions. It continues to draw in passionate viewers because it addresses important issues about identity, the nature of the cosmos, and the need for human connection and compassion. Each of its science fiction components is used as a device to address an important life issue: time travel is about remorse, forgiveness, and change; parallel universes acknowledge the double in each of us and the question of a road not taken; drastic genetic mutation and human cloning help us consider the consequences of playing God; and the Observers demonstrate the possibility that there is an invisible force at work in our fate. Even as we identify it as a classic work of science fiction, *Fringe* operates at the highest level of that genre, where fantasy, spirituality, and human psychology converge. Like the modern epic stories that preceded it — *Lord of the Rings*, *Star Wars*, *Lost*, and *The Matrix* trilogy — *Fringe* offers a deeper understanding of social and personal conflicts that cannot be as effectively addressed in fictional works of realism, personal self-help guides, or religious texts.

Season 1

1.1 Pilot
Original air date: 9/09/2008
Written by: J.J. Abrams, Alex Kurtzman, Roberto Orci
Directed by: Alex Graves

Olivia and Walter meet for the first time in the wake of a deadly incident that leaves no survivors among an airplane's passengers and crew.

1.2 The Same Old Story
Original air date: 9/16/2008
Written by: Alex Kurtzman, Roberto Orci, Jeff Pinkner, J.J. Abrams
Directed by: Paul Edwards

After a newborn rapidly ages to death, the Fringe team searches for the scientist responsible for growing human clones in his lab.

1.3 The Ghost Network
Original air date: 9/23/2008
Written by: J.R. Orci, David H. Goodman
Directed by: Frederick E.O. Toye

A man has visions of a strange terrorist attack shortly before a group of bus passengers are found trapped in a resin-like material.

1.4 The Arrival

Original air date: 9/30/2008
Written by: J.J. Abrams, Jeff Pinkner
Directed by: Paul Edwards

When a mysterious cylinder emerges from underground, Walter suddenly remembers a favor he owes someone.

1.5 Power Hungry

Original air date: 10/14/2008
Written by: Jason Cahill, Julia Cho
Directed by: Christopher Misiano

A deliveryman unknowingly generates his own electricity, wreaking havoc wherever the job takes him.

1.6 The Cure

Original air date: 10/21/2008
Written by: Brad Caleb Kane, Felicia D. Henderson
Directed by: Bill Eagles

When a disoriented young woman stumbles into a diner, the customers and staff are unprepared for what happens next: her head explodes and they suffer the same horrible deaths.

1.7 In Which We Meet Mr. Jones

Original air date: 11/11/2008
Written by: J.J. Abrams, Jeff Pinkner
Directed by: Brad Anderson

Olivia travels to Germany to solve the mystery of the giant parasite that has hold of Mitchell Loeb's heart, but the prisoner at the Wissenschaft facility is a difficult negotiator.

1.8 The Equation
Original air date: 11/18/2008
Written by: J.R. Orci, David H. Goodman
Directed by: Gwyneth Horder-Payton

When a boy is abducted, the only way that Walter can help is by returning to St. Claire's to speak to an old friend.

1.9 The Dreamscape
Original air date: 11/25/2008
Written by: Zack Whedon, Julia Cho
Directed by: Frederick E.O. Toye

A Massive Dynamic employee jumps out of a high-rise building when he encounters a swarm of lethal butterflies in the office.

1.10 Safe
Original air date: 12/02/2008
Written by: Jason Cahill, David H. Goodman
Directed by: Michael Zinberg

When a bank robber gets stuck in a solid vault wall, the Fringe team is called in to figure out how the man became embedded in the first place.

1.11 Bound
Original air date: 1/20/2009
Written by: Alex Kurtzman, Roberto Orci, Jeff Pinkner, J.J. Abrams
Directed by: Frederick E.O. Toye

Fast-growing deadly parasites and Olivia's abduction turn out to be closely linked.

1.12 The No-Brainer

Original air date: 1/27/2009
Written by: Brad Caleb Kane, David H. Goodman
Directed by: John Polson

After victims of a mysterious computer program are found dead, Olivia worries that her loved ones might be exposed to the brain-melting internet pop-up.

1.13 The Transformation

Original air date: 2/03/2009
Written by: J.R. Orci, Zack Whedon
Directed by: Brad Anderson

When an airplane passenger rapidly changes into a porcupine-like beast, the flight crashes. An investigation reveals a small, familiar-looking disc implanted in creature's hand, leading Peter and Olivia on a dangerous mission.

1.14 Ability

Original air date: 2/10/2009
Teleplay by: David H. Goodman
Story by: Glen Whitman, Robert Chiappetta
Directed by: Norberto Barba

The emergence of a strange orifice-sealing virus leads Olivia to search for the culprit: an old foe who knows more about Olivia that she can imagine.

1.15 Inner Child

Original air date: 4/07/2009
Written by: Brad Caleb Kane, Julia Cho
Directed by: Frederick E.O. Toye

Construction workers discover a boy sealed in an underground tunnel that's been closed off for seventy years. His extrasensory perception might be able to help the Fringe team solve a mystery.

1.16 Unleashed

Original air date: 4/14/2009
Written by: Zack Whedon, J.R. Orci
Directed by: Brad Anderson

When animal rights activists release a genetically mutated monster from a lab, the entire city is in danger. Meanwhile Walter grapples with a guilty conscience and a foggy memory.

1.17 Bad Dreams

Original air date: 4/21/2009
Written and Directed by: Akiva Goldsman

Olivia's nightmares are not fully her own, and she begins to think that she might be responsible for some horrific Pattern-related events.

1.18 Midnight

Original air date: 4/28/2009
Written by: J.H. Wyman, Andrew Kreisberg
Directed by: Bobby Roth

The team searches for a vampire-like killer preying on single men. Their investigation leads them to a ZFT bioterrorist cell.

1.19 The Road Not Taken

Original air date: 5/05/2009
Teleplay by: Jeff Pinkner, J.R. Orci
Story by: Akiva Goldsman
Directed by: Frederick E.O. Toye

Olivia begins to unearth more information about the cortexiphan drug trials as the investigation of a young woman spontaneously combusting brings Olivia closer to her own past.

1.20 There's More Than One of Everything

Original air date: 5/12/2009
Teleplay by: Jeff Pinkner, J.H. Wyman
Story by: Akiva Goldsman, Bryan Burk
Directed by: Brad Anderson

Walter's memory is jogged by a visit to an old familiar place; meanwhile the Fringe team hunts for the man who shot Nina, a search that leads Olivia to a whole new reality.

Season 2

2.1 A New Day in the Old Town

Original air date: 9/17/2009
Written by: Akiva Goldsman, J.J. Abrams
Directed by: Akiva Goldsman

When Olivia flies through the windshield an hour after the time of her car crash, the team is worried she will never recover.

2.2 Night of Desirable Objects

Original air date: 9/24/2009
Written by: Jeff Pinkner, J.H. Wyman
Directed by: Brad Anderson

There is something treacherous living in the underground tunnels beneath a Pennsylvania farm, and Olivia's heightened senses will help her figure out where it came from.

2.3 Fracture

Original air date: 10/01/2009
Written by: David Wilcox
Directed by: Bryan Spicer

A covert military experiment initiated in Iraq leads to human weaponization; the Fringe team investigates the mystery of a man who turns himself into a bomb.

2.4 Momentum Deferred
Original air date: 10/08/2009
Written by: Ashley Edward Miller, Zack Stentz
Directed by: Joe Chappelle

Frozen human heads are missing from a lab, and Olivia begins to regain her memory.

2.5 Dream Logic
Original air date: 10/15/2009
Written by: Josh Singer
Directed by: Paul Edwards

The patients of a sleep specialist suffer severe hallucinations — a waking nightmare — which drive them to murderous acts.

2.6 Earthling
Original air date: 11/05/2009
Written by: Jeff Vlaming, J.H. Wyman
Directed by: Jon Cassar

When a man is turned to pure ash in a matter of seconds, Broyles is compelled to follow up on an old case.

2.7 Of Human Action
Original air date: 11/12/2009
Written by: Glen Whitman, Robert Chiappetta
Directed by: Joe Chappelle

The son of a Massive Dynamic employee is kidnapped, and when the Fringe team investigates they discover why everyone who intervenes seems to attempt suicide.

2.8 August

Original air date: 11/19/2009
Written by: Jeff Pinkner, J.H. Wyman
Directed by: Dennis Smith

When a young woman is abducted just before a vacation, the Observers take center stage.

2.9 Snakehead

Original air date: 12/03/2009
Written by: David Wilcox
Directed by: Paul Holahan

Tragedy hits a ship full of Chinese immigrants; one survivor makes it to shore, unwittingly bringing a monstrous parasite with him.

2.10 Grey Matters

Original air date: 12/10/2009
Written by: Zack Stentz, Ashley Edward Miller
Directed by: Jeannot Szwarc

Mental patients make a sudden (and inexplicable) recovery, while a shapeshifter is on the move.

2.00 Unearthed*

Original air date: 1/11/2010
Written by: Andrew Kreisberg, David H. Goodman
Directed by: Frederick E.O. Toye

When a deceased girl returns to life only moments after her death, she appears to have more than one soul.

* Unearthed does not have a proper production number because despite it first airing in season 2, it was originally intended as a season 1 episode.

2.11 Johari Window

Original air date: 1/14/2010
Written by: Josh Singer
Directed by: Joe Chappelle

A small town in New York keeps to itself for good reason; the townspeople's secret is safe — until the Fringe team comes in to investigate.

2.12 What Lies Below

Original air date: 1/21/2010
Written by: Jeff Vlaming
Directed by: Deran Sarafian

Olivia and Peter are trapped in a quarantined office building where a deadly, fast-moving virus has been identified, as Walter frantically attempts to find a cure.

2.13 The Bishop Revival

Original air date: 1/28/2010
Written by: Glen Whitman, Robert Chiappetta
Directed by: Adam Davidson

Tragedy strikes a wedding as many of the guests suddenly die before the ceremony begins. Walter suspects the deaths are linked to his father's research.

2.14 Jacksonville

Original air date: 2/04/2010
Written by: Zack Stentz, Ashley Edward Miller
Directed by: Charles Beeson

Walter insists they revisit the site of his research in Jacksonville to help Olivia rekindle her ability.

2.15 Peter

Original air date: 4/01/2010
Teleplay by: Jeff Pinkner, J.H. Wyman, Josh Singer
Story by: Akiva Goldsman, Jeff Pinkner, J.H. Wyman, Josh Singer
Directed by: David Straiton

In a series of flashbacks, Walter reveals the secret of Peter's past to Olivia, confirming her suspicions that Peter is from the other universe.

2.16 Olivia. In the Lab. With the Revolver.

Original air date: 4/08/2010
Written by: Matthew Pitts
Directed by: Brad Anderson

When a man begins spreading cancerous cells to others, the Fringe team learns more about the cortexiphan trials.

2.17 White Tulip

Original air date: 4/15/2010
Written by: Jeff Vlaming, J.H. Wyman
Directed by: Tom Yatsko

An MIT physicist travels to the past, many times, to save the love of his life.

2.18 The Man From the Other Side

Original air date: 4/22/2010
Written by: Josh Singer, Ethan Gross
Directed by: Jeffrey Hunt

When the team sets up a trap for the shapeshifter, a man from another world appears.

2.19 Brown Betty

Original air date: 4/29/2010
Written by: Akiva Goldsman, J.H. Wyman, Jeff Pinkner
Directed by: Seith Mann

It's story time for little Ella when Walter spins a 1940s detective tale that features familiar characters.

2.20 Northwest Passage

Original air date: 5/06/2010
Written by: Nora Zuckerman, Lilla Zuckerman, Zack Stentz, Ashley Edward Miller
Directed by: Joe Chappelle

Angry with his father, Peter leaves Boston without a trace. He winds up in a small northwestern town where he meets a woman, but their relationship is short-lived.

2.21 Over There, Part 1

Original air date: 5/13/2010
Written by: Akiva Goldsman, Jeff Pinkner, J.H. Wyman
Directed by: Akiva Goldsman

Walter and the cortexiphan "kids" successfully cross over, only to be met with hostility by their doppelgängers.

2.22 Over There, Part 2

Original air date: 5/20/2010
Written by: Akiva Goldsman, Jeff Pinkner, J.H. Wyman
Directed by: Akiva Goldsman

Olivia and Fauxlivia face off. Peter discovers that Olivia wants to be with him. Walter and Bell must work together to return to their own universe.

Season 3

3.1 Olivia

Original air date: 9/23/2010
Written by: Jeff Pinkner, J.H. Wyman
Directed by: Joe Chappelle

Trapped in the wrong universe, Olivia must find a way to either convince her captors that she's not crazy . . . or start acting like Fauxlivia.

3.2 The Box

Original air date: 9/30/2010
Written by: Josh Singer, Graham Roland
Directed by: Jeff Hunt

A mysterious box leaves family members (and two burglars) bleeding from their ears and noses, as Fauxlivia begins to execute her mission.

3.3 The Plateau

Original air date: 10/07/2010
Written by: Monica Owusu-Breen, Alison Schapker
Directed by: Brad Anderson

Olivia joins the Fringe Division to solve a case in which a freakishly intelligent man predicts the outcome of certain events with surprising precision.

3.4 Do Shapeshifters Dream of Electric Sheep?

Original air date: 10/14/2010
Written by: Matthew Pitts, David Wilcox
Directed by: Ken Fink

When a woman discovers that her recently deceased husband is actually a mechano-organic hybrid, the Fringe team urges her to help them in their battle against the shapeshifters.

3.5 Amber 31422

Original air date: 11/04/2010
Written by: Ethan Gross, Josh Singer
Directed by: David Straiton

In the alternate universe an old quarantine victim is released from an amber zone, while Olivia begins to question her identity.

3.6 6955 kHz

Original air date: 11/11/2010
Written by: Robert Chiappetta, Glen Whitman
Directed by: Joe Chappelle

When listeners of the "number stations" suffer from the same kind of amnesia, the Fringe team is called in to investigate. Their findings lead to a strange device in the radio towers and a connection to the First People.

3.7 The Abducted

Original air date: 11/18/2010
Written by: Graham Roland, David Wilcox
Directed by: Chuck Russell

The Candy Man strikes again (in the alternate universe). Colonel Broyles must overcome his grief in order to solve the mystery of these bizarre kidnappings. Meanwhile, Olivia devises a plan of her own to escape her captor.

3.8 Entrada

Original air date: 12/02/2010
Written by: Jeff Pinkner, J.H. Wyman
Directed by: Brad Anderson

"Cover blown," writes Fauxlivia to a recipient in the alternate universe shortly after Peter discovers the truth. On the other side, Olivia has a plan for escape, if only she can find an ally in Colonel Broyles.

3.9 Marionette

Original air date: 12/09/2010
Written by: Monica Owusu-Breen, Alison Schapker
Directed by: Joe Chappelle

Victims of gruesome organ extractions lead to a suspect with a twisted notion of life after death. Meanwhile Olivia grapples with the emotional aftermath of having her life hijacked.

3.10 The Firefly

Original air date: 1/21/2011
Written by: Jeff Pinkner, J.H. Wyman
Directed by: Charles Beeson

With a grand demonstration of cause and effect, the Observer attempts to show Walter how seemingly insignificant actions can have far-reaching repercussions. It turns out that Walter's and Roscoe Joyce's lives are more interconnected than Walter could have imagined.

3.11 Reciprocity

Original air date: 1/28/2011
Written by: Josh Singer
Directed by: Jeannot Szwarc

Walter and researchers at Massive Dynamic begin to learn more about the machine and its origins. When shapeshifters are found "dead," Walter's own investigation leads to a startling surprise.

3.12 Concentrate and Ask Again

Original air date: 2/04/2011
Written by: Graham Roland, Matthew Pitts
Directed by: Dennis Smith

A man with extrasensory perception (one of Walter's past test subjects) agrees to help the Fringe team hunt down the suspects involved in acts of terrorism.

3.13 Immortality

Original air date: 2/11/2011
Written by: Ethan Gross, David Wilcox
Directed by: Brad Andersen

In the alternate universe Fauxlivia reunites with her boyfriend, Frank, shortly before she gets called in to investigate a Skelter beetle problem and a scientist hellbent on creating a vaccine.

3.14 6B

Original air date: 2/18/2011
Written by: Glen Whitman, Robert Chiappetta
Directed by: Tom Yatsko

A newly widowed woman does not realize that the visions she's been having of her dead husband pose a risk to every resident in her apartment building and perhaps to the entire universe.

3.15 Subject 13

Original air date: 2/25/2011
Written by: Akiva Goldsman, Jeff Pinkner, J.H. Wyman
Directed by: Frederick E.O. Toye

A flashback to the events of the Jacksonville daycare reveal more about Olivia's past and her and Peter's fateful relationship.

3.16 Os

Original air date: 3/11/2011
Written by: Graham Roland, Josh Singer
Directed by: Brad Anderson

A mysterious robbery leaves one of the suspects floating in mid-air. Further investigation exposes a grief-stricken scientist and father trying to concoct a cure for his wheelchair-bound son.

3.17 Stowaway

Original air date: 3/18/2011
Teleplay by: Danielle Dispaltro
Story by: Akiva Goldsman, Jeff Pinkner, J.H. Wyman
Directed by: Charles Beeson

A seemingly indestructible woman mysteriously appears at a suicide scene; she jumped off a building with the suicide victim, but she walked away unscathed.

3.18 Bloodline

Original air date: 3/25/2011
Written by: Alison Schapker, Monica Owusu-Breen
Directed by: Dennis Smith

In the alternate universe, Fauxlivia's pregnancy is accelerated by a clandestine medical team, while Walternate anxiously awaits his grandson.

3.19 Lysergic Acid Diethylamide

Original air date: 4/15/2011
Written by: Akiva Goldsman, Jeff Pinkner, J.H. Wyman
Directed by: Joe Chappelle

Peter and Walter enter the mind of Olivia in order to extract Bell's consciousness and figure out where she is hiding. Things get interesting when they find Bell awaiting them in his office.

3.20 6:02 AM EST

Original air date: 4/22/2011
Written by: Graham Roland, Josh Singer, David Wilcox
Directed by: Jeannot Szwarc

Both universes gear up to deal with the negative effects of Walter's breach and the possible destruction of all existence.

3.21 The Last Sam Weiss

Original air date: 4/29/2011
Written by: Monica Owusu-Breen, Alison Schapker
Directed by: Tom Yatsko

As the signs of an apocalypse increase, Sam Weiss reveals his secrets to Olivia as they race against time to undo the damage. Meanwhile a disoriented Peter disappears from the hospital.

3.22 The Day We Died

Original air date: 5/06/2011
Teleplay by: Jeff Pinkner, J.H. Wyman
Story by: Jeff Pinkner, J.H. Wyman, Akiva Goldsman
Directed by: Joe Chappelle

When Peter travels 15 years into the grim future, he discovers the truth about what he must do.

SOURCES

Asimov, Isaac. *The End of Eternity.* New York: Tom Doherty Associates, 1983.

Atwood, Margaret. *Oryx and Crake.* New York: Nan A. Talese, 2003.

Battlestar Galactica. SyFy, 2004–2009.

Brandspotters' *Fringe* Page. Brandspotters.com. 15 May 2011.

Burr, Ty. "A Fresh Frontier: In the best prequel ever, 'Star Trek' reboots the franchise and reminds us why we love it." *Boston Globe.* 8 May 2009.

Carroll, Lewis. *Alice's Adventures in Wonderland.* San Diego: ICON Group International, 2005.

—. *Through the Looking Glass and What Alice Found There.* New York: Classic Books International, 2009.

Carter, Bill. "DVRs Give More Shows a Lifeline." *The New York Times.* 24 April 2011.

Cockburn, Alexander, and Jeffrey St. Clair. *Whiteout: The CIA, Drugs and the Press.* London: Verso, 1998.

"Coming War, The." December 2010. Fox.com. Accessed January 2011.

"Determinism." *Stanford Encyclopedia of Philosophy.* 2010. Online. Accessed 20 February 2010.

Doctor Who. BBC Television, 2005–.

Dostoevsky, Fyodor. "The Double." *The Short Novels of Dostoevsky.* Ed. Thomas Mann. New York: Dial Press, 1945.

Early, Frances H., and Kathleen Kennedy. *Athena's Daughters: Television's New Women Warriors.* Syracuse: Syracuse University Press, 2003.

Fienberg, Daniel. "HitFix Interview: Jeff Pinkner and J.H. Wyman discuss the 'Fringe' finale and future." 11 May 2011. Hitfix.com. Accessed 25 May 2011.

Fox, Stuart. "J.J. Abrams Gets Lost Again." *Popular Science.* 27 August 2008.

Fringe. Fox, 2008–.

"Fringe Fan Thank You." April 2011. Fox.com. Accessed 26 July 2011.

Gellene, Denise. "Dr. Albert M. Kligman, Dermatologist, Dies at 93." *The New York Times.* 22 February 2010.

Goldenberg, Suzanne. "Mississippi floods threaten New Orleans." *The Guardian.* 15 May 2011.

Greene, Brian. "A Physicist Explains Why Parallel Universes May Exist." *Fresh Air.* Host Terry Gross. National Public Radio. 24 January 2011.

—. *The Elegant Universe: Superstrings, Hidden Dimensions, and the Quest for the Ultimate Theory.* New York: W.W. Norton, 1999.

—. *The Hidden Reality: Parallel Universes and the Deep Laws of the Cosmos.* New York: Knopf, 2011.

Gustafsson, Bengt, et al. "The Uppsala Code of Ethics for Scientists." *Journal of Peace Research* 21 (1984): 311–316.

Harty, Sheily T. "Absolute Nothingness and the Absence of Meaning." 2011. Accessed 12 May 2011.

Heinlein, Robert. "By His Bootstraps." First published October 1943 in *Astounding Science Fiction.* Accessed 1 April 2010 <http://pot.home.xs4all.nl/scifi/byhisbootstraps.pdf>.

Hibberd, James. "Joshua Jackson: 'Start the campaign' to save 'Fringe.'" *Entertainment Weekly.* 18 February 2011.

Huxley, Aldous. *Brave New World.* New York: Harper and Bros., 1946.

"J. Robert Oppenheimer." *A Science Odyssey: People and Discoveries.* PBS. 1998.

Johnson, Mike, and Tom Mandrake. *Fringe* (graphic novel). Wildstorm, 2008.

Kaku, Michio. *Parallel Worlds: A Journey Through Creation, Higher Dimensions and the Future of the Cosmos.* New York: Doubleday, 2005.

Keim, Brandon. "What Does It Mean to Be Human?" *Wired.* 1 June 2008.

Kurzweil, Ray. *The Singularity Is Near: When Humans Transcend Biology.* New York: The Penguin Group, 2005.

Lachonis, Jon. "How to Save Fringe." 19 November 2010. TVOver Mind.Zap2It.com. Accessed 10 May 2011 <http://tvovermind.zap2it.com/fox/fringe/save-fringe/39499>.

Lang, Gary. *The Science of the Soul.* Dir. Gary Lang. Prods. Kathryn Liptrott, et al. Associated Producers, Ltd., with TV Vision and History Television. 2009–2010.

Leigh, Phil. *Mobile Computing and Signal-Rich Media.* Tampa: Inside Digital Media, Inc, 2011.

Lieber, Fritz. "Catch That Zeppelin." *The Way It Wasn't: Great Science Fiction Stories of Alternate History.* New York: Carol, 1996.

Lost. ABC/Disney, 2004–2010.

Mazzetti, Mark, Sabrina Tavernise and Jack Healy. "Suspect, Charged, Said to Admit to Role in Plot." *The New York Times.* 4 May 2010.

McKibben, Bill. "Climate Change and Flood This Time." *The Los Angeles Times*. 10 May 2011.

McPherson, Sam. Interview with the Author. Email. 10 May 2011.

National Institutes of Health. "Willowbrook Hepatitis Experiments." NIH .gov. 2009.

Niven, Larry. "All the Myriad Ways." *The Way It Wasn't: Great Science Fiction Stories of Alternate History*. New York: Carol, 1996. 166–176.

Nordern, Eric. "*Playboy* Interview: Stanley Kubrick." *Playboy*. September 1968.

Postman, Neil. *Amusing Ourselves to Death*. New York: Penguin, 2005.

Rabkin, Eric S., Martin H. Greenberg and Joseph D. Olander. *The End of the World*. Carbondale: Southern Illinois University Press, 1983.

Roco. Interview with the Author. Email. 20 May 2011.

—. "Observers Are Here = Behave Seer Errors." 10 January 2009. FringeBloggers.com. Accessed 20 May 2011 <http://www.fringeblog gers.com/observers-are-here-behave-seer-errors/>.

Roffman, Marissa. "FRINGE: 'Bloodline' Teases, Plus EPs Jeff Pinkner and J.H. Wyman Talk Peter's Choice and the Other Universe." 25 March 2011. GiveMeMyRemote.com. Accessed 1 April 2011 < http://www.give memyremote.com/remote/2011/03/25/fringe-recap-bloodline/>.

Shelley, Mary. *Frankenstein*. San Diego: ICON Group International, 2005.

Simon, Anne. *The Real Science Behind the X-Files: Microbes, Meteorites, and Mutants*. New York: Simon and Schuster, 1999.

Stevenson, Robert Louis. *Dr. Jekyll and Mr. Hyde*. San Diego: ICON Group International, 2005.

Trials of War Criminals Before the Nuremberg Military Tribunals Under Control Council. Law. No. 10, Vol. 2. Washington D.C.: U.S. Government Printing Office (1949): 181–182.

Tucker, Ken. "'Fringe': Save this show! A guide (and a plea) for new fans." *Entertainment Weekly*. 11 March 2011.

—. "The 'Fringe' fourth-season renewal: 'It has begun,' and what 'it' means." *Entertainment Weekly*. 25 March 2011.

Vonnegut, Kurt. *Cat's Cradle*. New York: Dell Publishing, 1963.

—. *Slaughterhouse-Five*. New York: The Dial Press, 1969.

Wells, H.G. *The Island of Dr. Moreau*. New York: Tom Doherty and Associates, 1996.

—. "The War of the Worlds." *The Time Machine; The War of the Worlds*. New York: Oxford University Press, 1977.

Winston, Diane. "TV and Parables of Our Time." *Speaking of Faith with Krista Tippett*. American Public Media. 16 July 2009.

ACKNOWLEDGMENTS

I'd like to extend my sincere appreciation to Jen Hale at ECW Press, a gifted editor with a nose for good science fiction television. Many thanks to her — and her alternate universe self — for supporting this project all along. Thanks to Crissy Boylan and to everyone else at ECW who helped make this book happen.

I would like to express my appreciation for the help of bloggers Sam McPherson, Roco, and Jon Lachonis, and all of the *Fringe* fans who regularly offer their passionate insight into the show.

A special thank you to Steve (the person who first insisted I watch *Fringe*) for all of his support and encouragement. All of my love to Alexis, a heroine as serious and stunning as Olivia, and to Isaac, my little superhero.

As always, I'm deeply grateful for the support of my parents, Gary and Susan Clarke.

A special thanks to Jessie for inspiring me to take on the universe, both this one and the next.

SARAH CLARKE STUART teaches composition, literature, and popular culture at the University of North Florida and Florida State College at Jacksonville. She is the author of *Literary Lost: Viewing Television through the Lens of Literature*. Working closely with the producers of Lost University, Stuart was prominently featured as a lecturer of literature in *Lost*'s season 6 Blu-ray extra. Several national news outlets, including *USA Today*, have quoted Stuart on the subject of popular culture and education.